Creating a Female Dominion
in American Reform
1890–1935

Creating a Female Dominion
in American Reform
1890–1935

ROBYN MUNCY

New York   Oxford
OXFORD UNIVERSITY PRESS
1991

Oxford University Press

Oxford   New York   Toronto
Delhi   Bombay   Calcutta   Madras   Karachi
Petaling Jaya   Singapore   Hong Kong   Tokyo
Nairobi   Dar es Salaam   Cape Town
Melbourne   Auckland

and associated companies in
Berlin   Ibadan

Published by Oxford University Press, Inc.,
200 Madison Avenue, New York, New York 10016

Oxford is a registered trademark of Oxford University Press

Library of Congress Cataloging-in-Publication Data
Muncy, Robyn.
Creating a female dominion in American reform, 1890–1935 /
Robyn Muncy.
p.   cm.
Includes index.
ISBN 0-19-505702-3
1. Child welfare–United States–History.   2. Women social
reformers–United States–History.   3. Women social workers–
United States–History.   4. Women in the professions–
United States–History.   I. Title.
HV741.M82   1991
331.4′8136132′0973–dc20   90-38389   CIP

2 4 6 8 9 7 5 3 1

Printed in the United States of America
on acid-free paper

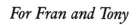

For Fran and Tony

Acknowledgments

During the several years I have worked on this book, I have had help from so many distinguished thinkers that I am overwhelmed when I take stock of my debt. I owe the largest intellectual portion to Robert H. Wiebe, who was, for me, the perfect dissertation adviser and who has proven an unerring guide to my writing and professional life generally. I cannot begin to express my gratitude for his wisdom, good humor, and generosity. Also members of my dissertation committee, Michael Sherry and Henry Binford, offered sound advice and good cheer. Elizabeth Payne and Joe Barton helped immensely in launching the project.

Others who have read the entire manuscript and shared their insights include Nancy Cott, Allen Davis, Karen Halttunen, Jane Hunter, Suzanne Lebsock, Regina Morantz-Sanchez, and Susan Ware. I thank them all for enriching the project and sharpening my analyses. Others who have commented on parts of the manuscript include Eileen Boris, Marjory DeVault, Meredith Muncy, Peggy Pascoe, Kathryn Kish Sklar, and Tony Speranza. Through their support for and contributions to this project, these scholars have welcomed me to the academic community and encouraged me to see my work as an expression of that community. I want to underscore my gratitude to Regina Morantz-Sanchez for her especially warm response to my work.

I also benefited from presenting parts of the manuscript before the Department of History at Le Moyne College in Syracuse, New York, the Upstate New York Feminist Scholars Workshop, and the Conference on Women in the Welfare State at Madison, Wisconsin. Moreover, I have enjoyed research support from the Alumnae of Northwestern University; the Colonial Dames of America; the National Endowment for the Humanities; and the Committee on Faculty Research and Development at Le Moyne College.

Among the other individuals who have facilitated my work, I want to thank Aloha South at the National Archives, who proved an especially undaunted and careful assistant. Sharyn Knight not only helped with word processing but also offered encouragement. I take special pleasure in acknowledging Judy Bachor Speranza, who joyfully and energetically helped with the tedious work of proofreading.

Penn State University Press has allowed me to publish in the Introduction and Chapter Three parts of my article, "Gender and Professionalization in the Origins of the U.S. Welfare State: The Careers of Edith Abbott and Sophonisba Breckinridge, 1890–1935," which appeared in *The Journal of Policy History* during the summer 1990.

Oxford University Press provided an editing team that made the publication process easy and enjoyable. Rachel Toor's support for the project kept my spirits high throughout the process of revision. Sheldon Meyer and Karen Wolny carried the project to completion. And thanks to Stephanie Sakson-Ford for engaging with the project as well as copyediting the manuscript.

Finally, thanks to those who have huddled close around me, providing warmth, encouragement, and confidence. Bob and Becky Muncy, my parents, and Meredith Muncy, my sister, believed in the project from the beginning just because it was mine. Their confidence in me has always been limitless, and nothing else in the world could possibly be so valuable. Frances Dolan, another whose love is unshakable, shared with me the thrills and woes of graduate school and our early professional lives. Some of my fondest memories of graduate school center on breakfasts with Fran at the Golden Waffle Restaurant in Chicago. There, over our scrambled eggs, she—and Alice, our infinitely patient waitress—let me read from my research notes. We would ooh, ah, and wonder over quotations from the letters of Jane Addams, Edith Abbott, Julia Lathrop. And somehow during those early morning sessions, I began to grasp the meaning both of those letters and of friendship. Always, always, Fran has helped me figure out the meaning of my work at its deepest level and to uncover its relevance to my own life. The first chapter especially is dedicated to her. Tony Speranza came into my life as I began to revise the manuscript for publication. He has added yet another dimension to my life and work, for which I thank him. To him and Fran, two on whose support I depend daily, I dedicate this book.

Syracuse, New York   R.M.
May 1990

Contents

Introduction

"I can hardly believe I have lived to see this day," exclaimed veteran reformer Molly Dewson in response to New Deal legislation. "It's the culmination of what us girls and some of you boys have been working for for so long it's just dazzling."[1] Indeed, Dewson and a host of her female contemporaries had inaugurated their reforming careers during the Progressive era (1890–1920), continued to fight their reforming battles through the 1920s–a decade that one activist called the "tepid, torpid years"–and stood ready with their program when the Great Depression bent Americans once again toward reform.[2] This book seeks to explain that continuity of reform activism among America's middle-class white women.

Previous historians have confirmed Dewson's judgment that female New Dealers had been hawking their agenda for a long time before Franklin Roosevelt's administration finally bought it. The earliest of these was Clarke Chambers, who showed that the 1920s were not tepid or torpid for activists in select voluntary organizations. For them, the decade provided time to fashion a reform program bound for popularity in the 1930s. Published in 1963, Chambers's book was full of women, but because it predated the renewal of feminism in the late 1960s, it did not ask why women were especially prominent among the diminished numbers of activists in the 1920s. Not until feminists swept into academe and offered gender as a primary category of historical analysis did a historian, J. Stanley Lemons, explicitly argue that women in particular sustained their commitment to reform through the 1920s.[3] Susan Ware subsequently supplemented the evidence and enriched the argument in her study of female policymakers in the Roosevelt administration and again in her biography of Molly Dewson.[4] Indeed, the trend among women's historians in the 1980s was to see the New Deal as, in part, a culmination of female reform activity since the Progressive era.[5]

What we lack now is an explanation for the dogged determination of middle-class white female reformers. Why, when so many Americans flocked to movie theaters and dance halls, when some renowned progressives publicly recanted their earlier beliefs, did a large contingent of women cling tenaciously to their reforming creed?[6] Why did women's organizations play a particularly prominent part in bridging America's two periods of reform, the Progressive era and the decade of the New Deal?

In this study, I offer an explanation of the continuity by identifying an interlocking set of organizatons and agencies that I have chosen to call a female dominion in the mostly male empire of policymaking. At the head of this dominion stood the Children's Bureau in the federal Department of Labor, an agency created by Congress in 1912 at the urging of child welfare advocates. Staking their claim to child welfare policy, women who had agitated for and staffed the Bureau went on to establish analogous public agencies in the states, and these agencies joined female voluntary organizations as the dominion's lower echelons of authority. An educational branch — represented in this study by the School of Social Service Administration at the University of Chicago — provided graduates trained specifically for the dominion's work, and a lobbying auxiliary — the Women's Joint Congressional Committee — offered critical support with federal legislation. I argue that within this network of organizations, female professionals and their followers preserved for the New Deal the reform values and strategies of the Progressive era.

By using the metaphor of a dominion, I want to evoke a combination of autonomy and circumscription. Like a self-governing member of the British Commonwealth, this female dominion exercised considerable control over its territory, which was child welfare policy. But at the same time, its power was always limited by the higher authority vested in male legislatures, cabinets, and courts. Indeed, the continual renegotiation of those limitations provided one of the critical dynamics in the dominion's history.

Although for convenience I shall often refer to the child welfare dominion as *the* dominion, I do not mean that it was the only female policymaking network in the United States. Women also took control of policy regulating female workers in the early twentieth century. To do so, these female policymakers built an organizational nexus very similar to that of the child welfare dominion. The Women's Bureau in the federal Department of Labor led this sister administration; many female voluntary organizations participated in both polities; and certainly the two shared educational and lobbying resources. Moreover, personnel passed easily and often between them especially because their common values and strategies had grown out of similar experiences in the Progressive era.[7]

As this study will show, these female policymaking bodies emerged from the unique needs of women who were seeking channels to professionalism in the Progressive era. As historians of women have demonstrated, gender was an important determinant of experience in the professionalization process, which was part and parcel of the Progressive era. Prescriptions for female behavior directly contradicted the solidifying requirements of professional conduct: lingering nineteenth-century feminine ideals urged women toward passivity, humility, and self-sacrifice, while professionalism demanded activity, confidence, and self-assertion. By validating behaviors traditionally associated with men, professionalization put aspiring women into perpetual conflict. If they donned the behavioral garb appropriate to professional life, they invited criticism for being unfeminine. If they refused to wear the suit, they lost the aura of professional authority. Women thus endured unique conflicts in the professionalization process, devised unique strategies for coping with those conflicts, and often followed unique career paths as a result.

Within this broad field bounded by gender, female experience divided into smaller sections corresponding to the sort of profession a woman entered. For example, women in male dominated professions like law, ministry, the social sciences, the physical sciences, and many medical specialties encountered blatant discrimination in education, hiring, promotion, and salaries. Moreover, the entrance of some intrepid women into these professions did not represent an opening wedge for younger women. Often, the struggle to maintain their own positions was so exacting and uncertain for pioneers or the profession so structured that these women could not serve as mentors to younger women or in any way help ease them into professional life.[8]

Women's experience in female-dominated professions revealed different patterns. Entrants to these fields did not have to tough out discrimination just to obtain a job, and they could count on female mentors. Nevertheless, women in professions such as nursing, teaching, or librarianship found their entire professions dependent on and circumscribed by separate male groups—for instance, doctors or school administrators. As a result, these female professions simply could not develop the autonomy necessary to full professional privilege.[9]

Somewhere in between these two groups lay the experience of women in new female professions created during the Progressive era. Here I include especially social work, public health nursing, and home economics, in addition to a large proportion of doctors in female specialties. In these professions, women were freer in their attempts to reconcile professional ideals with values from female culture, which produced uniquely female ways of being professional.[10] This book provides a study of the origins, character, and products of this peculiarly female professionalism.

Furthermore, this book will argue that this understanding of professionalism had profound implications for the continuation of reform in the early twentieth century. I believe that the female professions created during the Progressive era contained as part of their professional creeds many of the commitments of the progressive reformers who gave them birth. So long as those reformers and their protégés controlled their professions, they were able to use their power and patronage to socialize subsequent generations of women into a common reform culture. For many women in these professions, professionalization itself sustained reforming commitments.

This is not the usual reading of the relationship between professionalization and reform. In the literature on social work, for instance, the 1920s are often seen as a time when the weight of professionalization suffocated the impulse to reform.[11] The literature on feminism correctly blames professionalization for dividing the community of women and distracting professionals from their commitment to public activity on behalf of their sex.[12] Within the history of the social sciences, scholars have detected a tension that pitted professionalization (with its requirement of objectivity) against the expression of political convictions.[13]

I do not want to challenge these readings of the conflict between professionalization and reform. I do insist that professionalism was not a monolith, that different groups involved in the professionalization process produced varied versions of the professional code and that some women involved in creating social work, public health nursing, home economics, and some female medical specialties formed a peculiar variant that was not only less hostile to reform than some others but that actually embraced reform, nurtured it, and cradled it across the 1920s.[14] The relationship between reform and professionalization in the first half of the twentieth century varied among professions, varied among reforms.

Because the particular reforms promoted by dominion-builders ultimately shaped the U.S. welfare state, this study also provides a new perspective on the relationship between gender and the construction of that policy system.[15] I see one source of New Deal policies—the foundation of the U.S. welfare state—in the peculiar predicament of turn-of-the-century women searching for professional niches. While creating their new professions in the Progressive era, these women discovered that their male counterparts were much more willing to cede professional territory, to acknowledge the female right to expertise in instances where women and children were the only clients. This encouraged creators of new female professions—unconscious of their motive I am sure—to define certain social problems in ways that made women and children central.[16] They felt mothers caused the need for child protection, but also provided the solution, for instance, which *empowered* female caseworkers, policymakers, and bureaucrats because if fathers were responsible then professional women would have had a harder time claiming jurisdiction over the issue.

The special tragedy of this was that as female professionals were wrangling desperately for a spot in the professional world, their interest thus encouraged them to blame their nonprofessional sisters for all children's ills, if anything to increase the burden of female responsibility for child care, to shorten the leash that tied most women to home and children. Insistence on the primacy of the mother-child relationship in child development, the obligation of mothers to stay home, and fathers to earn a family's living were critical tenets in shaping welfare policies oppressive to women. And there is no denying the central role that female policymakers played in perpetuating those tenets and drafting those policies.

Nevertheless, I see no reason to castigate dominion builders for either their insensitivity or ambition. Far from it. I want rather to expose and mourn a society in which the perfectly legitimate desires for respect, a steady income, and a base of effective action in the world could be satisfied only at the expense of others. Professional women at the turn of the century were constrained by a culture that increasingly granted respect, financial resources, and effectiveness to those who could convince their public that they possessed esoteric knowledge on which the public's welfare depended. Thus only by rendering somebody else powerless could professionals justify themselves. And given the particular constructions of gender at the turn of the century, female professionals could succeed in satisfying their needs for respect, autonomy, and effectiveness only at the expense of other women. This is no reason for condemning the women in this book; it is reason for reconstructing society.

My study proceeds through five chapters. Each chapter follows the development of the dominion's distinguishing characteristics: its femaleness, its monopoly over child welfare policy, and its commitment to public service.

Chapter One investigates the origins of the dominion in the female community at Hull House. Students of the Progressive era recognize that social settlement as a community of reformers, a social laboratory, and an institution of separatist feminism. In this book, we will see Hull House as an incubator for new female-dominated professions and a peculiarly female professional culture that held public service to be its supreme value; as a place where women struggled to find a public voice; and as a setting in which some women began to satisfy their will to dominate.

After developing the values and strategies of their professions and professional culture, women from Hull House—and other, similar female communities—needed a base of operations from which to achieve a national influence. They created that base in the Children's Bureau, which provides the subject of Chapter Two. Before World War I, the Children's Bureau had begun to establish a monopoly over child welfare policy, and the dominion had materialized. Because the dominion comprised a system of interconnected government bureaus and private organizations, its emergence and subsequent operation speak directly to historian Daniel Rodgers's plea for an understanding of "the tissue of connections" among private and public agencies in the Progressive era. Without this understanding, historians of the early twentieth century have, according to Rodgers, been incapable of spelling out the meaning of Progressivism itself.[17] As Chapter Two begins to illuminate public/private connections, it contributes to Rodgers', "search for progressivism."

Perpetuating the dominion required a continuing supply of professionals trained specifically for its tasks. Chapter Three shows that the supply flowed from such places as the School of Social Service Administration at the University of Chicago, where a generation of female reformers socialized younger women into reform culture. This middle chapter closely investigates the creation of social work, and it highlights the role of professional schools in the network of reform organizations in the early twentieth century.

Between 1918 and 1924, the dominion consolidated and expanded its monopoly over child welfare policy. That process occupies the pages of Chapter Four, which shows how the dominion operated during the peak of its power. This climactic chapter, by concentrating on the history of the Sheppard-Towner Maternity and Infancy Act, offers an opportunity both to explore the ways that reformers used World War I to advance their program and to analyze issues of social control in the drawing and implementation of that program.

After 1924, the dominion's expansiveness ended; later in the decade it actually contracted; and finally in the mid-1930s, the dominion crumbled. Chapter Five explains the initial decline especially as a stalemate between a male and female understanding of professionalism and explores the implications of these understandings for the formation of public policy. The final destruction of the dominion was caused, however, not by opposition to its policies but by the success of its agenda in the passage of New Deal legislation. When the Great Depression convinced male policymakers that the federal government should indeed be involved in the provision of social services, child welfare policy ceased to hover on the fringe of federal concerns. As it slid into the mainstream of public policy, women lost their exclusive hold on child welfare programs, and thus the dominion dissolved.

Creating a Female Dominion
in American Reform
1890–1935

CHAPTER 1

Origins of the Dominion: Hull House, 1890–1910

"There's power in me, and will to dominate which I must exercise," wrote Jane Addams in 1889, "they hurt me else."[1] In late-nineteenth-century America, frustrated ambition was injuring other college-educated women as well. Consequently, when Addams eased her own pain by founding a social settlement in Chicago, her venture attracted a group of women similarly bruised by constraints on their aspirations and ready to unfetter their capacities for personal independence and public authority. The desire to unlock the shackles that would have bound them to obscure, private lives provided Addams and her followers with a motive for creating a female dominion within the larger empire of policymaking; their experiences at Hull House supplied the values and strategies that made their creation possible.

The precondition for opening Addams's settlement in 1889 lay in a transformation of female experience that had occurred during the previous half-century. Middle-class Americans had, in the early nineteenth century, invented a set of prescriptions for female behavior and assumptions about women's nature that largely excluded women from the competitive arenas of politics and business. Called the cult of true womanhood, this belief system proclaimed women the natural harbors of spiritual and moral values in the wildly acquisitive seas of Jacksonian America and further apotheosized women as that half of the human race motivated only by concern for others. In all she did, woman was to sacrifice individual ambition in order to serve. She served best through childrearing, charitable activities, and nursing the wounds sustained by both individual men and communities in battles for political and economic advantage. To fulfill this

3

responsibility for preserving familial and social relationships, women were to cultivate piety, purity, submissiveness, and domesticity. But the first two of these qualities almost immediately subverted the latter two: If men tended to corruption and women to moral perfection, some women reasoned, then the Republic needed women for duties other than cooking and cleaning and even childrearing.[2]

Thus justifying their escape from domesticity and submissiveness, free antebellum women broke into the public sphere. Barred from political parties and business enterprises, they operated especially through all-female, voluntary organizations that promised, by a variety of means, to lift their communities from sin and degradation. Some of these bodies, for instance, sent female missionaries to the American West and to China; others claimed elementary school teaching for women by arguing that women had an affinity for children. While the more aggressive petitioned for temperance laws, attempted to save prostitutes from the uncontrolled passions of men, or condemned slavery, the more timid published religious tracts and founded Sunday Schools. Whether bold or cautious, though, middle-class antebellum women did not stay home. Moreover, in their public lives, most of them avoided organizations run by men. They preferred separate societies because only within segregated groups could they certainly resist male domination.[3]

After the Civil War, middle-class women used the cult of true womanhood not only to build ever larger voluntary organizations but also to justify their admission to higher education. They argued that if they were to be the best possible mothers and wives—the repositories of culture in a materialistic society—then they needed the finest educations. This argument inspired the opening of several women's colleges. Vassar College opened in 1865, followed by Wellesley and Smith in 1875. During the 1880s, Harvard founded its annex for women; Columbia University opened Barnard; and Brown created Pembroke. In 1893, Bryn Mawr started classes. At the same time, many American colleges and universities became coeducational, partly in response to female demand for higher learning but mostly because the proliferation of such institutions created stiff competition for students. In 1870, one-third of American colleges and universities admitted both women and men; by 1890, two-thirds did. Before the turn of the century, women accounted for 36 percent of America's undergraduates and 13 percent of its graduate students.[4]

Especially in the close-knit communities of women's colleges, students, faculty, and administrators produced a unique variant of middle-class female experience. Precisely because nineteenth-century culture defined women and men as radically different and attempted to assign them to separate spheres of activity, middle-class women spent a great deal of their time in the company of other women. Moreover, since no cultural constraint prevented these women from expressing themselves freely and passionately to each other, they regularly formed profound romantic friendships that lasted a lifetime. Even while married, middle-class women often drew their emotional sustenance from other women and shared their most intimate experiences — such as childbirth — only with female friends. Within this world of female friendships and duty, middle-class women nursed a peculiarly female culture that emphasized humility, relationships, care, and service.[5]

Women's colleges created space for ever more passionate attachments. After all, students and faculty studied, dined, slept, and played together. Administrators encouraged their young scholars to think of each other as family, and many students suffered miserable crushes on each other during the course of every school year. Because Victorian constructions of femininity cast doubt on female intelligence and strength, a sense of mission further united the first generation of collegiate women as they set out to prove the intellectual abilities and physical stamina of their sex. Forged in a crucible this hot, relationships among students were bound to endure: many pairs of students lived together until death in what became known as Boston marriages, while alumnae in general remained loyal to each other and their schools.[6]

Life after college came as a shock to women steeped for several years in a mission and a rich communal life. For men, the paths out of college led toward independence through business or the professions. For women, they either stretched toward elementary school teaching or wound back to the family, where graduates were expected to throw themselves into the endless round of social visits that filled the days of middle-class ladies. These options could not satisfy all female graduates, many of whom suffered a period of disorientation and depression after graduation. They were fitted for greater challenges than pouring tea and teaching the alphabet, but society closed most other options to them. Responding to their isolation and the lack of a meaningful outlet for their talents, these women formed organizations such as the Association of Collegiate Alumnae in order to recapture the community and purpose they shared in college. In their clubs, the alumnae discussed the latest literature on female education, raised scholarships for younger women, and enjoyed the companionship of those shaped by similar experiences. For many, however, club meetings did not extinguish the ambitions that college had kindled.[7]

Such aspirations burned in the souls of Jane Addams and Ellen Gates Starr, two women who met in 1877 at Rockford Female Seminary in Rockford, Illinois. Addams, destined to become the better known, had been born in 1860 to Cedarville, Illinois's wealthiest family. At his daughter's birth, John Huy Addams had already served as a Republican state senator for six years and would represent his district for another decade. He owned saw and grist mills in addition to substantial parcels of land. In 1864, he would become president of the Second National Bank of Freeport and would eventually leave an estate worth $250,000. Perhaps because her mother died when Jane was only two, she idolized her father, cherished her time with him, and strove for his approval. Fortunately for Jane, her father supported female education, but unfortunately he made no parallel commitment to a daughter's independent decisionmaking: despite Jane's longing to attend Smith College her father sent her to nearby Rockford Female Seminary.[8]

At the Seminary, Jane Addams blossomed. She achieved popularity with faculty and students and excelled in virtually everything she undertook. Here, too, she began developing her ideas about new roles for women. Of a collegiate woman, Addams wrote in 1880: "She wishes not to be a man, not like a man, but she claims the same right to independent thought and action." And the action that Addams alluded to subsisted especially in service to the world, which she argued had always been woman's duty: "So we [collegiate women] have planned to be 'Bread-givers' throughout our lives; believing that in labor alone is happiness, and that the only true and honorable life is one filled with good works and honest toil, we have planned to idealize our labor, and thus happily fulfill Woman's Noblest Mission."[9] With this reasoning, Addams was attempting to reconcile her ambition for independence with conventional female roles. The necessity for this reconciliation would continue to mold Addams's thought, self-presentation, and career.

As a student, Addams revealed other traits that would also follow her through life. Her popularity, for instance, seemed to result from her considerable intellect, a zestful enthusiasm for learning, and genuine engagement with every project, but she lacked warmth in personal relationships. In these, she seemed always to hold something back, to be detached, careful, deliberate. Addams wanted to control situations, and she seemed to believe that control required that she play her cards close to the chest. Even in letters to close friends, the seminarian refused to disclose too much of herself. In one such missive, she apologized for "how shallow my religion is"; and then suggested that she and her friend not discuss religion any more.[10] Later she would open a paragraph, "I will not write of myself . . . ," which might well have been her motto.[11] Too profound a self-revelation apparently threatened Addams's sense of independence and control, neither of which she was willing to relinquish.

In these ways, Addams could not have been more different from her closest college friend, Ellen Gates Starr. Born in 1859 to an Illinois farmer and small businessman, Ellen Starr craved intimacy and surrendered herself unself-consciously to passionate attachments. During her first year at Rockford, she opened herself to Addams, and, when a financial shortfall prevented her return thereafter, she continued her self-disclosures through the mail.

Though she would have much preferred to remain at Rockford, Starr bravely accepted the family's need for her labor. Of the break in her formal education she wrote to Addams: "I do not say I am not sorry, but I do this voluntarily . . . for when duty calls and bread and butter . . . it behooves me to respond."[12] In 1878, she took up school teaching and the next year received an offer to teach in Chicago at Miss Kirkland's School for Girls, an offer she felt she could not refuse. One of the enticements to the midwestern capital was proximity to her unmarried Aunt Eliza Allen Starr, who had made a reputation writing books on Christian art.[13]

At first, Starr was happy in Chicago. She enjoyed her teaching, her aunt, a group of close friends, and preparation for Harvard's entrance exam. Especially dear to her was the friendship of Mary Runyon, whom Starr described thus: "She is so *beautiful*. The first handsome friend I ever had."[14] In mid-1882, however, Runyon had to leave Chicago, and her departure occasioned Starr's expression of intense romantic communion with her friend: "The first real *pain* I had in parting, came with separation from her. I began to think myself incapable of that kind of feeling, finding that I am not is worth much more than the price." She went on to confide: "I don't speak of it [this feeling], because people don't understand it. . . . 'People' would understand if it were a man."[15] Starr's love for Runyon was one example of an ardent relationship between women that, though perhaps incomprehensible to the world at large, seemed perfectly acceptable in the world of middle-class women. Jane Addams certainly accepted Starr's profession of love for Runyon, as did other of Starr's female friends.[16]

Just as Mary Runyon's departure from Chicago signaled a deterioration in the quality of Starr's life, graduation from Rockford in 1881 sent Addams on a downward spiral. Though in February before her graduation, she reported that her "former vague dream to study medicine for a year in

Edinburgh is growing into a settled passion," by the following year, her father's sudden death and her own illnesses combined to thwart Addams's attempts to continue her education.[17] Now, she settled into the family fold, where for a decade she managed her late father's estate, helped to rear her nieces and nephews, and accompanied her stepmother on extended visits to Baltimore and Europe.[18]

Both Addams and Starr originally tried to enter professions through the same doors that admitted men, and both failed. Illness and family obligations blocked Addams's approach to medical school.[19] Harvard's discriminatory rules obstructed Starr: when she arrived to take the entrance exam in Chicago, proctors told Starr that women could take the test only in Cambridge, New York, and Cincinnati, even though women took precisely the same exam as male applicants.[20] Robbed of a specific object for her ambition, Starr grew weary with grading "huge piles of worthless compositions," and Addams showed even deeper dejection when she warned: "I will not write of myself or how purposeless and without ambition I am, only prepare yourself so you won't be too disappointed in me when you come."[21] Two years later, Addams complained that she remained "low in mind."[22]

Supposing a change of scenery might at least lift their spirits, the two women set out for a European tour with a mutual friend—Sara Anderson—in December 1887.[23] Both Starr and Anderson were in large part Addams's guests on this trip, and the three women spent some time together, some time separated. Several months into their tour, when Addams was off on her own, Starr revealed that she had developed the same fierce passion for Addams that she had earlier felt for Mary Runyon. Addams did not reciprocate. Referring to the big double bed that she and Anderson were sharing in Pompeii, Starr wrote to Addams: "I wonder if I am wicked to wish that you were on one edge of it, & I in the middle, comme toujours. I didn't know I was going to miss you so much." Starr continued in a characteristically passionate passage: "I knew well enough in Munich that I was going to sacrifice our old relation & never get it back. . . . but I'm too old now to say that I will never love anybody again as much as I can. It's about all there is worth doing, & if it pulls you to pieces a good deal when you have to give up what you've had & got dependent on—why let it!"[24] It is impossible to know how Starr sacrificed her previous relationship with Addams, but it is clear that the pair successfully reformed their understanding—probably in accordance with Addams's less ardent desires. Their friendship remained strong and central for several years yet, and they would never make a final break with each other.

Indeed, during their European trip, the couple lighted on a joint project that would cement their relationship as it suggested a way around the roadblocks in their careers. While in London, they visited the first settlement house in the world. Toynbee Hall, founded by Samuel A. Barnett in 1884, invited university men to live in the midst of a working-class neighborhood. The purpose of the settlement was to bridge the gap between London's educated and laboring classes, to promote understanding between those groups, and especially to provide education and culture to working people. Though Addams and Starr had surely witnessed similar poverty in American cities, the very unfamiliarity of London permitted them to see the suffering of working-class life with new eyes. So impressed were the two women by both the living conditions of working-class London and the settlement's response to those conditions that they determined to open their own settlement in Chicago.[25]

Addams and Starr were not the first American women to be intrigued by the settlement idea. Also inspired by trips to Toynbee Hall, a group of graduates from Smith College founded the Settlement Association in 1887. Chapters of the Association formed at Vassar, Smith, Wellesley, Bryn Mawr, and Harvard Annex. Opening its first settlement on Rivington Street in New York City, the Association began with seven female residents, and received over eighty applications for residence by the end of the first year.[26]

Relocating in working-class neighborhoods attracted educated women in America because it offered them wholly new opportunities in public life that could be justified as an extension of accepted female activities. On the conventional side, settlements appeared simply to extend female philanthropic activities. After all, the cult of true womanhood had slated women for leadership in charitable service, and because settlements required women to surrender themselves to the needs of others, they seemed to fulfill the imperative to female self-sacrifice.[27] On the innovative side, settlements promised women independence from their families, unique possibilities for employment, and the sort of communal living arrangement they had cherished in college.

More radical still, life in the American settlements would turn gender relationships upside down: women on top; men on the bottom.[28] Because men had alternative routes to independence, they did not flock to the settlement movement in the numbers that women did. Indeed, by 1911, the first year for which a measure of male and female participation was available, 53 percent of the 215 settlements reporting to investigators housed women only; less than 2 percent only men. The rest accommodated both sexes.[29]

But numbers only began to suggest the degree of female superiority in the settlements: women also dominated by strength of character. Beatrice Webb, who visited Addams's sex-integrated settlement in 1898, wrote in her diary that "the residents consist in the main, of strong-minded, energetic women, bustling about their various enterprises and professions, interspersed with earnest-faced, self-subordinating and mild-mannered men who slide from room to room apologetically."[30] To appreciate fully the significance of Webb's observation requires a listing of the individual men she described. During the late 1890s, Hull House's male residents included MacKenzie King, who would later become prime minister of Canada; Gerard Swope, the future president of General Electric Company; Earnest Carroll Moore, destined to co-found the University of California at Los Angeles and to serve as its vice president and provost; and George Hooker, a journalist and longtime director of the Chicago City Club.[31] In their own professional worlds, none of these men would have seemed "self-subordinating" or "mild-mannered." But in the settlement world, even aggressive and successful men deferred to women.

Female dominance at Hull House matched the blueprint that Addams and Starr had drafted for their project. Intending to create a predominantly female community, they recruited volunteers through Chicago's female organizations and philanthropic societies. They found the Chicago Woman's Club especially receptive. In 1889, the settlement project spoke directly to the emerging interests of such groups because they were in the process of shifting focus from literary and charitable pursuits to increasingly political activities. As these organizations enlisted college-educated members already well read and dissatisfied with their post-collegiate lives, the clubs themselves began to participate in a search for innovative female roles in American society. In 1890, isolated, local clubs gave their search a nation-wide base by uniting in the national General Federation of Woman's Clubs.[32] Very much a part of this national trend, the Chicago Woman's Club saw the settlement as potentially broadening women's opportunities.

This warm reception confirmed Addams's and Starr's suspicion that other women shared their discontent. Indeed, by May 1889, Addams could easily support her contention that the settlement idea had become "a fashionable fad"[33] among Chicago's leading ladies: an activist in the Chicago Woman's Club had invited thirty young women to hear Addams expound on her plan, and on the spot, several had offered to take up residence at the settlement and others to volunteer in its programs.[34] Furthermore, an article in one of Chicago's newspapers announced that the plan had won the support of "several rich ladies," and on first hearing the scheme, a male supporter insisted that he knew at least three young women who would jump at the chance to join Addams because they were "dying from inaction and restlessness."[35]

Addams later identified that female "inaction" as a subjective motive for the settlement movement in America. In her famous essay, "The Subjective Necessity for Social Settlements," Addams argued that America's middle-class women were "taught to be self-forgetting and self-sacrificing, to consider the good of the whole before the good of the ego." But "when the daughter comes back from college and begins to recognize her social claim . . . the family claim is strenuously asserted. . . . " As a result, according to Addams, "the girl loses something vital out of her life to which she is entitled. She is restricted and unhappy; her elders, meanwhile, are unconscious of the situation and we have all the elements of tragedy."[36] Settlement life offered a worthy vocation for these tragic figures, who otherwise languished in a society that had little use for them.[37] The success of the settlement movement at the turn of the century thus represented the middle-class female quest for a new place in American life.

In addition to the subjective necessity for settlements, Addams identified an objective need: the great chasm that separated America's working and middle classes. In fact, Addams defined a settlement as "an experimental effort to aid in the solution of the social and industrial problems which are engendered by the modern conditions of life in a great city."[38] And in 1889, when Addams and Starr were recruiting for their settlement, Chicago certainly exhibited all of "the social and industrial problems" that "the modern conditions of life" could hope to produce. Many problems of housing, transportation, and sanitation stemmed directly from Chicago's phenomenal rate of growth in the late nineteenth century. Representative of urban centers all over the country, Chicago more than doubled its population in the decade between 1880 and 1890.[39] Mushrooming from 503,000 to over a million inhabitants, the midwestern city admitted immigrants from Germany, Scandinavia, Poland, and Italy to such an extent that by 1890 almost 78 percent of Chicagoans were either born abroad or were children of parents born abroad.[40] Also indicative of national trends, Chicago had become an industrial center with almost one-half of its working population engaged in manufacturing and mechanical trades.[41] Moreover, as Chicago's cultural diversity increased, the city's work force embraced not only more ethnic groups but also more women. Between 1870 and 1890, the number of women in the city's work force quintupled, with 41 percent of the total in domestic service and 31 percent in manufacturing.[42]

As these workers moved the United States past all other countries in industrial production—by 1900, the United States produced more than Britain, France, and Germany combined—their employers grew richer and more aloof. In Chicago, such men as George Pullman, the railroad-car manufacturer, meat-packers Philip and Joseph Armour, and Cyrus McCormick, the maker of agricultural equipment, benefited from a trend toward the consolidation of industrial enterprises that could monopolize huge sectors of the national economy. Marshall Field and Potter Palmer made fortunes respectively in retailing and real estate. The opulent lives of these magnates, expressed in magnificent homes on Prairie Avenue in the 1880s and on the Gold Coast in the 1890s, stood in stark contrast to the poverty of their employees. Chicago's immigrant working classes crowded around factories and stockyards in tenements often unsafe and always lacking the amenities enjoyed by Chicago's elite.[43]

It was especially the contrast between these groups that concerned Jane Addams, Ellen Starr, and growing numbers of middle-class Americans. As railroads, mail-order houses, and business mergers brought America's far-flung communities closer together, those same advances seemed to split individual communities into hostile classes. America, once divided by distance and region, now appeared to be dangerously divided by economic class. Embodied especially in over 23,000 strikes that punctuated the century's last two decades, class conflict seemed constantly to threaten national unity.[44] Perhaps the most famous and anxiety-producing conflict of all occurred right in Chicago, where several police and workers were killed in the Haymarket Riot of 1886.

Thus, driven by their own need for meaningful work and drawn by the social problems they might solve, Addams and Starr opened their settlement at 335 South Halsted Street on September 18, 1889. Located in an immigrant neighborhood on the southwest side of Chicago, the mansion of the late Charles Hull provided enough space for a start and promised more room in the future. The women originally rented only part of the house because several businesses operated out of the ground floor. Dilapidated houses and commercial strips suggested that Halsted Street was a perfect place to begin what one columnist called an "interesting departure in humanitarian work."[45]

When Addams and Starr first settled into the Hull mansion, their plans were vague. No one knew exactly how the women intended to bridge the gulf between classes or provide a "people's parlor."[46] Addams herself referred to the first year as "experimental," a time during which she and Starr would get to know their neighbors' needs.[47] Until familiarized with the neighborhood, the women followed Toynbee Hall's example: they organized social clubs for the young according to age and sex; parties for all according to nationality; lecture series for adults; concerts and exhibits. From the beginning, the settlement housed a kindergarten and sponsored a visiting nurse.[48]

During the next few years, the settlement proved a remarkably flexible institution, devoted especially to serving women and children. As Addams and Starr acquainted themselves with immigrants from southern and eastern Europe, who constituted the bulk of their neighbors, they witnessed the problems encountered by these newest groups of America's working class. When the women became aware of a specific problem, they endeavored as best they could to solve it. Having discovered by 1891, for instance, that mothers in these families often worked outside the home, Addams and Starr opened a day nursery. By then familiar with the vagaries of wage-paying employment, they started a free labor bureau for men and women. Remembering with nostalgia the fresh air and wide-open spaces of their rural childhoods, the women opened Chicago's first public playground. Growing concerned about the horrid working conditions and low pay suffered by working-class women, Addams began to invite female labor unions to meet at the settlement, and she raised funds to build a cooperative living club for working women just down the street from Hull House. Grateful residents named it the Jane Club. In addition, the settlement experimented with a public kitchen to offer cheap meals to working parents and a cooperative coal association for the neighborhood. In those early years, the residents also sought in individual cases to support deserted women, widows, and injured workers.[49]

To operate these programs, Addams and Starr steadily increased the number of residents at the settlement. During the first year, most of the help came from non-resident volunteers. Cramped quarters, continuing repairs on the house, and uncertainty as to the future of the venture prevented an immediate flood of permanent residents from joining the founders.[50] By fall 1891, however, Addams and Starr had taken over the entire Hull mansion, and several other women moved in with them. Two years later, with more property and programs, the settlement housed 15 permanent residents, and in 1896, it boasted 25. After the turn of the century, that number more than doubled.[51] Throughout the 1890s, women dominated the residential force: in 1894, it comprised 13 women and two men; in 1896, 20 women and five men; in 1899, 18 women and six men.[52]

These residents were handpicked by Addams and her growing cast of permanent residents. Every woman who wished to reside at Hull House had first to apply for admission, then to submit to a probationary period, and finally to face the decision of current residents as to whether she should receive the privileges of permanent residency. During this process, the community scrutinized novitiates especially for the "settlement spirit," which, because it was never defined, gave current residents the power to exclude anyone they did not like. This exclusivity assured the settlement some degree of cohesion and internal peace, as it resulted in the selection of an elite group of highly educated, middle-class women and men.[53]

Once ordained to permanent residency, a woman was beholden to the settlement community at every turn. She must, for instance, either attend the weekly meetings at which residents decided domestic as well as programmatic matters or present Addams with an excuse for her absence. She must participate in the full spectrum of settlement activities, which ranged from staffing the settlement's programs to cleaning the dining room. In the early years, she must also take her turn at supervising the playground, answering the front door, and serving the communal meals.[54] No resident could claim much time as her own, and because she lived and worked with the same group of people, most aspects of her life were subject to her colleagues' evaluation.

Not every opinion mattered equally, however, for within this community of women, a hierarchy emerged. Satisfying her need to dominate, Addams reigned supreme. She presided at all meals and residents' meetings; she represented the residential force on the board of trustees after it formed in 1895; and she controlled other residents' professional opportunities by assigning them jobs at the settlement. With very few exceptions, residents knew that the settlement belonged to Addams, that without this one woman, there was no Hull House. One male resident described Addams's ascendancy this way: "The essential fact of Hull-House, the dominant fact, was the presence of Miss Addams." He admitted that this sense of her overladyship was "strange because while one was living there Miss Addams was away a good deal of the time, and when she was there one did not have a great deal to do with her; yet Hull-House," he went on, "was not an institution over which Miss Addams presided, it was Miss Addams, around whom an institution insisted on clustering."[55] A close friend of Addams later contended that her refusal to relinquish any power to other residents prevented them from developing their full potential. She said that one long-term resident of Hull House "would be even better [at her job] with a little more responsibility, more than J.A. has ever been willing to give anyone."[56]

In the settlement, then, women created a social structure that allowed women to dominate men but did not make all women equal. In fact, Addams's position was so powerful that other women's authority depended on the degree of intimacy they established with her. Those residents, volunteers, and trustees who won Addams's confidence and formed the closest friendships with her occupied the second rung of authority in the settlement's hierarchy. They enjoyed the prerogative of calling her Jane or J.A. and could even tease the great woman, a liberty no others dared to take.[57]

Especially as Hull House grew in size and Addams's leadership extended beyond her own institution, new residents found it difficult to forge solid ties with her. Consequently, from 1895 to about 1910, Addams's group of intimates remained pretty much the same, thus freezing the ruling caste. Mobility occurred among the lower ranks of permanent residents, who could distinguish themselves from each other by impressing Addams's familiars rather than Addams herself. Julia Clifford Lathrop, one of the founders' closest friends, proved particularly committed to identifying gifted residents and drawing them through the ranks to hold authoritative positions. Recognizing Lathrop's commitment, Addams wrote: "From her very first years at Hull-House Julia Lathrop most brilliantly displayed her genius for friendship with the very young residents. . . . "[58] Many women would later attribute their successful careers to Lathrop's sponsorship, and surely no woman at Hull House doubted that her position within the settlement depended on support from other women farther up the ladder.

While mentorship and professional need bound together the various strata at Hull House, warm personal relationships united women within each stratum. Some pairs—like physicians Grace Dewey and Josephine Milligan—left the settlement to live together permanently.[59] Others, eventually separated by marriage or their own careers, remained intimately connected until death, meeting as often as possible, spending holidays together, and always depending on each other through correspondence.[60] One settlement resident would later say of her roommate at Hull House: "Clara and I have lived together, in the same room, for eighteen years more or less, and I have the tenderest affection for her, and so close a knowledge of her that nothing she could do would antagonize me for long. I could not think of a life in which Clara did not have a great part. . . . "[61] Another resident could write that "we were a kind of family group."[62]

In the earliest years at Hull House, Addams herself formed a very intimate relationship with a devoted volunteer, Mary Rozet Smith. In a short time, their friendship took on the character of a marriage as Smith performed as wife to Addams until Smith's death in 1934. Smith, the daughter of a wealthy Chicagoan, thus replaced Ellen Starr in Addams's affection, a replacement that Starr accepted reluctantly. "I have always—at any rate for a great many years—been thankful that Mary came to supply what you needed," she wrote to Addams late in their lives. "At all events, I thank God that I never was envious of her in any vulgar or ignoble way." She continued in her brutally honest vein: "The envy I did feel of others' gifts & graces & their just fruits which I know was a great treat to you, I have repented of for a good many years. . . . "[63] What Addams needed and received from Mary Smith was an uncritical, unchallenging, quiet, and utterly reliable sort of love. For Addams, Starr was too passionate and demanding. Starr wanted to get too close; she would not admire from a distance, she would not be satisfied with the shadows. Smith, by contrast, was much gentler and satisfied by the role of helpmeet to a great woman. One mutual friend described Smith's devotion this way: "Mary was in the habit of following her [Addams] around with a shawl, pocket handkerchiefs, crackers if she thought Miss Addams might be hungry, or anything else she might want, and was always ready to supply Miss Addams' needs, whatever they were."[64]

Just as a Victorian wife was supposed to do, Smith took her identity strictly from her relationship with Addams. Only one year before her death, Smith wrote to Addams: "You know that you have made my life—all its meaning and its color have come from you. I bless you for it and wish I could ever show you how much I care."[65] Another mutual friend recognized Smith's supportive role when she said to her: "In all of Miss Addams' triumphs and achievements, I associate you, you who 'clear the way' from constant obstacles, you who give love and devotion and inspiration. . . . "[66] Mary Rozet Smith was the great woman behind a great woman.

Such private, life-sustaining relationships as the one between Addams and Smith were not unrelated to the public success of turn-of-the-century women. Most college-educated women in the 1890s saw their options as career or marriage.[67] To combine the two—especially given the unreliability of contraception—seemed nearly impossible. But the choice against marriage was not a foreclosure on rich, emotional partnerships; indeed, quite the opposite. For women living in settlements, a life without husbands or children allowed them not only freedom to pursue careers but also the opportunity to live in communities where they might form a particularly strong relationship with one woman while continuing numerous other crucial friendships. No single relationship had to bear the burden of all the partners' needs because each lived amidst so many like-minded women. As other historians have concluded, this foundation of personal support that women provided each other in the settlements made their public lives possible.[68]

Less intimate female relationships also supported work in Addams's settlement. These were collaborations with rich matrons who helped Addams to pay for the services of settlement workers. The kindergarten at Hull House, for instance, depended on funding from Chicago's Kindergarten Association. Women of means formed the Association and raised funds for kindergartens all over the city. Although the Association's primary interest was the education of children from disadvantaged homes, its financial support not only helped children but also paid the salaries of aspiring kindergarten teachers. At Hull House, two of the four kindergarten teachers were paid directly by the Association and could not have plied their trade without the support of their wealthier sisters.[69] The development of kindergarten teaching as an alternative for these professional women rested on the willingness of monied women to fund the professionalization process.

Where there were not existing organizations to support a resident's work, Addams sought individual patrons. At first Addams had drawn from her own independent income to pay the salaries of a few workers, but as the settlement grew, she began to ask wealthy friends to help finance the work of individual residents. By 1895, Addams had ordered the process. Whenever she identified a need in the community and found a woman ready to meet the need, Addams went in search of an individual donor to pay the worker's monthly salary. This Addams called the fellowship system. While soliciting a fellowship for Anne Withington, Addams described the system to Anita McCormick Blaine. Anne, she said, "is obliged to be self-supporting, and could not possibly give her time for less than $50.00 a month. It would cost her about $25.00 a month to live at the house, and as her mother is particularly dependent upon her, she could not possibly come for less. Several people—Miss Coonley, Mrs. Wilmarth, Miss Mary Rozet Smith, and Miss Colvin—pay sums of $50.00 a month, which are known as fellowships. The person receiving these sums devotes herself to a special sort of work and reports to me, of course, but directly to the persons giving the money."[70]

fellowship and women employees

Individual donors thus supported many of the budding professionals at Hull House. Ellen Starr herself was paid by fellowship. The four women who directed the settlement's day nursery received fellowships, as did the women who ran the labor bureau. Art, music, and gym teachers were usually beholden to a specific patron. When the settlement opened a model lodging house for dependent women, a fellowship paid the director, and even women who read to sick children in their homes earned fellowship money.[71]

The fellowship system allowed women to experiment with and to begin defining new professions. Many of the services provided by fellowships were supplied previously by volunteers in charitable organizations or not at all. Before 1890, no one could have earned her living by reading to sick children or minding the neighbors' kids. Schools did not yet hire teachers specifically to offer music or art lessons or to exercise their students. Unemployment did not earlier provoke the intervention of a professional devoted to nothing else save finding one a job, and few homeless women could have sought shelter in a lodging home whose director received a salary. Often, after a period of definition and testing, women convinced established institutions to incorporate these services into their regular programs. During the early twentieth century, public schools, for instance, began to hire kindergarten teachers, art teachers, and gym teachers as part of their permanent educational staffs. Municipalities and state governments established employment bureaus, and even charitable organizations replaced volunteers with salary-earning professionals.[72]

In other areas, too, this process allowed women to create altogether new professions for themselves. Originating outside of Hull House in the 1890s, a group of women in Chicago united to agitate for the establishment of a Juvenile Court. These women had been indignant to learn that young legal offenders were routinely locked up in the same jails and tried by the same procedures that shuffled adults in and out of the justice system. In keeping with a new view of childhood and adolescence as distinct stages in individual development, the women insisted that the justice system should treat juvenile offenders in ways appropriate to their age. Because the young remained impressionable, their mode of detention and their court itself should simulate the home, nurturing the youthful charges toward a responsible and respectable adulthood. In 1899, the women won the country's first Juvenile Court. To their dismay, however, the law called for clerks and probation officers but allocated no funds for salaries. Determined that women who filled these positions should not be volunteers but self-supporting professionals, the women who had lobbied for the court raised funds to pay the court's probation officers and clerks. The president of the committee resided at Hull House, and the group moved its meetings to the settlement. The first probation officer hired by the committee was also a resident of Hull House, and the fundraisers met with the clerks and officers regularly to discuss their mutual responsibilities and performance. Not until eight years later did the committee convince the county government to pay these officials from the public coffers.[73]

Visiting nurses had the same sort of help from non-professional women. In the 1880s and 1890s, wealthy women in American cities formed Visiting Nurses Associations. The purpose was primarily charitable: to provide nursing care to those who could not otherwise afford it. As with kindergarten teachers and probation officers, however, the nurses themselves were equally beneficiaries of this charity. Paid by generous women, nurses demonstrated the value of their services. After the turn of the century, nurses and their benefactors convinced schools, municipalities, counties, and even states to hire women to conduct public health programs.[74]

In New York City, Lillian Wald founded a settlement for visiting nurses. Born in 1867, Wald graduated from the nursing school at New York Hospital in 1891. After practicing for a year at the Juvenile Asylum in New York, Wald entered the city's Women's Medical College, where she was asked to go to a Sabbath School on the Lower East Side to teach a mothers' class on hygiene. Stunned by the poverty she found during her visit to the immigrant neighborhood, Wald determined to quit medical school and to live among those who seemed to need her special nursing skills. To finance her move, she approached Mrs. Solomon Loeb, who had funded the health lessons at the Sabbath School. Wald, with another nurse in tow, stayed at the College Settlement on Rivington Street while looking for an apartment among Russian and Rumanian immigrants on the Lower East Side. She and her friend began immediately to build a practice among patients who could not pay them. Overwhelmed by the need, the women recruited two more nurses, moved into a larger place, and by 1900 housed fifteen nurses and several other residents who staffed the Nurses' Settlement, soon made famous as the Henry Street Settlement.[75] Lillian Wald was later credited with creating the first independent public health nursing service, establishing the independence of nurses from doctors, and defining nursing as a dignified profession for American women. Without the salaries paid by other interested women, however, Wald could never have defined public health nursing for female professionals.[76]

This process, whereby elite women funded the professionalization process for other women, was widespread and would continue through the early twentieth century. Historian Margaret Rossiter has identified what she called "creative philanthropy" as a strategy that women used to open educational opportunities in the sciences. Groups of fundraising women involved in these schemes slid their opportunity-seeking sisters into all-male educational programs on scholarships, bequests, and post-doctoral teaching fellowships specified for women only.[77] Moreover, wealthy women like Josephine Shaw Lowell in the late nineteenth century and Lucy Sprague Mitchell in the twentieth financed the careers of other women in philanthropic work, educational administration, pre-school education, and child development.[78]

In the 1890s, women were thus creating a professional culture different from that of the older, male professions. One reason for the difference was that women entered the professional world most successfully when they carved out wholly new areas of expertise in which they did not compete with men for jobs or training. Their successes increased when they could justify their professional ambitions as fulfillments of the Victorian imperative for women to serve children and the poor. Because this clientele could not afford to pay for services, female professionals looked to wealthy women for financial support. The incomes of female professionals, unlike those of men in law, medicine, or business, consequently came not from a fee-paying client but from wealthy benefactors who vicariously fulfilled their own missions through the professionals they supported.[79] This peculiar position required professionals to draw non-professional women into their work and to convince both client and patron that their services were important. Under these circumstances, the female professions could not develop the exclusivity of the older male professions. At precisely the time when those traditional male professions were seeking to increase their fees and status by emphasizing their esoteric knowledge, women were creating professions that depended on the cooperation of lay people.[80] Though specialization and specific training increasingly characterized those female professions, the women who claimed expertise had continually to interpret that knowledge to their lay sisters. They had to be popularizers as well as professionals.

These relationships provided a socio-economic motive for the peculiarities of the new female professions emerging in the early twentieth century.

But there were other motives as well. Recent research has shown that even before the late nineteenth century, women in America often performed the task of popularizing scientific knowledge in their voluntary organizations and women's magazines.[81] Moreover, female doctors in the nineteenth and early twentieth centuries saw as their special mission the dissemination of medical knowledge.[82] Thus, women in older, male-dominated professions and female amateurs, as well as women in the newer, female-dominated professions, were inclined toward this position as a bridge between the producers/practitioners of scientific knowledge and the utterly naive laity. The persistence of this inclination suggests that the educating role suited Victorian ideals of womanhood. The cult of true womanhood had envisioned women as the healers of divisions in communities. By popularizing technical knowledge, women were fulfilling their obligation to pull groups together, to heal the divisions between the educated and uneducated, between professionals and potential clients, between elite and mass. Thus, cultural constructions of femininity and the socio-economic location of aspiring women in the late nineteenth century provided the motives for the relative inclusiveness of new female professions and their propensity for popularizing.

Popularization was not, however, an exclusively female element of professions at the turn of the century. Simultaneous with the creation of female professions, men were shaping new service professions, many of which also aimed to ameliorate problems coughed up by industrialization and urbanization. Men were elbow-deep in the clay they were using to sculpt, for instance, innovative forms of engineering, social scientific research, city planning, journalism, and scientific management. Many of these new male professions—especially journalism—committed themselves to popularizing expert knowledge. Popularizing, then, was not a quintessentially female characteristic of professions at the turn of the century, but new female professions were nonetheless quintessentially popularizing. Furthermore, the *sources* of the popularizing element in the female professions were peculiar to women: the specific socio-economic and cultural position of women in the 1890s encouraged them to embrace popularization as a defining characteristic of the professions they were creating. Men drew the same commitment from different sources, and in both cases the refusal to hoard esoteric knowledge lowered the prestige of the new professions relative to the older male professions.[83]

In addition to popularizing scientific knowledge, the emerging female professional ethos valued self-sacrificing service. Whether in male- or female-dominated professions, women could not escape the cultural imperative to submerge their egos in service to others. While male professionals were also expected to serve, their professional culture did not define service as self-sacrificing. One historian has written: "The professional concept of service essentially required no more than competent performance; its altruism was general and abstract, a vague commitment to a disembodied, 'public interest.'"[84] This definition of service held true for professional men at the turn of the century. But for women, service continued to imply self-abnegation.

This peculiar element in the female professional ethos arose not only from turn-of-the-century constructions of femininity but also from the social positions of women creating professions. In order to maintain the sponsorship of their benefactors—those wealthy women funding the professionalization process—professional women had to direct their individual ambitions toward service. After all, the true object of the patronage of elite women was to aid the downtrodden—not to subsidize individual careers. Only by justifying an occupation in terms of service to the dispossessed could professional women solicit such support. In some sense, these professionals were conduits of charity: their labor *was* the charitable contribution of one class to another, and this position required an erasure of self on the part of women defining new careers.

Contrasting the experience of two female doctors at Hull House illuminates the power of this requirement in shaping the careers of female professionals. The first was Dr. Harriet Rice, a black physician who joined the residential force during the early 1890s and whose very presence at Hull House attested to the degree of social experimentation among middle-class women in the 1890s. After the turn of the century, the trend would be to support settlements specifically for African-Americans, and by 1910, there would be ten settlement houses in America specifically for blacks.[85] Hull House would support the Wendell Phillips Settlement, which housed both black and white residents and served a racially mixed neighborhood.[86] But in general, the settlement movement was white, and Harriet Rice was an exception.

From the beginning of her residency, Rice posed problems for Jane Addams not because of her color but because Rice showed no enthusiasm for serving the needy. Rice wanted to succeed in private practice. However difficult it was for white female doctors to establish private practices in the 1890s, the task proved doubly Herculean for black women. One study has shown that even the black middle classes usually chose white doctors, and if they did hire an African-American physician, sexism prevented their choosing a woman.[87] Racism and sexism thus combined to make private practice nearly impossible for black female doctors.[88] Nevertheless, Harriet Rice might have overcome the obstacles to a career in medical practice in the context of the settlement community if she had bowed to the requirement of self-sacrificing service. Residents of Hull House and the Jane Club provided the core of her practice, but she resisted supplementing that work with charitable service to the needy. In January 1895, Addams wrote to a friend: "Dr. Rice is . . . desperate about her financial situation, she has no practice save the Jane Club & H.H."[89] Referring to Rice's refusal to care for the settlement's "sick neighbors," Addams later insisted that Rice did not show "the settlement spirit."[90] Addams confessed: "I am constantly perplexed about her."[91] Other residents, concerned about Rice's situation, nevertheless dreaded discussing it with her. Of one resident who volunteered to suggest that Rice hire on with a hospital for blacks, Addams wrote: "Sister Lathrop has taken her life in her hands and is trying to induce her to go to the colored hospital. She said that I might find her in fragments upon my return."[92] Finally, Addams convinced Rice to accept a fellowship, but this grated on the independent woman, who—perhaps because of race—could see the fellowship only as charity.[93] Years later, Rice left Hull House over a mysterious dispute and tried elsewhere to realize her dreams.[94] She failed. In a 1933 announcement of her lay-off from the lab at Columbia University Medical Center in New York, Rice herself blamed sexism for her plight: "This is a man's world," she wrote, "and they won't let a woman get any farther than they can help—or hinder."[95]

Dr. Alice Hamilton, because she ultimately accepted the imperative to self-sacrificing service, had a very different experience from that of Harriet Rice. Hamilton—sister of Edith, the famous student of ancient mythology—took her M.D. from the University of Michigan's medical department in 1893. Four years later, she moved to Chicago to teach at the Woman's Medical School of Northwestern University and became a resident at Hull House. While earning her bread as a teacher and researcher, she opened a well-baby clinic at the settlement and conducted research on diseases in the neighborhood. But increasingly she suffered a conflict between the detached world of scientific research and the demands for social usefulness at Hull House. As she tried to balance her scientific ambitions and her desire to fulfill the female imperative to service, she found herself torn in so many directions that she felt she was not doing a good job of anything. Addams had defined the settlement as a place that would "translate knowledge in terms of life," and Hamilton wondered how "pathology could ever be ap-

plied to Polk street."[96] Because she was a behind-the-scenes sort of person who
enjoyed her scientific work and resented the settlement's distractions from it,
Hamilton feared that she did not have the settlement spirit and determined
at one point to leave. By that time, however, her personal qualities had
endeared her so to Addams and other settlement residents that they convinced her to stay on and promised to restrict their demands on her time.[97]

Ten years after her struggle began, Hamilton resolved the conflict between her duties as a scientist and as a woman. In 1908, the Governor of
Illinois asked her to join the state Commission on Occupational Diseases.
Through her pathbreaking research on lead poisoning in industry, Hamilton found her niche: she became the country's leading expert on—indeed
the founding mother of—industrial medicine. Industrial medicine satisfied
both Hamilton's desire to serve and her need to do medical research. Hers
was research aimed at exposing the health hazards in various industries and
at minimizing those dangers. So successful were her pioneering efforts in the
field that in 1920, Harvard Medical School hired her as its assistant professor of industrial medicine.[98] As with visiting nurses, probation officers, and
employment counselors, Hamilton created a new profession that reconciled
her professional ambitions and her desire to serve.

Within the settlement, success crowned only those who subscribed to
the ideal of service. Had Rice relinquished hopes of a lucrative private
practice, accepted the financial support of a patron, and bent her career
toward the needy, her biography might have read like Hamilton's. But Rice
rejected those terms and consequently isolated herself from the female
professional community, which was the only group that might have sustained her. Hamilton, who resented the demands of service, nevertheless
fulfilled them, and thus won the enthusiastic endorsement of the most
important women at Hull House. With their encouragement, Hamilton
endured her conflicting desires until she discovered a way to reconcile them.
The reconciliation brought her professional success as well as a peaceful
soul. Conformity to the service ideal was the price of her success.

Indeed, the service ideal itself exacted a price. Serving a clientele that
could not pay for professional services, the women at Hull House constantly searched for sources of funding. Because voluntary contributions continued only at the pleasure of individual donors who might at any time find a
more attractive cause for their largess, female professionals began to look for
more constant and reliable funds from the very beginning of their occupational experiments at Hull House. Usually, their patrons searched with

them, and often the most obvious source of continuous support was government. Soon after the settlement opened its employment bureau, for example, it began to lobby the state government for the establishment of publicly funded bureaus. In 1899, such legislation passed.[99] Services to young legal offenders finally found a continuous source of funding through the county government, and recreational specialists won municipal support for playgrounds. Even Alice Hamilton's success depended on governmental intervention because workers could ill afford to pay for studies of industrial diseases and employers did not care to.

In some cases, government was the first place that Hull House residents turned for financial support. The career of Florence Kelley serves as a case in point. Kelley arrived at Hull House in December 1891, a mother of three, immigrating to Illinois because of its relatively lenient divorce laws. Motherhood and divorce set her apart from the average Hull House resident, as did her association with radical politics. After graduating from Cornell University in 1881 and suffering rejection by the graduate school at the University of Pennsylvania, she eventually made her way to the University of Zurich. While there, she became a socialist and translated into English Friedrich Engels's *The Condition of the Working Class in England in 1844*. In 1884, she married a Russian medical student, Lazare Wischnewetzky, and the next year bore her first child. In 1886, the young family moved to New York City, where two more children were born and Wischnewetzky threw herself into the projects of the city's socialist party. When her marriage disintegrated, she took her children to Illinois, obtained a divorce, and resumed her maiden name. While lecturing at the College Settlement in New York, she had heard of Hull House and in 1891 decided to rebuild her life there.[100]

As this simple narration of Kelley's early life indicates, she was a strong and fascinating character. "Indomitable" probably described her best.[101] Unlike Addams, Lathrop, or Hamilton, Kelley refused to be cautious in her self-presentation: she was bolder, angrier, less bound by Victorian notions of womanhood. Moral passion ruled her, and what made this headstrong, incautious woman especially attractive was that she knew exactly who she was. She described herself as a "raging furnace" and as a person "consumed with burning indignation."[102] She wrote further: "I must warn you that my friends think my criticisms more candid than kindly, and must beg you to make allowance for an inborn brusqueness which has brought me much trouble."[103]

Though her ferocity never diminished, Kelley experienced a subtle transformation during her eight years at Hull House. She metamorphosed from a male-identified into a female-identified woman. The most crucial influence on her before her sojourn to Europe was her politician father, Congressman William "Pig-Iron" Kelley.[104] She later made an intellectual and political break from the congressman when she discovered the world of international socialism in Zurich, a male-dominated community in which she found other male mentors. Not until her marriage dissolved and she entered the female world of Hull House did Florence Kelley have colleagues and mentors predominantly female.[105]

As for her sister residents, Hull House provided Kelley with the resources she needed to define a new position for herself within American society. Because Kelley's special interests lay with industrial workers, Addams put her on a fellowship in the Labor Bureau.[106] Of this experience, she wrote to Engels in 1891: "I am . . . conducting a bureau of women's labor and learning more in a week of the actual conditions of the proletarian life in America, than in any previous year."[107] In 1892, Kelley convinced the Illinois Bureau of Labor Statistics to hire her to study the sweatshop system in Chicago's garment industry, and at the same time, Kelley's research as an undergraduate at Cornell and a socialist in New York convinced the federal commissioner of labor to recruit her to survey Chicago's slums for a larger investigation of workers' living conditions.[108]

Kelley drew her fellow residents into her research and appalled them with her findings. Especially touched by the miserable conditions under which women and children worked in the sweatshops, residents joined her and the Illinois Woman's Alliance (a cross-class umbrella organization for thirty women's unions and voluntary societies) in an effort to persuade the state legislature to regulate the sweating industries.[109] Every night for three months, the lobbyists scattered over Chicago to publicize their findings at meetings of trade unionists, benefit societies, churches, and social clubs.[110] With a group of prominent women and union leaders, Hull House residents moved their lobbying efforts to the state capitol, where the coalition convinced lawmakers in 1893 to pass a law prohibiting child labor, limiting the hours of work for women, and regulating conditions at the sweatshops. Under pressure from the Hull House community, laboring women, and allies among wealthy female Chicagoans, the governor appointed Kelley to enforce the new law. She thus became Illinois's first Chief Factory Inspector.[111]

Here women had turned to government for help in solving a social problem and in the process had carved out a new professional field for themselves with continued financial support from the state. As Illinois's Chief Factory Inspector, Kelley had her first steady job. She wrote to a friend that her appointment "assures us [her family] of permanent useful employment."[112] And that appointment allowed Kelley to open opportunities for other women as well. As her assistant chief inspector, she hired Alzina Stevens, another Hull House resident. Among her ten deputy inspectors, she employed four women, one of whom lived at the Jane Club.[113] Though Kelley's original interest in protective legislation flowed from her indignation at the industrial exploitation of women and children, her own need for paid employment surely solidified her commitment to governmental solutions to that set of problems. Concern for others and for self simply could not be separated.

Because their professional situations thus predisposed them to see governmental intervention as the solution to social problems, women at Hull House counted among America's first progressives. Historians refer to the first two decades of the twentieth century as the Progressive era because they constituted a period of vital response to the social and economic changes wrought by industrialization in the previous half-century. Literally millions of Americans organized in local, state, and national bodies to push for reforms of the industrial order.

Though members of many of those bodies would unite in the new and temporary Progressive party in 1912, there existed no truly unified progressive movement in these years but rather a hodgepodge of coalitions working for changes that often contradicted each other. Different social groups had different ideas about how the new industrial order should look, and in many cases, the same individual lobbied simultaneously for changes that now seem antithetical to each other. For example, in an effort to democratize government, reformers mounted campaigns for the direct elections of senators, women's suffrage, the use of referenda, and the right to recall representatives thought to betray voters' interests. At the same time, groups of reformers sought to streamline local governments by replacing political machines with expert administrators ostensibly responsible to no other bosses than efficiency and economy. Rule by unelected experts, of course, flew in the face of democratic ideals and in many instances represented the attempt of native-born middle classes to wrest control of city governments from immigrant groups.

As problematic for reformers as democracy were the gigantic corporations that had engulfed the American landscape during the late nineteenth
century. While some progressives—convinced that huge corporate entities
threatened the economic competition on which American mobility and
democracy depended—devoted themselves to busting trusts, others—cherishing the efficiency of larger enterprises—urged various levels of government simply to regulate industries so as to prevent rank exploitation of
either consumers or workers. From the latter motive came legislation to
guarantee the purity of food and drugs, to regulate railroad rates, and to
ensure the sanitation of manufacturing establishments and city streets. Often enough—as in the case of the first progressive president, Theodore
Roosevelt—reformers favored trust busting in some cases and regulation in
others.

Toward the plight of industrial workers progressive reformers took wildly different approaches as well. Some believed that government should take
the lead in ameliorating the suffering of the working classes by requiring
unemployment and disability insurance, public employment agencies, and
legal safety standards for industries. Others saw the salvation of the workers
in unionization; yet others, in the ever-increasing scientific management of
industry, which would reputedly so increase productivity that every worker
would earn a decent wage under clean and safe conditions. Distrustful of
management's good will, still other reformers organized consumers who,
through socially conscious buying, would force employers to do justice to
their workers. Some progressives advocated all of the above, attesting to the
difficulty of identifying any unifying motive or political agenda for the
various people agitating for change between 1900 and 1920.

In addition to the near impossibility of defining a single political agenda
for progressivism, historians face the confusion of trying to distinguish the
era of progressive reform from the late nineteenth century, which after all
faced the same problems as the early twentieth and also spawned enormous
and energetic reforming organizations. The Knights of Labor, the Women's
Christian Temperance Union, and the national farmers' alliances stood as
worthy examples of Gilded Age reform organizations. Was progressivism
simply the relocation of their agenda to the city? Certainly the three groups
listed here, along with the Populist party of the 1890s, espoused some goals
similar to those ringing through the Progressive era. They, for instance,
asked the federal government to regulate or own the railroads; they wanted
some sort of public control of the finance industry; they especially wanted
to create cooperative economic ventures that included consumers' coopera-

tives as well as cooperatively owned and run industries. In part, however vaguely, these reform groups were agitating against the centralization of private wealth and power that industrialization was creating, and they envisioned, however hazily, an economy based on cooperative ventures, some large-scale and centered in the federal government, some small-scale and centered in local communities.

In these ways, reformers in the Gilded Age sought to preserve democracy itself insofar as democracy meant that people should control their own lives. Seeing that laissez-faire individualism was rendered obsolete by corporations that swallowed individual entrepreneurs and located financial decisions in a small area of New York City, reformers tried to create a new economic basis for democracy in cooperative economic enterprises.

Sometimes progressive reformers sounded a lot like these Gilded Age agitators: the younger activists often echoed the call for a more democratic order and for governmental regulation of industry. In addition, some progressive reformers used the language and ideals of Christianity as the basis for their reforming zeal just as the older generation of reformers did. On the other hand, the Progressive era brought something new to the fore: a constellation of ideals, values, and methods revolving around the word "efficiency." The heralds of efficiency—those social scientists, managers, and businessmen who aimed to rationalize and systematize American life—preached control by experts, created bureaucracies to manage problems, and preferred the sleekness of commissions to the roughness of elections. Both sets of ideals—democracy and efficiency—joined to produce Progressive reform.

In fact, the Progressive era might be seen as a beach on which the wave of Gilded Age democratic ideals had broken, surged, and just begun to recede when the wave of efficiency had broken and only begun to surge. Both waves were on shore, one overlapping the other; one surging, the other receding. Unlike the action of actual waves, however, neither would ever wash entirely away. Older democratic ideals continued to create an undertow that never allowed efficiency an entirely dry shore to saturate.

At times, the drives both for efficiency and democracy encouraged the expansion of government into the social and economic life of the country. Accordingly, one hallmark of the Progressive era was the growth of federal policy beyond tariffs and treaties. During these years, the federal government reached into communities to form more intimate relationships with individual citizens and corporate enterprises. The distance between public and private institutions shrank, and the relatively passive and transcendent governments of cities, states, and the nation grew increasingly active and imminent in citizens' lives. That activity occurred largely in new government bureaucracies that studied and ultimately aimed to manage social problems.[114]

Insofar as progressive reform meant the expansion of government especially into areas of social welfare, women loomed large in progressive reform. As the early years at Hull House show, female participation in that area of reform grew out of a set of needs and values peculiar to middle-class women in the late nineteenth and early twentieth century. Settlement workers did not set out to become reformers. They were rather women trying to fulfill existing social expectations for self-sacrificing female service while at the same time satisfying their need for public recognition, authority, and independence. In the process of attempting to weave together a life of service and professional accomplishment, they became reformers as the wider world defined them.

Indeed progressive reform cannot be fully understood without the specific study of female reformers. Even if middle-class women worked closely with and shared many ideals with their middle-class male counterparts, women and men came to those common enterprises from different motives and with different experiences. Surely the peculiar situation of aspiring professional women in the 1890s—as exemplified by the women at Hull House—should be counted as one of the causes of Progressive reform and as one explanation especially for the early twentieth century's enthusiasm for governmental solutions to social problems.

As other historians have concluded, Florence Kelley more than any other resident transformed Hull House from a philanthropic organization into an engine of social reform, and her approach to social problems became the model for the settlement's reformers.[115] Drawing on the experience of a small group of early social scientists, Kelley taught her sisters to begin their crusades with investigations into specific problems; armed with these facts, to publicize the issues and offer solutions; supported by public opinion, to lobby the government for programs to enact the solutions; based on their expertise in the area, to demand their own appointment to administer the new program. This was a route to reform and to professional success for women.[116]

After completing Kelley's slum survey, Hull House residents undertook their next major research project under her direction. In 1895, that effort produced *Hull-House Maps and Papers*, a survey of the settlement's neighborhood based on ethnic group, occupation, and income. Various residents took responsibility for different chapters, and Addams carefully negotiated the publication process.[117] This team effort put Hull House itself on the map of social research institutions and lured new kinds of residents to the settlement. Increasingly, residents and volunteers came from universities with strong social science departments, and the prominence of Hull House as a "social laboratory" inspired many such departments to open their own settlements both to offer service to working-class families and to provide students with unique opportunities for research.[118]

Just as commitment to social research thus became a hallowed tenet of the Hull House professional code — and to the residents' version of reform — so did opposition to political patronage. Kelley's experience as a factory inspector explained why. While she was inspecting factories for Illinois, the courts declared several provisions of her law unconstitutional, and in 1897 a new governor replaced her with a political crony who cared very little about enforcing the remaining provisions.[119] Based on such experiences, Kelley and her colleagues grew disgusted with the practice of political patronage. Not only did they hate to see their cherished laws gutted by the appointments of lackadaisical administrators, but they stood to lose professional opportunities when patronage ruled. Because women could not yet vote and were not welcome in political parties during the 1890s, patronage effectively blocked them from competition for any position within governmental agencies. Only by replacing the patronage system with hiring based on expertise could women hope to gain and hold jobs in public administration.

Middle-class women were certainly not the only people to oppose patronage in the Progressive era. Indeed, many groups agitated for a governmental service based on skill and merit, and civil service reform moved from the fringes to the center of political discourse in the early twentieth century. Nevertheless, female interest in the issue had meanings peculiar to middle-class women especially because of their complete exclusion from political parties.

Though professional and political self-interest encouraged women to support civil service reform, self-interest certainly was not their conscious motive. Genuine and profound concern for those disadvantaged by unregulated industrial capitalism was their conscious motive for commitment to civil service reform as it was for their devotion to social research and to governmental activism. Nevertheless, that concern could have taken many forms. The very same concern might have expressed itself in a commitment to revolutionary Marxism, trade unionism, or scientific management, to name a few alternatives. Professional and political self-interest explain why women at Hull House largely disregarded those options and chose instead a reforming strategy that expanded the state into social welfare through bureaucracies filled by experts. That strategy not only promised some relief of working-class suffering but also increased opportunities for middle-class women.

Julia Lathrop was one Hull House resident who made her name in local reform circles by heroically opposing patronage. Born in Rockford, Illinois in 1859, Lathrop attended Rockford Female Seminary for one year and then Vassar College, from which she graduated in 1880. Like Addams, Lathrop returned to her hometown after taking her degree. There, for a decade, she played secretary to her father's legal practice. She met the young Addams while helping to produce a play at Rockford, and when her acquaintance later advertised a venture on Chicago's southwest side, Lathrop migrated to the promise of broader opportunities.[120] Almost immediately, Addams hailed her as "the best resident we've had all winter" and substantiated the accolade by drawing Lathrop into the circle of favored residents.[121]

For Lathrop, as for others, Florence Kelley and the depression of 1893 proved formative. Lathrop and Kelley, both intelligent, witty, and energetic, formed a profound friendship during their early years at Hull House.[122] Intimates of Addams, they played leadership roles in the settlement's community. Kelley introduced Lathrop to the plight of laboring women and children, social research, and methods of reform; the depression of 1893 acquainted her with public institutions for the dispossessed. During the depression, Lathrop served as an agent investigating applicants for relief from the county. More interesting to Lathrop than the applicants, however, were the institutions charged with offering relief. Asylums for the insane and the disabled particularly disgusted her and supplied fertile ground for a Kelleyesque approach to reform. Lathrop's opportunity to put the process in motion opened during the depression, when the Governor of Illinois appointed her to the Illinois Board of Charities, a commission charged with oversight of the county institutions that Lathrop already abhorred. While a commissioner, Lathrop visited every county institution in the state and publicized her findings in articles, annual reports, and speeches. To increase her expertise on the subject, she read widely in the field of mental health and twice toured Europe to broaden her knowledge of the options for treating the mentally ill. In 1905, she firmly established her reputation by publishing *Suggestions for Visitors to County Poorhouses and to Other Public Charitable Institutions*. In this work, she suggested the segregation of patients based on age and disability and the replacement of county institutions for the insane with "more responsible humane and intelligent care" in state hospitals.[123]

From the start of her investigations, Lathrop railed against political appointments to executive positions in public charitable institutions. In discussions with administrators of Illinois's 102 poorhouses, she discovered what she considered an appalling lack of knowledge about the problems that the institutions were supposed to treat, and as early as 1895, published her contention that appointments to the charitable institutions should occur not in closed political caucuses testing for loyalty to the party but "in the open labor market, for fitness, by examination."[124]

Later experience only increased Lathrop's antipathy toward patronage. After she had spent eight years persuading institutional directors to implement changes in their treatment of public charges, a new governor ransacked the states' charitable institutions for jobs to give his political supporters. Lathrop resigned from the Board of Charities in protest against the move. In 1905, she resumed her seat under a more amenable governor, and in 1909 won a coup when the state abolished the voluntary Board of Charities and established a salaried Charities Commission, which supervised three inspectors for each of its institutions. By that time, Lathrop herself was so deeply involved in the Juvenile Court movement that she gladly relinquished her position on the Board.[125]

Through this sort of leadership in the cause of research and reform, Hull House residents achieved national as well as local fame. In Chicago, Addams and Starr had won widespread publicity even before their settlement opened. Through women's magazines like the *Woman's Journal*, the venture caught national attention. Naturally, journalists followed their story to see whether it would meet success or failure. Because residents needed publicity to fund their programs and to lobby for their legislation, they continually fanned out to speak and debate before existing women's societies, civic clubs, labor organizations, and reform groups. Furthermore, the residents regularly published articles, pamphlets, and eventually books containing their research findings and suggestions for reform.

At the national level, residents helped to form new reform organizations and to transform older organizations into tools for change. As early as 1892, when only a handful of settlements existed, Addams and Lathrop represented Hull House at a conference on applied ethics in Plymouth, Massachusetts. There, Addams read two papers on the meaning of settlement life before a group that included those already active in the settlement movement. The lectures established her unquestioned leadership in the as yet small movement, and the conference itself established a precedent for informal annual meetings of America's settlement workers. Although they would not found the National Federation of Settlements until 1911, residents all over the country stayed in close touch, copied each others' programs, and formed a national community of mutual interest and support.[126]

Eventually, settlement residents transformed an older organization, the National Conference of Charities and Corrections. Because the settlements wanted to distinguish themselves from charitable organizations, their leadership at first shied away from the Conference of Charities. Though Addams used the popular image of a philanthropic institution to attract funds and residents to her settlement, she and her colleagues insisted that they did not distribute alms but rather provided a meeting ground in which middle- and working-class people learned from each other and combined their resources to solve public problems. The connotations of charity contradicted the mutuality of the relationship that settlement residents claimed characteristic of their endeavor. Still, many of the settlements' programs reached the same population that the charities touched, and settlements regularly served as referral depots to those distributors of benevolence. During economic crises, the settlements provided convenient locations for temporary service centers sponsored by local charities, and settlement residents were among the first to urge reform in the concept and delivery of services to the indigent. The settlements and charities could not ignore each other; they constantly collided.

As a consequence, the settlements' leadership began attending the conventions of the National Conference of Charities during the late 1890s. At first the newcomers did not feel comfortable with the implications of their attendance and were not at all sure they were welcome, but soon settlement residents attended in ever greater numbers, presented papers, and led discussions. They did in this forum what they did best—persuaded audiences of the virtues of their approach to social problems. By 1909, the leadership of the Conference represented the settlements, with Addams elected its first female president. During the next few years, the Conference became a prime mover on the progressive scene: it urged governmental regulation of child labor, mothers' pensions to support dependent children, unemployment and disability insurance, and other reforms. In the Conference, later the National Conference of Social Work, settlement workers increased the breadth of their reforming network.[127]

Settlements also hooked up with other reforming organizations when residents from the settlement moved on to head those groups. In 1899, Florence Kelley, for instance, accepted an offer to serve as executive secretary of the National Consumers' League. Recently formed, the Consumers' League sought to influence industrial working conditions by educating consumers to purchase only those goods produced under humane conditions. Under Kelley's leadership, the League increasingly advocated legislation to control those conditions and took the lead in coalitions opposed to child labor. In order to take her new job, Kelley moved to New York City and lived at the Henry Street Settlement with Lillian Wald. As often as possible, she returned to Chicago to roam the halls of Hull House, and even years later Addams would bemoan the loss of Kelley from her residential force.[128] But Kelley's move provided an especially strong link between Hull House and the Henry Street Settlement, between the Consumers' League and the settlement movement.

Settlement workers played leadership roles in the National Women's Trade Union League as well. Two former Hull House residents, William English Walling and Mary Kenny O'Sullivan, founded the NWTUL in 1903. With the blessing of the American Federation of Labor, the two activists set out to create an organization for all working women, modeled on the British Women's Trade Union League. Addams served as vice president of the new group; Lillian Wald as a member of the board. Branches of the League opened first in Boston, Chicago, and New York, each at a settlement. Because middle-class women were invited to join the Union and often held the highest executive positions, men in organized labor distrusted the new group. Nevertheless, in the years before World War I, the NWTUL proved an effective organizer of female workers and a strong advocate of protective legislation for women in industry.[129]

In a variety of ways, then, women in the settlements were reaching out to form an informal, national network of reformers. Most prominent in the network were Addams, Kelley, and Wald, who never failed to support each other and who provided a solid connection between the reforming communities in Chicago and New York. Their connections with women's organizations such as the General Federation of Women's Clubs and the Mothers' Congress (later the Parent-Teachers' Associations) drew the leadership of those bodies and their millions of members into the network as well.

As these women played increasingly visible and important roles in America's public life, they continued to justify their activism through argu-

This would limit participation

ments based on Victorian assumptions about woman's nature. Women, they insisted, were born to nurture, and American society itself, torn by industrialization, needed nurturing. Middle-class women had always been mediators between classes as they voluntarily went into poorer districts to convert heathens, staff missions, and offer charity. No one, they argued, was better qualified to mediate between the working and middle classes in 1900 than America's women. Moreover, urbanization and industrialization had increased every family's dependence on forces outside the home. Addams argued that in the country a woman could keep her home clean by washing her own walls and sweeping her own stoop. But in the city, the filth of the streets invaded the home so that in order to fulfill her household duties, a woman must be interested in public services that kept streets clean and garbage collected. Similarly, on the farm, women controlled the quality of the milk, meat, and produce they fed their families, but in the city, where women purchased food from places far away, they had no control unless they convinced companies and legislatures to ensure unadulterated products.[130] "Woman's place is Home," proclaimed one female reformer, "but Home is not contained within the four walls of an individual house. Home is the community."[131] And community increasingly connoted the nation.

Given the persistence of Victorian ideas about female interests, women succeeded best in winning professional positions and in influencing public bodies when they addressed issues that affected women, children, and the poor. Legislators would listen attentively when women urged regulations of the milk supply but not nearly so earnestly when they discussed foreign policy. Male unionists expected their female comrades to organize women workers and not to play a significant role in larger union decisions. Female reformers might just have something when they advocated minimum wages and maximum hours for female laborers or children, but the value attributed to their suggestions often decreased where male workers were involved. Juvenile delinquency, deserted mothers, and infant mortality were issues on which women could speak with authority; they could staff women's prisons and judge in juvenile courts. But they were finding no place in the larger justice system, on trade commissions, or on committees reforming the tax laws.

The doctrine of separate spheres thus followed women into public life. Though women tried to influence policies and break into professions traditionally dominated by men—as had Addams and Starr and Harriet Rice—they were often turned back. Men who held that ground did not care to relinquish any part of it to ambitious women. Consequently, women began to create within the public realm a new territory they could rule themselves: it was that territory of policy and professional expertise which affected women and children exclusively.

During the 1890s, middle-class American women developed values and strategies that would permit them to build their dominion. They formed female communities bound together by a common commitment to new roles for women in the larger society. They proved themselves tireless social researchers and publicists. They made public issues of private matters that had always fallen under female authority and thus convinced men that they had a right to positions of power. To support their initial excursions into professional life and policymaking, professional women called on their wealthier sisters for support and grew accustomed to working with and depending on lay women. But at the same time, professionals were seeking to end their dependence on private benevolence and to convince established institutions, often government, to fund their services to an indigent clientele. This professional need led them to combine their search for individual opportunities with campaigns for the expansion of governmental involvement in social welfare, and through the national networks they formed, these women were gaining the strength of numbers and perspective needed to move these strategies from the local to the national level.

CHAPTER 2

A Dominion Materializes:
The Children's Bureau, 1903–1917

In 1905, Florence Kelley claimed: "The noblest duty of the Republic is . . . so cherishing all its children that they . . . may become self-governing citizens. . . . The care and nurture of childhood," she continued, "is thus a vital concern of the nation."[1] These assertions indicated the direction that Hull House women would take in the early twentieth century: they and their growing network of reforming women would begin seeking national influence, and child welfare policy would provide the field for their broader authority.

Representing the success of this new, national focus was the creation of the Children's Bureau in 1912. Situated in the Department of Commerce and Labor, the new agency became the first female stronghold in the federal government, and it provided the widening circle of female reformers an official leadership. In fact, by the time America entered World War I, the Children's Bureau presided over an interconnected set of organizations that joined the Bureau in attempting to control child welfare policy in the United States. Thus materialized a female dominion in policymaking, the evolution of which illuminates the continued interrelationship between the professional interests of white, middle-class women and their participation in progressive reform.

Settlement culture was partly responsible for the idea of a federal bureau devoted exclusively to children. Legend holds that, in 1903, Lillian Wald and Florence Kelley were enjoying breakfast as usual at the Henry Street Settlement, and in the habit of settlement breakfasts, residents were reading their mail and exchanging the morning papers. By this time, settlements had achieved reputations for their interest in social welfare and so received all sorts of letters seeking information and advice on current social problems. To Kelley fell the task of opening a letter that asked why nothing was done about the high summertime death rate among children. Tossing the letter to her colleague, Kelley suggested that Wald answer the inquiry. As Wald mused that she knew no source of information on variable death rates among children, Kelley read aloud an article from the morning paper, which announced that the federal government was sending the Secretary of Agriculture to investigate damage inflicted by the boll weevil in southern cotton fields. Wald is purported to have retorted: "If the Government can have a department to take such an interest in what is happening to the cotton crop, why can't it have a bureau to look after the nation's child crop?"[2]

Given the times, there seemed no reason at all. Two years before the fateful breakfast, Theodore Roosevelt had replaced the assassinated William McKinley as President of the United States. Already by 1903, the robust Roosevelt was urging the federal government to exert itself in new ways. Roosevelt believed that the national government should be interested in a wide variety of social and economic problems that it had previously avoided, and he created the machinery for such interest by convincing Congress to establish new executive agencies, by appointing special investigative commissions, and by calling for national conferences to debate and pass resolutions on specific issues. In the year of Wald's brainstorm, for instance, Roosevelt won congressional approval for a new cabinet-level Department of Commerce and Labor and appointed a public lands commission to study the consequences of public land laws. Whether Roosevelt's new executive agencies received mandates strictly to gather information or to manage some economic problem, they represented the arrival of progressive reform at the federal doorway.

Wald's proposal for a federal bureau to harvest data on "the child crop" fit perfectly into this new scheme of federal activity. She argued that children represented the future of the Republic and that the national community consequently had a legitimate interest in their well-being. Industrialism, the source of so many Progressive-era maladies, exploited children in numerous ways, according to Wald: sometimes through their own employment at early ages, other times through poverty resulting from their families' low wages. In order to know exactly what ills afflicted the nation's youngest citizens, to learn the causes of those ills, and to know whether any existing programs had yet remedied the sicknesses, reformers needed information gathered from all over the country. They needed comprehensive and continuous studies that only a federal agency could conduct.

This reasoning—in the context of Roosevelt's presidency—made sense of Kelley's legendary response to Wald's spontaneous suggestion. The ever-confident Kelley reportedly picked up her colleague's idea and marched it into the office of Edward T. Devine, sociologist at Columbia University and general secretary of the Charity Organization Society in New York. Devine operated at the center of reform activities in New York City and among the group of social reformers who were reaching out to form national networks. He edited *Charities*, a journal deeply involved in reform causes, and he had connections in high places. As Kelley had predicted, Devine responded enthusiastically to Wald's proposal and even wired President Roosevelt to arrange a meeting between Wald and the chief executive. In that first lobbying session, Wald is said to have won the President's support for a federal children's bureau.[3]

Although this legend squeezes events into a briefer time period than actually contained them, the tale accurately reflects the spirit of Wald, Kelley, and their reforming cohort. The confidence displayed by characters in the story is consonant with the real-life assurance of this generation of reformers. Kelley's prompt call on Edward Devine and Devine's subsequent cable to the President exemplified a faith that would remain unshaken during a nine-year drive for a federal children's bureau.

From 1903 forward, Kelley and Wald made the creation of a children's bureau one of their top priorities. They opened this crusade as they had opened many others—with a search for public support. In this instance, the crusaders had to reach a national audience instead of the usual local elites, and by this time they were ready for that challenge. They began by tapping into their organizational network. Jane Addams, of course, allied immediately with her friends and hooked them into Chicago's reform circles. As general secretary of the National Consumers' League, Kelley represented a national group dedicated to the reform of working conditions for women and children. Its support for Wald's idea was never in doubt. Edward Devine's backing won the cause editorial support in *Charities*, a powerful generator of favor among the nation's reformers, and eventually Wald and Kelley garnered endorsements from the settlements, the National Conference of Charities and Corrections, the General Federation of Women's Clubs, the Mothers' Congress, and local child welfare societies such as Chicago's Juvenile Protective Association.[4]

To draft legislation for the creation of a children's bureau and to steer the bill through the maze of congressional procedure, the women approached the National Child Labor Committee. Both women belonged to this temporary union of northern and southern opponents of child labor. At a convention of the National Conference of Charities and Corrections in 1903, members of the New York Child Labor Committee—organized by Kelley and Wald in 1902—heard Alabama's leading opponent of child labor call for a national movement against the employment of children. In response, the New Yorkers joined the Alabaman Edgar Gardner Murphy to organize the National Child Labor Committee on April 15, 1904.[5] Although the NCLC's southern contingent remained extremely small, the association's urge to expand reform efforts beyond local boundaries was very much in keeping with the times.

Wald and Kelley were leaders in the NCLC, but it was not a women's organization. Indeed, in October 1904, the general committee of the NCLC comprised 35 men and only five women.[6] As its first general secretary, the Committee hired Samuel Lindsay, a sociology professor at Columbia University whose distinguished resume included service as the Commissioner of Education in Puerto Rico. Both of the NCLC's full-time assistant secretaries were also men, Alexander J. McKelway from the South and Owen Lovejoy from the North. When, in the spring of 1905, Wald and Kelley convinced the NCLC to sponsor the fight for a federal children's bureau, they entrusted their idea to a sex-integrated organization concerned primarily with child labor.[7]

Female dependence on male help in this particular endeavor revealed the special stage of women's public involvement at the turn of the century. On issues regarding children, powerful men listened to women and were willing to act on female advice. But women as yet had little experience with the national government. Female campaigns for reform had previously succeeded at the local and state levels, where reformers used the influence especially of their wealthy sisters to pass legislation. At the national level, women had not yet established reputations compelling enough to assure a hearing without help from prominent men. Wald reached President Roosevelt, for instance, only through the intercession of Edward Devine, and the pattern continued when Wald and Kelley chose a sex-integrated organization to carry their program for a federal children's bureau into the all-male national Congress.

Their choice was a good one. By fall 1905, Samuel Lindsay had drafted a bill to establish a bureau for "the collection of information and the dissemination of the results of the latest scientific work on the care and protection of children—thus furnishing to the several states the basis for wise legislation and to the officers of state boards the information necessary for efficient administration of laws relating to the welfare of children."[8] In January 1906, Winthrop Murray Crane of Massachusetts introduced the Lindsay bill in the Senate. In May, Representative John J. Gardner introduced it in the House. Although both bills died in committee, the NCLC saw that a new bill appeared before Congress every year until its passage in 1912.[9]

While the NCLC intensified its lobbying through these years, the broader Wald/Kelley network strove for recognition as a national policy-making body. Only since the 1890s had reformers wrenched child welfare out of parental hands and subjected it to public authority. They had made juvenile delinquency, recreation, education, and child labor the subject of municipal and even state legislation. Such successes, however sporadic and tentative, had established child welfare as a legitimate public issue and thereby identified experts in child welfare as local policymakers. At the national level, however, these identifications had yet to be made. So far, children had not been scooped into the basket of federal concerns, an omission that left experts in child welfare outside the assembly of national policymakers. Through their campaign for a federal children's bureau, Wald and Kelley were thus edging child welfare onto the federal stage for the first time, and of course *female* reformers were inching onto the national platform simultaneously.

The first big break for these relative unknowns came in January 1909, when President Roosevelt allowed them a national audition. Just as he had called experts together to discuss issues relating to business practices, country life, and natural resources, Roosevelt invited over two hundred delegates representing the country's child welfare agencies to the first White House Conference on the Care of Dependent Children. The primary purpose of such conferences was to arouse public interest in a particular set of problems and, if participants agreed on the solutions to those problems, to build support for the solutions.

For the conferees on dependent children, the central substantive issue was how best to care for children whose parents could not provide for them. On that question, the conference was simply to provide a set of opinions that Roosevelt could then offer to the states to guide their care of needy children. Well before the conference, organizers clearly intended to recommend against institutional care and urge that whenever possible children be supported within their own families or in foster homes. Dominant opinion in the child welfare community weighed heavily on the side of keeping children with their biological parents, which explained that group's support for a variety of income maintenance programs that would allow parents to keep their children in spite of poverty.[10]

Roosevelt's invitation to the conference also asked, however, that attendees offer a recommendation on the creation of a federal children's bureau. By convening this meeting, Roosevelt meant to increase the pressure on Congress to create such a bureau and thereby to recognize children as an appropriate ongoing concern for the federal government. The President himself had failed to convince the Congress; now it was up to child welfare advocates themselves.

The stakes for female reformers were especially high. If the conference could persuade Congress that children should become a subject of federal legislation, then women would have their main chance for joining the national policymaking establishment. Jane Addams herself insisted that the convening of this conference alone gave child welfare work "a dignity and a place in the national life which it had never had before."[11] And by association, it gave child welfare workers—women included—a wholly new authority in national life.

At the conference, female delegates deported themselves well. They constituted a distinct minority at the conference—representing only 30 of the 215 members—but they made themselves heard on nearly every issue. Indeed, Addams and Wald delivered two of the key addresses to the group, and the proceedings show that though most agenda items sparked differences of opinion, the federal children's bureau was a striking exception. Not a single voice objected to the proposal for the bureau, a tribute to the success of Wald's and Kelley's outreach to the prime movers in child welfare work.

Disagreements did erupt, however, over the job description for a federal bureau. Wald pictured her agency as more than a data-gathering machine: "The Children's Bureau would not merely collect and classify information, but it would be prepared to furnish to every community in the land information that was needed, diffuse knowledge that had come through experts' study of facts valuable to the child and to the community."[12] Wald imagined the children's bureau as a national consensus builder, actively publicizing its findings, drafting recommendations, and working directly with local organizations to pass legislation that embodied its proposals.[13] In these ways, Wald's vision, affirming the popularizing commitment of the female professions, would elevate her federal agency to leadership in a national movement on behalf of child welfare.

Several of Wald's male colleagues at the conference argued passionately that the United States Constitution would not allow a government agency to do what one participant called "promotion work."[14] This contingent—and it constituted the majority of the conference—maintained that child welfare experts should create a voluntary organization to shadow the federal agency, interpret its findings, and lobby the states for programs.[15] As Homer Folks, secretary of the State Charities Aid Association of New York and co-organizer of the conference, put it: "There is, and must always be, a difference between the work that is proper to an organization which is a part of the machinery of the government, which is bound to represent all the people, and that of a society which is not bound to represent anything except its own members and its own particular views." He went on to insist that a government bureau's "possibilities would be greatly enlarged by the existence of a voluntary group of citizens, free to express their views on all subjects at all times, and thereby to make possible the molding of public opinion which later on would permit official action and official expression, which might not safely be taken at an earlier date."[16] Several important matters animated this debate between Wald and the (male) majority of the conference. One of the most significant was the nature of social scientific research. At the turn of the century, men who were in the process of creating the social sciences wrestled with the relationship between their emerging disciplines and politics. In many ways, the Gilded Age desire to reform American life had produced the social sciences, but as the new professions matured, their most powerful practitioners decided that they must avoid the appearance of passionate attachment to any particular political ideals. In the interest of establishing unassailable professional authority, the social scientists ultimately eschewed political ends, but allowed each other to serve as technical experts for organizations explicitly political. In other words, by the time of the Conference on Dependent Children, male social scientists had agreed that if they openly combined research and advocacy, they cast doubt on the objectivity of their research and thus lost credibility for themselves and their professions. As researchers, therefore, they must appear politically disinterested.[17] Wald's opponents were in part simply upholding this resolution to the supposed conflict between scientific objectivity and political engagement.

To Wald and her settlement colleagues, this bifurcation of research and advocacy seemed false. Since the early 1890s, they had combined data-gathering and lobbying to achieve some measure of public authority, just as had the earlier social scientists.[18] In fact, Wald and company were sustaining the older marriage between research and activism in their professions, politics, and institution-building.

The history of female professions easily explained this special refusal of women to divorce social investigation from political engagement. Because women in the newer female professions had defined their mission as self-sacrificing service, because they had won support for their public lives by offering themselves as funnels of aid from one class to another, they did not have the freedom to withdraw their research from some immediately useful end. Even the beloved Alice Hamilton could not rest secure in the developing female professional culture at Hull House until her medical research aimed explicitly to solve social problems. Women coming through the settlement network of the 1890s had a gender-specific need to reconcile their professional goals with Victorian ideals of womanhood, and this need produced a version of professionalism and a justification for public participation peculiar to women. Wald's insistence on the bureaucratic union of research and advocacy was one of the implications of that justification for female professionals and reformers in the early twentieth century.

Moreover, as these women moved their reforming strategies to the national government, their inclination to combine investigation and promotion encouraged them to advocate a more activist government than some of their male counterparts. Here Wald began to locate her place on the spectrum of opinion about how to involve the state in solutions to social and economic problems without creating an oppressive, homogenizing, state machine. As argued by historian James Kloppenberg, part of the progressive project was a search for the *via media* between nineteenth-century socialism and liberalism, and Wald along with most of the settlement community fit the description of progressives who aimed to increase equality and "social cooperation" without sacrificing individual freedom.[19]

Within the exploration for a *via media*, however, seekers disagreed over the allowable degree of state power, and the conflict between Wald and Folks suggested that gender played a part in determining positions on the issue. Wald's location on the side of greater state power resulted in part from peculiarly female experiences in the 1890s and early 1900s, because, for her, to advocate a research agency was at the same time to argue for a bureau that also made recommendations for policy and actively organized public support for those recommendations. This was not true for Homer Folks, whose experiences allowed him to separate research and advocacy. Of course, in 1909 not all women agreed with Wald or all men with Folks because gender did not alone shape experience. Nonetheless, along the *via media*, gender-specific professional cultures helped to define opinions on the proper role of the state and therefore to account for the political options available to Americans in the early twentieth century.[20]

Despite differences of opinion, the Conference on the Care of Dependent Children proved a great success and inspired congressional hearings on the children's bureau bill. During January and February 1909, both the House and the Senate heard testimony on the proposal, and women increased their visibility in Washington by counting among the witnesses called. Jane Addams, Florence Kelley, and Lillian Wald took the stand alongside Edward Devine, Samuel Lindsay, and Homer Folks. During subsequent hearings, too, the women bolstered their reputations as experts in a field struggling to enter the federal government's domain.[21]

On April 19, 1912, President William Howard Taft signed the children's bureau bill into law.[22] Although Taft himself was hardly a reformer, it was no accident that Congress finally passed the children's bureau bill in 1912. That year saw progressive reformers achieve their greatest cohesion with the formation of the Progressive party, whose presidential candidate was none other than Theodore Roosevelt, and they probably enjoyed the support of more Americans than at any other moment. Jane Addams, a key player in the Progressive party's first convention, described the exhilaration of 1912: "At moments we believed that we were witnessing a new pioneering of the human spirit, that we were in all humility inaugurating an exploration into the moral resources of our fellow citizens."[23] Progressive party members had a sense in 1912 that they were setting the intellectual and political agenda for the entire country. As Addams later explained: "During the Progressive campaign, measures of social amelioration were discussed up and down the land as only party politics can be discussed, in the remotest farmhouse to which the rural free delivery brought the weekly newspaper; certain economic principles became current talk and new phrases entered permanently into popular speech."[24]

Some of the new phrases that Addams referred to came straight from the list of social justice reforms that her crew of reformers had advocated for years and that had now found their way onto a political party platform. The Progressive platform advocated child labor laws, old age pensions, minimum wage and maximum hour legislation, workmen's compensation programs, and factory inspections.[25] It was a settlement worker's dream.

Although the Democrats soundly defeated the Progressives in the presidential election of 1912, the victorious Woodrow Wilson ultimately supported much of the Progressive agenda, and his first term as President certainly represented the culmination of progressive reform in the national *Woodrow* government. Wilson's administration created two of the most important *Wilson* regulatory agencies of the early twentieth century: the Federal Trade Commission and the Federal Reserve Board. Moreover, the staunch Presbyterian eventually advocated a federal child labor law, workmen's compensation for federal employees, and the eight-hour day for railroad workers.[26] He also appointed the progressive Louis Brandeis to the Supreme Court and a former official in the United Mine Workers as Secretary of Labor.[27] Thus, despite its loss at the polls in 1912, the Progressive party actually won much of its agenda during the Wilson years.

Congress finally created the Children's Bureau during the reforming fervor of 1912. The new agency received a broad mandate, which was to "investigate and report upon all matters pertaining to the welfare of children and child life among all classes of our people." Among the issues suggested for study were "infant mortality, the birth rate, orphanage, juvenile courts, desertion, dangerous occupations, accidents and diseases of children in the several States and Territories."[28]

With this wide range of issues from which to choose, the Bureau's chief had extraordinary discretion in determining the character of the new agency. The Bureau might become the leading opponent of child labor and harass employers the country over. Concentrating on orphans, it might advocate more efficient and humane institutions for dependent children. It might focus on the birth rate, become the chief herald of race suicide, and condemn educated women for not bearing enough children. Or, serving as an adjunct to the Census Bureau, it might simply compile vital statistics on the child population and advocate nothing in particular. The predilections of the Bureau's first chief, therefore, took on great significance.

As it turned out, that appointment held other importance as well. When President Taft signed the children's bureau bill, no one could have predicted that the new agency would establish the primacy of women in its area of public policy. After all, the Bureau enjoyed the support of a good mix of male and female reformers. Moreover, many congressmen expected that the Bureau's chief would be male, and the NCLC considered several men, including Samuel Lindsay, Homer Folks, and Alexander McKelway, for the position.[29] All were qualified candidates. Only three days after the children's bureau bill became law, however, female reformers made their move: Jane Addams wired both Lillian Wald and President Taft to say that "the Chicago group" supported Julia Lathrop's appointment to the new office. Lathrop, she said, would not actively seek the appointment but would serve if the President appointed her. That same day, Addams wrote more elaborately to Wald: "It does seem to me a pity not to have a woman, and a very able one in this position. . . . Let's try hard for a woman first."[30] Wald agreed, and she persuaded the NCLC to support Lathrop's candidacy. On April 17, 1912, Taft sent Lathrop's appointment to the Senate, where it received confirmation that same day. Thus, Lathrop became the first woman to head a federal bureau.[31]

Female settlement workers were following their pattern. Rather than competing with men for positions of authority in established areas of policy, they led in the creation of a brand-new field. When the logic of separate spheres encouraged men to cede this particular territory—child welfare—to women, female reformers were able to win their first bid for a position of official authority in the national government. Female reformers did not, of course, lobby for a children's bureau in hopes of gaining professional and political power for themselves, but in this case as in others, professional advancement for women was intimately connected to progressive reform.

In her own words, Lathrop was "dazed to find myself appointed" as chief of the United States Children's Bureau, and dazed was an appropriate response.[32] Although the new bureau chief had pioneered in the juvenile court movement and the creation of psychiatric facilities for children, her most spectacular achievements had occurred at the state level in her work on behalf of the insane.[33] Only because of support from the likes of Jane Addams could she have found herself in the country's most prominent child welfare position.

Addams surely recognized that, despite her vita, Lathrop's personality suited her perfectly for this sensitive post. Described by intimates as "sparkling," "full of humor," and "brilliant," Lathrop had proved above all to be diplomatic.[34] She rarely offended anyone, not because she kept quiet but because she listened before she spoke and then carefully but firmly stated her own case. Alice Hamilton once accompanied Lathrop on an investigation of a public asylum in Illinois and described Lathrop's *modus operandi*: "We were met by the Superintendent who was sulky and suspicious. . . . gradually under the influence of Miss Lathrop's cordial and uncritical attitude he thawed out; and presently he was pouring out all his troubles to her, going out of his way to point out what was wrong. . . . "After the tour concluded, "Miss Lathrop sat down in the office and proceeded gently but with devastating thoroughness to go over the whole situation and point out to the superintendent that after all he was the one in authority; if things were rotten it was he who must shoulder the responsibility. . . . We left him evidently impressed and promising to do his best, certainly not resentful in spite of her severity."[35] From an entirely different quarter came confirmation of Lathrop's diplomacy: Dr. Adolf Meyer, eventually head of the Henry Phipps Institute at the Johns Hopkins University Hospital, claimed that Lathrop was among the people who "[t]hrough an ability to bring together elements who otherwise could hardly blend . . . create a meeting ground for achievement."[36]

Lathrop herself later hinted at the source of her success: "I have been a most courteous & patient lady & a new *pose* will now be mine."[37] In public, Lathrop carefully constructed herself as a lady. She never put people on the defensive, and she tailored her dealings with each individual to fit her always shrewd assessment of their positions. Unlike Kelley, who came on like gangbusters, she was cautious; unlike Addams, who stood aloof, she was accessible. In her public persona, she brilliantly kept in tension expectations for Victorian ladylike behavior and those for intelligent, public authority. Holding that "pose" accounted for much of her popularity and accomplishment.

One of those accomplishments subsisted in Lathrop's use of her new public power to open professional opportunities for other women. Just as Addams had initiated Lathrop's elevation to head the Children's Bureau, Lathrop determined to lift other women. The process by which she accomplished this uplift is especially interesting because it exposes the meaning of Lathrop's—and other civil service reformers'—vehement opposition to patronage and helps to define her understanding of the value of civil service reform: even from her earliest days in office Lathrop used the civil service code on the one hand to protect her independence in hiring and on the other to support her own sort of patronage system based on gender and culture.

To fill the highest positions on her staff, Lathrop enjoyed the freedom to administer "unassembled" civil service exams. An unassembled exam required no written test but rather depended on candidates' fulfilling educational and experiential requirements and receiving a certain number of recommendations. Because the chief of a bureau could make the qualifications as specific as she liked, she might identify a promising candidate and *politics* then tailor the requirements to fit that candidate's resume. A master of that option and feeling no compunction about it, Lathrop once said of an unassembled exam: "A careful investigation of each candidates' fitness was made and *personal elements* were weighed in a manner hardly practicable by the assembled method" (emphasis added).[38]

Personal elements included gender. When Lathrop's first assistant chief—appointed by the Secretary of Labor—left the Bureau, Lathrop's own choice for the spot was female, and for decades to come, the assistant chief would be a woman. In 1914, when an increased appropriation from Congress allowed Lathrop to reorganize the Bureau into five divisions, all but one received a female director.[39] Later, as the number of divisions expanded to include a Division of Child Labor and a Chicago office, Lathrop gave each a female head.[40]

While the unassembled exam allowed Lathrop a completely free hand in appointing decisionmakers, she had only slightly less freedom to feminize hiring at lower levels. The Civil Service rules—ostensibly written to assure that merit alone qualified an applicant for government jobs—explicitly allowed the heads of agencies to specify the sex of candidates for all positions.[41] Once in power, Lathrop took full advantage of that permission to promote female hiring. In 1914, for instance, she wrote to the Civil Service Commission: "Most of our field agents must be women."[42] She argued that, to investigate many issues, the Bureau (emulating the door-to-door technique introduced by Hull House residents) intended to conduct frank interviews with mothers, which would include questions about childbirth, breast-feeding, and child care. Lathrop insisted that it was inappropriate for men to ask women such questions.[43]

This argument illuminates the complexities of Lathrop's motives for hiring women. Certainly she preferred women in part because she wanted to increase female participation in America's public life, and this commitment amounted to a rejection of nineteenth-century prescriptions for female behavior. But equally as supportive of her exclusively female hiring was Lathrop's acceptance of those aspects of the Victorian gender system that deemed it improper for men to talk to women about such personal experiences as breast-feeding. In the context of hiring at the Children's Bureau, then, even a sort of prudishness inadvertently advanced the cause of middle-class women.

Indeed, Lathrop obtained permission from the Civil Service Commission to accept only female eligibles from existing civil service lists for most of her hiring. Asserting that none of the men on the list for special agent or research assistant had the requisite knowledge of child welfare, Lathrop convinced the Commission in July 1914 to allow her to qualify all female eligibles for those positions and to disqualify all male eligibles.[44] She refused to hire men as statistical machine operators, statistical clerks, experts in child welfare, factory inspectors, stenographers, clerks, or typists.[45] Finally, it became her practice simply to return civil service lists with a note saying that "it was not deemed advisable to employ the services" of male eligibles.[46]

Lathrop thus ensured that women dominated the Children's Bureau. The overwhelming majority of its special agents, researchers, experts, and clerks were women.[47] By March 1919, the Bureau listed only 14 men among its 169 staff members, and women outnumbered men in every occupational category except that of messenger.[48]

Women whom Lathrop hired would have passed muster at Hull House, in the process revealing the other bases for her patronage system. Most of the women she employed were white, middle-class, well-educated, and unmarried.[49] Many were also midwesterners and formed by the same reform traditions and institutions that Lathrop herself had helped to fashion. Emma O. Lundberg, for instance, who joined the Children's Bureau staff as head of the Social Service Division in 1914, had graduated from the University of Wisconsin before doing graduate work at both the New York School of Philanthropy and the Chicago School of Civics and Philanthropy, where Lathrop was an officer. She had already proven her research abilities in her work for the Wisconsin Industrial Commission.[50] Lundberg's good friend and protégé, Katharine Lenroot, followed her to Washington and served first as a special agent for the Children's Bureau (beginning in January 1915) before moving through the ranks finally to become chief of the Bureau in the 1930s. Like Lundberg, Lenroot came out of Wisconsin's reform culture and had hooked into the national progressive network through her congressman father in 1910. Thereafter, she matriculated at the University of Wisconsin, where she studied social science with old-timers—Richard Ely and John Commons—who continued to tie research and reform together, and as a student Lenroot wrote a brief supporting Wisconsin's minimum wage law. From there, she served on the Wisconsin Industrial Commission, where she met Lundberg.[51]

Other employees of the Bureau had similar profiles. Dr. Grace Meigs, hired in 1915 to head the Division of Hygiene, had earned her M.D. in Chicago where she had made contact with the Hull House cohort.[52] Evelina Belden, hired as a special agent in 1915, had done graduate work at the Chicago School of Civics and worked in the city's juvenile court.[53] All of these early hires had some experience with the tradition of social research and advocacy that Lathrop had helped to mold. Thus the ardent opponent of patronage systems based on affiliation with political parties actually began to build her own sort of patronage system based on gender and culture. In fact, the kind of ideological patronage that other historians have

associated with Franklin Roosevelt's administration in the 1930s was already in full operation in the Children's Bureau as early as 1912.[54]

Because women were privileged in Lathrop's system, men who served
on the Bureau's staff were, as at Hull House, marginalized.[55] None occupied
decisionmaking positions, and even when they held the same title as a
woman, they were assigned the least responsible tasks. In a study of infant
mortality in Johnstown, Pennsylvania, for example, one male and three
female agents conducted the field work. The women actually visited mothers, completed surveys, and tabulated results, while the lone male "assisted
in the preliminary work of copying the birth and death certificates" on file
at a registrar's office.[56] The man's assignment, requiring no special skill,
prevented him from earning promotion. Only women were entrusted with
work that permitted them distinction and mobility in the Bureau.

In other ways, too, Lathrop's Bureau re-created life in the settlements.
Some women formed close personal as well as professional relationships.
Sometimes they lived or at least dined together. Most workers lived in
boarding houses or apartment hotels. Hotels provided individual kitchens
but also supplied meals in a common dining room. Women who lived in
either a boarding house or a hotel thus enjoyed many of the advantages
offered by settlements: private rooms, freedom from cooking, and a communal dining arrangement. Lathrop herself lived in an apartment hotel and
took most of her evening meals in the dining room. Dr. Anna Rude, who
eventually replaced Grace Meigs as head of the Hygiene Division and lived
in the same hotel as Lathrop, ate breakfast each morning in Lathrop's
apartment. Lenroot and Lundberg lived together for years while they were
both in Washington. Evelina Belden rejoiced when she moved from her first
home in Washington to a building where other workers lived. She especially
liked dinners with her colleagues and socialized exclusively with them.[57]

Close friends showed special concern for each other on the job. One
employee, for instance, intervened to protect the health of an overworked
friend: in a private note to Lathrop, she recommended that her friend be
granted a long vacation and forbidden during that time to conduct any of
the Bureau's work. The chief complied.[58] When Evelina Belden had stomach trouble during one of her research assignments, Lathrop wrote to her: "I
am sure I need not advise you as to the value of a supply of plain biscuits
and sweet chocolate in your traveling bag."[59]

Bureau workers also showed warm concern for the countless women
who wrote letters to them. Having read about the Bureau in a local newspaper or received one of its pamphlets, women often turned to the Bureau

for personal advice and material aid. The Bureau's files became repositories
for innumerable supplications that revealed the most intimate details of
women's lives, a testimony to the Bureau's popularity among women and to
the lonely, fragmented lives of many American wives and mothers. Women
wrote to the Bureau to confide beatings, ignorance about birth control,
menstrual problems, and pregnancies outside marriage.[60]

Just one heart-rending example of these pleas for help came from a
twenty-two-year-old woman in Wisconsin. She was pregnant at the time of
her first letter and was by her account "very thin and sick which makes my
husband disgusted and very cruel to me." She continued: "He always tells me
about other women who are built nice and don't look sick . . . he is not
satisfied with me at all, he said he would go out with some better looking
and better built women than I am." Such treatment, she confessed "almost
breaks my heart . . . for I try everything in my power to make him happy."
She wanted especially to know if Lathrop thought that her pregnancy was
her fault—as her husband insisted it was—and whether all of her worry
about her marriage would hurt her baby. She closed with, "I beg, Miss
Lathrop, to be a friend. . . . "[61]

Such letters revealed the Children's Bureau's reputation for responsiveness, which was a reputation well deserved. Every plea for help elicited a
personal reply from the Bureau's staff and often involved long hours attempting to ensure adequate care. Usually that care came from an appropriate local agency to which the Bureau referred the supplicant.[62]

In this way, the Children's Bureau carried the settlement ethos into the
federal government and with it the culture of female professionalism created
in the settlements.[63] Even here in Washington, workers needed to show "the
settlement spirit" through their immediate and personal responses to needy
individuals. Though they could rarely meet the needs before them, their
attempts far exceeded the legal mandate, which required no attention at all
to individuals's personal problems. Here, the Bureau contradicted latter-day
preconceptions about bureaucracies: it was not simply an impersonal machine cranking out studies and forms according to standard operating procedures but also a flexible institution, responding to problems outside its
official ken.[64]

The peculiarity of this ethos was confirmed by several problematic
episodes in Emma Lundberg's career. While supervising field work for an
investigation in 1916, for instance, Lundberg apparently had trouble with
her underlings. This she attributed to the unique standards controlling
professional relationships among women. "I seem to have an unfortunate

way of expressing myself," she wrote to Lathrop, "perhaps due in large part
to the fact that most of my past work has been with men who have
encouraged my natural instinct for free and frank discussion of things that
concerned the job."[65] According to Lundberg, female colleagues required a
gentler approach to direction and criticism.

No amount of gentility, however, could mask the competition that
sometimes strained relationships in the Bureau. In the context of a government agency, even Julia Lathrop could not precisely duplicate settlement
life. While the hierarchy at Hull House had operated informally, lines of
authority at the Bureau were formally delineated: every employee had a
title that proclaimed her place in the structure and controlled her salary.
Status descended from the chief to the assistant chief; from there to the five
division heads; next to the special agents and research assistants; and so on.
Women who filled these slots were ambitious. To reach the Bureau, they
had beaten out a good many applicants and, once there, competed against
equally capable women for the best assignments, promotions, and admission to Lathrop's inner circle of favorite daughters.[66] Imperatives dictated by
the job market and governmental structure modified female professional
culture as they set limits on the possibilities for simply shifting to this federal
agency the values and strategies of the settlements.

Also pulling at the seam of intraoffice intimacies were bureaucratic
procedures. Memoranda and travel vouchers hardly promoted close, personal relationships. Moreover, the staff had an enormous amount of work
to do and little space in which to do it. Consequently, Lathrop tried to
enforce a strict code of behavior in the office. In May 1918, she circulated a
memo reminding the staff of paragraph 3b in the Bureau's General Regulations. The memo quoted 3b's exhortation: "That when conversation is
necessary, it be carried on in such a manner as not to interfere with the
work of others in the room." Lathrop asked all carefully to observe the rule
and went on to interpret it. "The conversation referred to in the regulation,"
she averred, "is that made necessary by official business. Personal conversation, of course, is not to be carried on during office hours."[67]

These strictures were a far cry from the flexibility ruling settlement
houses. Office ambience militated against the gentility expected of the
workers and may have made some feel torn between two, sometimes conflicting, sets of expectations. Though these tensions between competition
and community, between personal relationships and impersonal procedures,
were central to professional experience and had certainly existed before the
founding of the Children's Bureau, they intensified for women with the

increasing bureaucratization of professional life and the opening of greater
professional opportunities for women. The point needs to be clear, however, that bureaucratic structure did not utterly control the working lives of
women in the Children's Bureau; it acted as a tube through which female
professional culture was forced and thereby modified. Within the limits set
by bureaucratic rationality, women in the Bureau created a work space that
valued responsiveness, individual initiative, and personal relationships.

Indeed, while bureaucratization eroded some settlement traditions, it
increased the effectiveness of others. Once women had taken control of the
Children's Bureau, they used the agency to promote their reform agenda on
a national scale, just as Lillian Wald had hoped. During her first months in
office, Lathrop settled her strategy. Because child labor attracted controversy, she had her staff quietly compile child labor laws and concentrated the
balance of her precious resources on infant mortality studies and a drive to
improve birth registration in the states. In addition, she determined to begin
publishing a series of popular pamphlets on prenatal and infant care.[68]

In her implementation of this strategy, Lathrop employed such tactics of
female professional culture as popularizing technical information. As she
mulled over the possibility of pamphlets on prenatal and infant care, for
example, she resisted colleagues who suggested that male physicians author
them. "[I]n the series we now contemplate on the care of the mother and
child," she argued, "there is a real strategic advantage in having them come
from a woman who has herself had the experience of bringing up a family
of children. . . . we can keep the thing simpler than if it were written by a
professional person."[69] Though Lathrop involved doctors in the preparation
of the series, she chose Mary Mills West to write the pamphlets. West, a
widow with five children to put through college, proved worthy of Lathrop's confidence.[70]

West's publications became the best-selling pamphlets of the Government
Printing Office in the 1910s. The first edition of West's pamphlet, *Prenatal
Care*, sold out in two months. Only six months later, the Bureau had distributed 30,000 copies and could have sent out twice that number but for the
inability of the printers to keep up with the demand.[71] Indeed, so overwhelmed was the Bureau by requests for the pamphlet that one worker wrote
to Lathrop: "The demand for prenatals is perfectly appalling."[72] Nearly a
million and a half copies of West's second pamphlet, *Infant Care*, were
disseminated between 1914 and 1921.[73] When the Bureau added *Child Care*
and *Milk: The Indispensable Food for Children* to its list of popular dodgers, it
was distributing hundreds of thousands of pamphlets each year and was never

able to meet the demand. To help satisfy some of the need, local women's groups began to print up excerpts for local distribution.[74]

The Bureau's pamphlets struck a resonant chord with middle-class women. One historian has called the years between 1900 and 1920 the era of educated motherhood because women were professionalizing their maternal work just as they were systematizing their charitable activities. Colleges began to offer courses in home economics and child care, which warned against rearing children the way previous generations had and insisted that unsuspecting mothers could drive their youngsters toward delinquency. Mothers needed special knowledge to form responsible adults from the raw material they received at birth.[75] Anxious to do their job right, middle-class mothers welcomed the Bureau's guidance with relief and gratitude.

But middle-class mothers were not the only group that the Bureau reached with its childrearing advice. Lathrop, trained in self-promotion by her settlement experience, extended the Bureau's influence by establishing excellent relationships with the press. The importance that Lathrop attached to these relationships was summed up in her claim that "the Bureau lives by publicity. . . . "[76]

This assertion placed Lathrop squarely in her era. During the earliest years of the twentieth century, Americans invented the press release and professionalized public relations; propaganda had yet to carry any pejorative meaning.[77] In fact, reformers sometimes saw publicity as a panacea for the country's ills insofar as they believed that the American public simply needed reliable information on social problems in order to make good decisions about their solutions. Lathrop herself once said: "A fruitful fact needs no compulsory legislation nor military sanction; nothing but a chance to be used."[78] The confidence that Lathrop and her colleagues had in publicity inspired them not to settle for the use of print media alone to disseminate their advice but to pioneer in the use of public exhibits, demonstrations, eventually radio spots, and motion pictures.

Women in the Children's Bureau used each method of publicity in several ways. First—and most obviously—they distributed information from the Bureau's research. Sometimes that information aimed toward the reform of childrearing; sometimes toward the reform of public policy. But in either case, that publicity served a second purpose: it drew attention to the Children's Bureau itself. And as it spotlighted the Bureau, it began to establish the agency as the national authority on matters of child welfare. Strategies at Lathrop's agency thus continued the trend developed at Hull

House. In the process of responding to demonstrable material problems, for example, maternal and infant death, middle-class women created new professional opportunities for themselves and increased their own authority in national life. *emergence of the professional women*

The Bureau's relationships with the press help both to illuminate the route that the agency took to pre-eminence in the field of child welfare and to prove its success. Well before World War I, magazines and newspapers competed for the latest word from the Bureau. Reform journals and leading women's magazines were among these publications, but interest in the Bureau's work stretched well beyond the readership of *The Survey* and the *Ladies' Home Journal. Woman's World,* a magazine with two million rural subscribers, approached the Bureau for advice to appear in its monthly column on maternal and infant health. Smaller journals like *Mother's Magazine* in Elgin, Illinois, offered the Bureau similar publicity. Newspapers as diverse as *Atlantic Tri-Weekly Journal*, the *Delineator*, and the *East Tennessee News* requested information from the Bureau for articles and editorials on prenatal and infant care.[79] Solicitations also came from national and local religious communities. R. R. Wright from the Book Concern of the American Methodist Episcopal Church, for instance, asked if the Bureau could provide a weekly letter for his department's newspaper. The dean of St. Paul's Cathedral in Fond du Lac, Wisconsin, asked for permission to print information on the Bureau in his monthly church magazine.[80] The editorial secretary of the Baptist Sunday School Board offered occasionally to use Bureau material in his weekly paper for young people.[81] A representative of the Sunday School Publications of the Methodist Episcopal Church wrote: "Every time there is an opportunity to make reference to any of the activities [of the Bureau] . . . we are glad to do so."[82]

Reformers, journalists, church leaders, and individual mothers recognized the Bureau as the nation's leading expert on children, and were helping Lathrop's agency to establish a monopoly in child welfare. The number of inquiries sent to the Bureau by individual mothers revealed its increasing acceptance among the nation at large as, in the words of one historian: "Women from every geographic region, social class, and educational background wrote to the Bureau as many as 125,000 letters a year."[83] Another has concluded that "the bureau was seen as the official values setter and standards setter in the child welfare field during its early years of activity."[84]

To extend the Bureau's influence into America's policymaking bodies, Lathrop needed even more help than the media could offer. In the early twentieth century, the country's significant public policymakers in the area of child welfare were municipalities and state legislatures, and, in order to insinuate the Bureau's preferences there, Lathrop used the national network of female voluntary organizations which she knew through her work in the settlements. Thus, the interdependence of professional and lay women, a salient feature of settlement life, continued.

The chief self-consciously wooed these voluntary groups because she believed that the Children's Bureau "will need as perhaps no other bureau of the government will need, the continuance of the popular pity which demanded and secured it."[85] Already a member of the General Federation of Women's Clubs, Lathrop joined many more women's groups after becoming head of the Children's Bureau.[86] She often spoke before the women's societies and paid her staff members to attend regular meetings. She added women's groups to her mailing list so that they received all of the Bureau's publications and news releases.[87] In response, groups ranging from the General Federation of Women's Clubs to the Illinois Society for the Prevention of Blindness asked the Bureau to "map out" their annual programs or to suggest "a line of work that we could do."[88] In return for the help, they offered the Bureau further publicity and support.[89]

Capitalizing on those offers, Lathrop drew the voluntary organizations under her leadership, testing them first in her campaign for better birth registration. Discussions with the Census Bureau early in her tenure revealed the inadequacy of birth registration in the United States. For its own purposes, the Census Bureau constructed a Birth Registration Area, which included all states that registered 90 percent of their births. Most states did not meet the 90 percent requirement. Some states simply had inadequate registration laws; others had good laws but failed to enforce them. Lathrop believed that all other efforts to improve the lives of children depended on adequate birth registration. Without it, the country could not collect reliable statistics on infant mortality or discover its causes; officials could not document a child's age and thereby enforce school attendance or child labor laws. Lathrop, therefore, made birth registration one of the Bureau's top priorities.[90]

The Bureau's strategy for improving birth registration bore the mark of the agency's dual commitments to bureaucratic procedure and personal relationships. In 1913, it published *Birth Registration: An Aid in Protecting the Lives and Rights of Children*, printed up thousands of registration certificates, and decided that a house-to-house canvass would best expose the inadequacies of current registrations.[91] In addition, personal calls on mothers would give the Bureau's representative a chance to build public support for more effective registration procedures.

With an original staff of only fifteen people, Lathrop could not hope to conduct a national campaign, so she called in the female voluntary associations. Florence Kelley committed the Consumers' League and the National Child Labor Committee to the cause in 1913, and the two groups carried the crusade into the South, where they were working against child labor.[92] In 1914, the General Federation of Women's Clubs took up the standard. In 1915, the Association of Collegiate Alumnae joined, and in 1916, so did the Women's Christian Temperance Union.[93] By 1918, women's organizations were vying for the honor of helping the Bureau. The chair of Child Hygiene for the Congress of Mothers and Parent-Teacher Associations, for instance, reminded Lathrop that her organization comprised 8000 groups devoted "to the interests of childhood" and was very well-organized. According to the chair, the large membership and effective organization of the Congress better qualified it than the General Federation of Women's Clubs to aid the Bureau.[94]

Despite competition between groups, the Bureau was able to coordinate their activities. In November 1914, Alice Day Marston informed Lathrop that she had just been elected chair of the Iowa Daughters of the American Revolution (DAR) Committee on the Welfare of Women and Children. Marston announced that she would like to put the resources of that committee at the disposal of the Children's Bureau. The committee offered to help with investigations, lobbying, anything the Bureau needed.[95] Lathrop responded that a birth registration law was to go before the Iowa legislature that winter. The DAR, she suggested, might want to work with the Iowa Federation of Women's Clubs and the Iowa State Board of Health in seeking passage of that law. Lathrop gave Marston the names of women spearheading the lobbying effort and assured her that they would welcome the DAR's aid.[96] Marston then joined the lobbying effort and convinced one Iowa senator to distribute copies of the Children's Bureau pamphlet on birth registration to every member of the Iowa Congress.[97] When, in the fall of 1915, the registration bill failed to pass, Marston broadened the lobbying effort by activating the entire Iowa State Conference of the DAR.[98]

The birth registration drive also enabled the Bureau to draw women unconnected to prominent organizations into the network. In the summer of 1915, Mrs. Maud Hemingway of Ganado, Texas, asked the Bureau how she might join the campaign. A staff member wrote that so far Texas had not participated but that the state's health officer was lobbying for a model registration law and needed the support of a good canvass. The letter described in detail how to conduct a canvass and suggested that Hemingway contact the secretary of either the Texas Federation of Women's Clubs or the state's Congress of Mothers.[99]

Thus, female volunteers all over the country joined the Bureau's force. By October 1914, the Ohio Federation of Women's Clubs had already returned to the Bureau 1300 reports from seventeen cities, including Akron, Cleveland, and Dayton.[100] The Vermont Federation of Women's Clubs in that same month boasted the largest number of reports returned to the Children's Bureau in proportion to the numbers sent to them.[101] A year later, the Bureau reported that over 3000 club women had participated in birth registration surveys and issued over 13,000 reports.[102] The Association of Collegiate Alumnae conducted tests of birth registration in Denver, Colorado; Huntington, West Virginia; Providence, Rhode Island; Eugene, Oregon; Lawrence, Kansas; Missoula, Montana; and Ann Arbor, Michigan.[103] From the state of Washington to Florida, club women marched door-to-door to do the Bureau's bidding.[104]

The loyalty and commitment of the Bureau's volunteers drew attention. State health officials and legislators knew that if they wanted an immediate force of lobbyists on behalf of better birth registration laws, they need only write to Lathrop, and the lobby would materialize.[105] One Kentucky senator was so impressed by the volunteers' efforts that he asked Lathrop how she managed to win such cooperation from the women of his state.[106]

Following a Kelleyesque approach to reform, the birth registration drive succeeded. After each door-to-door canvass had provided volunteers with a list of babies recently born to a neighborhood, the women checked their records against official documentation in local registrars' offices. Most found the public registry deficient, sent the Bureau their results, and lobbied state legislatures for better laws, local officials for better enforcement, and both doctors and midwives for compliance with the laws.[107] Pressure from women and the publicity they gave to the issue of birth registration prompted state health officials to back the movement and to plead for help from the Bureau in achieving the 90 percent registration rate.[108] Mothers and fathers anxiously wrote the Bureau to ask how they could obtain birth certificates for their children.[109] And before 1920, the women's efforts had added fifteen states to the Birth Registration Area, with more states qualifying every year thereafter.[110]

Lathrop's bureau was proving itself true to Wald's vision of an activist agency, and was, in the process, creating a female dominion within the larger empire of policymaking. The loose network of female reformers, connected in various ways to the settlements, found a single, national leadership in the Children's Bureau. Organized, non-professional women were increasingly looking to the professionals in Washington to set their agenda and recommend a method for reform. Volunteers functioned as active partners in the Bureau's work, and in this early stage of the dominion's history, the voluntary organizations served as the lower echelons within the dominion's hierarchy. To fulfill their charge, the national women's groups formed child welfare committees and encouraged their state associations to do the same. The national chair then worked directly with the Bureau and sent orders down to her state chairs, who would finally direct the activities of local branches.[111]

Even in specialized investigations, the Bureau sustained the earlier reliance of professional women on their lay sisters by activating the lower echelons of the dominion. In 1915, for example, the Delaware Cooperative Education Association asked the Bureau to help with a study of "mental defectives" in Delaware. The purpose of the study was to discover the number of learning disabled children in the state and to detail their inadequate care. The Bureau agreed to help, and Emma Lundberg coordinated the study.[112] In the absence of state agencies or a great federal bureaucracy that reached into the states, Lundberg needed local residents to introduce her to the individual communities, institutions, and schools that housed information on Delaware's disabled children. Without that help, she could not locate such children much less investigate the effects of different methods of care.

By entering the state through local, female activists, Lundberg gained access to information that private administrators, suspicious of outsiders and free to ignore them, might never have unveiled. To devise her tentative outline for the study, Lundberg contacted 25 people in Delaware whom she believed might help her to identify her targeted children and gain access to institutions and agencies that cared for them. The list embraced superintendents of schools, doctors, private asylums for destitute or sick children, philanthropic societies, settlements, and women's organizations. Of the 25 potential aides, 15 were women, and Mrs. Frank M. Jones, chair of the Committee on Civics and Health for the Delaware Federation of Women's Clubs, proved most valuable.[113] She supplied Lundberg with a list of Delaware citizens interested in the problem of "mental defectives," a list that included 17 men and 57 women.[114]

The results of the Delaware study underscored the effectiveness of the

dominion's approach to reform. When Lundberg completed the preliminary report in December 1916, she sent copies to the Delaware Cooperative Education Association, the Federation of Women's Clubs, and the governor. At the request of the Federation, she then mailed copies to every
Delaware legislator and press releases to all Delaware newspapers. Local
women used the study to lobby for better public facilities for learning-
disabled children, and by March 1917, they had won legislation providing
new institutions for these children.[115] The pillars of Kelley's strategy for
reform — research, publicity, organization, and lobbying — were now guiding
Lathrop's emerging national dominion.

By allying itself with female voluntary organizations, the Children's
Bureau was marking child welfare as the preserve of female policymakers. In
the Delaware study, a sex-integrated group, the Delaware Cooperative Education Association, had first solicited the Bureau's help and followed the
Bureau's work throughout the investigation. But the Bureau had shifted its
reliance to the state's Federation of Women's Clubs and treated the women's
group as its true partner in the enterprise. The women had then been
responsible for legislation implementing the Bureau's recommendations.
Like the birth registration drive, local studies directed by the Bureau quickly
became associated with women's groups and established the primacy of
women in the area of child welfare.

The legislative victories of these alliances between the Children's Bureau
and local women's organizations exposed the potential power of even a
small, federal agency lacking any legal right to coerce states or individuals, a
power that lay primarily in what one historian has called "the tissue of
connections" between public and private agencies in the Progressive era.[116]
To uncover the relationships and methods of the early Children's Bureau is
to discover a world in which the barriers between public and private agencies were permeable — in those places where barriers could be said to exist at
all. And though other small federal agencies also joined forces with private
groups to further their work — so much so that historian Robert Cuff has
referred to "that imaginary line separating business and government, private
and public institutions" — the depth and breadth of the Children's Bureau's
reliance on and partnership with volunteers was remarkable.[117] Since the
New Deal, progressives' enthusiasm for what appeared to be powerless,
data-gathering agencies has seemed a bit naive. But as it turns out, some
progressives saw those little, fact-finding government agencies not as isolated
entities in a growing government but as integral parts of a closely knit
community of organizations, and as part of that nexus, small government
bureaus actually did act as significant agents of reform.[118]

Lathrop's female dominion – the most striking example of such a web – effectively influenced the federal government as well as states and municipalities. It first proved itself at that level in an episode occurring two years after the Bureau's establishment. In her annual report for the fiscal year ending June 30, 1913, Lathrop proposed that, for the 1914–15 fiscal year, her appropriation be increased from $25,640 to $164,640 and her staff from 15 to 76. In spring 1914, the House Appropriations Committee voted not to recommend the increase.[119]

Lathrop had only to contact Lillian Wald and Florence Kelley in New York and Jane Addams and Mary McDowell in Chicago to obtain the full support of her troops. On April 3, Wald and Kelley wired Owen R. Lovejoy, general secretary of the NCLC since 1907, asking him to notify Congress of his organization's support for the increased appropriation. By April 9, Lovejoy reported to Lathrop that he had sent letters to every member of his organization and wired the 25 state committee secretaries "to get their people and all their machinery to action." He also commanded McKelway to notify the American Federation of Labor about the Appropriations Committee's unfavorable report, and he announced that the General Federation of Women's Clubs had begun contacting its state federations.[120] In Chicago, Mary McDowell, president of the National Federation of Settlements, got "the machinery of the settlements going."[121] Settlement workers not only wrote to their congressmen and the members of the Appropriations Committee but also activated the local networks at which they were so often the center. By April 17, for instance, the headworker at Madison House, a New York settlement, informed Lathrop that he had contacted every settlement in New York City, a number of "social agencies," the Joint Board of Sanitary Control, the Board of the Cloak, Suit and Shirt Makers' Union, and the Board of the International Ladies' Garment Workers. All had sent cables and letters to the appropriate legislators and urged their memberships to do so as well.[122]

Once Wald and Kelley had alerted the organizational network, they opened the campaign to reach the general public. On April 13, Wald explained to Addams that she and Sister Kelley had "divided up the tasks" and assigned Addams to the *Ladies Home Journal*.[123] By the end of April, editorials appeared in newspapers and magazines all over the country. *The Survey*, the *New York Times*, Chicago's *Inter-Ocean*, the *Boston Transcript*, the *St. Louis Republic*, and the *American Federationist* were but a few of the heralds of Lathrop's distress.[124]

No sooner had Lathrop's four generals alerted their forces than supportive letters and telegrams deluged Congress. Charitable organizations from

Pennsylvania to Minnesota responded to the call. Local women's clubs from all over the nation shot off letters to their congressmen. The state committees of the NCLC began their letter-writing campaign within days of receiving Lovejoy's telegram. Private citizens from Utah, Michigan, and Colorado protested the committee's decision. By early May, the diocese of Chicago had denounced the parsimony of Congress as had the Mother's Congress, World Book Publishers, the YMCA, the Russell Sage Foundation, and several juvenile court judges.[125]

The storm of cards and letters worked. On April 15, Lathrop notified Wald that the outpouring of constituents' protest had convinced Congress to consider an amendment to the budget, which would increase the Bureau's appropriation. She wrote: "I think publicity has turned the trick."[126] The House approved Lathrop's full request, 276 to 47.

Throughout her tenure as chief, Lathrop relied on this kind of support. In 1916, Lathrop's appropriation was again threatened, and again the lower echelons of the dominion saved her.[127] Earlier that year, the corresponding secretary of the General Federation of Women's Clubs had reminded Lathrop that "the General Federation always receives cordially any advances from the Children's Bureau."[128] And Lathrop received the same assurances from the American Association of Collegiate Alumnae, the National Council of Women's Organizations, the Home Economics Association, the American Association for the Study and Prevention of Infant Mortality, and the Woman's Foundation for Health.[129] Jane Addams was right when she wrote that Lathrop "had learned to explore women's organizations for that moral enthusiasm which she constantly needed to back her official undertakings."[130]

Before America entered World War I, a female dominion had materialized within the larger empire of policymaking. With the Children's Bureau at its head and female voluntary organizations serving as second in command, this group of associations was establishing a monopoly over child welfare policy and childrearing advice. Moreover, in the process of reforming America's treatment of children, white, middle-class, female progressives were increasing their own professional opportunities and public authority.

Into the governmental arena, these women carried the female professional culture that had emerged from experiences in female communities such as Hull House. They maintained commitments to the combination of research and advocacy; to public service; to popularizing expert knowledge; to the interdependence of professionals and laity; and to the integration of their private and public lives. But all of these values were modified by integration into an increasingly bureaucratic order and an ever-more competitive job market. In turn, bureaucratic operations took on a peculiarly female cast at the Children's Bureau, where personal relationships both within the Bureau and with volunteers outside the agency carried great weight, and where standard operating procedure included door-to-door visits with mothers of new babies.

Crucial to the persistence of female professional culture in the Children's Bureau and therefore to the survival of this nascent dominion was the ability of leaders to hire women who shared their values. As it happened, that capacity was guaranteed by the development of new forms of professional training which imparted to younger women the commitments of Lathrop's generation. One such training ground was the University of Chicago's School of Social Service Administration, the history of which occupies the next chapter.

CHAPTER 3

Staffing the Dominion:
The School of Social Service
Administration, 1903–1930

In 1926, a woman long associated with Hull House wrote: "As I look back over the years I have been connected with Hull-House . . . I feel that . . . I received there from Miss Addams the training and education in social work which is now given at the Schools of Civics and Philanthropy. My instruction, however, did not come from text books or lectures, but from Miss Addams' teaching and from my personal experience with the many people with whom I came in contact."[1]

This author properly observed the continuities between her experiences at Hull House and later programs for social work that formally professionalized female service values. One of the places where this process occurred most dramatically was in Chicago, where women from Hull House joined other settlement workers in creating the Chicago School of Civics and Philanthropy and its successor, the School of Social Service Administration. Within these schools, female reformers inscribed their progressive commitments on the profession of social work, and through leadership in professional education for social work were then able to socialize aspiring, younger women into their culture of reform. Thus, professional training at the School of Social Service Administration specifically fitted a new generation of women to staff the female dominion.

The professionalization of social work had a long and complicated history that began in the late nineteenth century. A first phase of professionalization opened in the 1870s with the formation of the charity organization movement, which aimed above all to systematize the delivery of social services to the needy and to minimize material aid to the poor by offering instead the spiritual and moral uplift of personal relationships with respectable people. Representing so-called respectable society in these relationships, middle-class, white women functioned as friendly visitors who called on applicants for charity and, while investigating their need, offered encouragement to self-improvement.[2]

In the 1890s, the professionalization of social work entered a second phase. During this decade, with its several years of severe depression, members of the charity organization societies began to acknowledge that poverty was not always—or even usually—a result of individual moral failing but more often the consequence of economic forces over which those impoverished had no control.[3] Workers in settlement houses were discovering the same thing and were especially keen on documenting the discovery through social scientific research, which brought together settlement workers and social scientists in a variety of studies and reform campaigns.

As these middle-class groups determined that alms and advice to individual families simply did not strike at the root of poverty, the identity of social work blurred. If the mission of social work was to aid the poor, and poverty resulted from pervasive economic relationships, then social work should—it seemed to some—train practitioners to understand and devise ways to alter those relationships. For these practitioners, social reform should be the purpose of social work. Others, even if they believed that individuals were victims of an unjust economic system, believed that the duty of social workers was to aid the currently suffering who, after all, could not wait for massive economic restructuring. These social workers advocated a much less political role for their profession, one that instead concentrated on material and psychological aid to individual families. Although some leaders in the new profession insisted that the two sides were reconcilable, the first two decades of the twentieth century saw factions within the social work community wrestle with the different ways of defining their young profession and ultimately create two distinctly different identities, both of which managed to survive—however uncomfortably—under the rubric of professional social work.[4] One arena in which the battle for the identity of social work was most dramatically fought was at the Chicago School of Civics and Philanthropy.

The Chicago School represented a movement toward formal education for social work. The first full-time training ground was the New York School of Philanthropy, which opened its doors in October 1904. As its affiliation with the city's Charity Organization Society would suggest, its original faculty sought especially to teach students how systematically to assess a family's needs, keep orderly records of friendly visits, and deliver services efficiently. Under the auspices of Simmons College and Harvard University, the Boston School for Social Workers also opened in the fall of 1904; and in 1908, the St. Louis School of Philanthropy and the Philadelphia Training School for Social Work offered their first full-time programs. By 1915, would-be social workers had their choice of five independent schools and two programs with university affiliations. Like the New York School, most were connected in some way with private, charitable organizations that wanted especially to rationalize the methods of their own friendly visitors.[5]

In 1903, a program in Chicago had begun with a similar purpose: "to aid in supplying the demand for trained workers in the social phases of [city welfare work]."[6] At first, the program was only an extension course on philanthropy taught by Graham Taylor, who was a minister, founder and head-resident of the Chicago Commons Settlement, and a teacher of Christian sociology at Chicago Theological Seminary. The next year, the course expanded to become the Institute of Social Science and Arts Training for Philanthropic and Social Work, the stated purpose of which was "to provide a basis of general knowledge for intelligent interest and participation in whatever promotes the welfare of the community" and "to offer a more technical preparation for professional and voluntary service in specific lines of organized effort."[7]

By 1907, the program—now called the Chicago School of Civics and Philanthropy—had expanded through a five-year grant from the Russell Sage Foundation to include a research department "for social investigation on a scientific basis."[8] Several other schools, including the New York School, received comparable grants, but the Chicago School provided the base for three women whose work would soon distinguish it from all others.[9] To head the research department, Taylor first hired Julia Lathrop, who—always on the lookout for fresh talent—recruited Sophonisba Preston Breckinridge as her assistant. In 1908, when Lathrop moved into the School's vice presidency, Breckinridge took up the reins of the research department and convinced Edith Abbott to join her staff.[10]

To the extent that constructions of gender determined professional opportunities at the turn of the century, gender motivated both Breckinridge and Abbott to participate in the development of social work and in reform. Both women tried first to take the customary male paths to professionalism, and all evidence indicates that, had they been men, they would have succeeded brilliantly. Success would have left neither woman a reason for building a new profession or entering the reform fray: only because gender discrimination blocked them did the two women continue to grope for the innovative channels to professionalism that would eventually lead them toward careers in reform.

Breckinridge, born in 1866 to a prominent Kentucky family, belonged to the first generation of college-educated women. Her father was a lawyer and congressman; a great-grandfather had served as Attorney General in Thomas Jefferson's administration; and a distant relative, John C. Breckinridge, ran for the presidency against Abraham Lincoln.[11] Later described by a colleague as "sweetness and light," Breckinridge proved that she was born to study. While at Wellesley College, she wrote of one set of exams: "They have been so very lovely that I have enjoyed every one."[12] At Wellesley, too, she developed a self-image and ambition that would carry her through a long and productive life. A sentence from her father's pen summed up perfectly Breckinridge's own self-evaluation: "You don't know how glad I am that you are not a genius; but a hard-working, dutiful, trained intellect, capable of doing anything because you are willing to undergo the necessary labor and submit to the request[ed] discipline."[13] Confidence in her abilities and joy in hard work gave Breckinridge a sort of grace even in her career ambitions. "I ache to get out and work," she confided as she neared her 1888 graduation, "I shall be glad to go fight— glad to feel some times the delight that must come from doing something hard."[14]

Abbott was born in Grand Island, Nebraska, a decade later than Breckinridge. Much scrappier than Breckinridge, Abbott had to work her way through the University of Nebraska over a nine-year period because of the heavy losses her lawyer-father sustained in the depression of 1893. Having taught from age sixteen to meet her family's expenses as well as those for her own education, Abbott developed an abrasive sort of independence fixed especially on her pay check. "No self-respecting American woman of the middle classes is any longer willing to be supported by her masculine relatives," she wrote, misrepresenting the truth in 1905 but clearly revealing her own values.[15]

After college, both Breckinridge and Abbott experienced the frustrations of trying to find professional satisfaction in a male world. The older Breckinridge endured frustration longer. As for so many of her sister graduates, the years following commencement presented Breckinridge with no obvious plans for the future.[16] She tried high school teaching, studied law, and became the first woman to pass the Kentucky bar. But even the latter achievement brought little satisfaction because potential clients avoided this female attorney. Indeed, her failing practice so discouraged Breckinridge that she gave it up in 1895 to become secretary to Marion Talbot, then dean of women at the University of Chicago.[17]

In Talbot, Breckinridge met a friend indeed. Recognizing her secretary's promise, Talbot secured Breckinridge a fellowship in political science at the University of Chicago, from which she earned her Ph.D. in 1901. From there, she took the J.D. degree in 1904, and finally, decorated with stellar credentials in the social sciences and law, Breckinridge became an instructor in Talbot's department of household administration, teaching courses on economic and legal aspects of the home.[18]

This denouement to Breckinridge's stunning educational drive underscored the power of gender in controlling her professional options. No man with her resume taught home economics. Women who received the same training as men, rather than compete with men, were expected to employ their expertise in areas related to women's traditional sphere.

Coming along a little later than Breckinridge, Abbott represented a new generation of college-educated women whose professional paths had been partially cleared in advance. She suffered no long period of indecision and confusion after college. In 1902, only one year after graduating, she attended graduate summer school at the University of Chicago and met Breckinridge, who at the time was head of Abbott's dorm and about to become assistant dean of women. In 1903, a fellowship supported Abbott's full-time study of economics at the university, and two years later she received her Ph.D. Both Breckinridge and J. Laurence Laughlin, a Chicago economist, pulled strings to secure Abbott's first employment as a researcher studying women's wages and the cost of living in Boston and Washington, D.C. After researching for a year, she won a fellowship to study at the London School of Economics, and in the fall of 1907 took up a teaching position at Wellesley. For an older woman, the professorship would have been a plum of a job, but Abbott was dissatisfied. She missed the excitement of research, shared her cohort's disdain for single-sex colleges (an attitude that seemed to reflect the larger society's tendency to assume anything connected with men superior to that associated only with women), and felt less comfortable in the East than in the Midwest.[19]

Even after achieving the highest academic degrees available, neither Breckinridge nor Abbott was able to obtain employment commensurate with her training, ability, or expectations. And these two women were, of course, not alone. Studies in the 1910s showed that although coeducational universities were hiring more women, female pedagogues were stranded at the bottom of faculty ladders unless they accepted appointments in home economics.[20] Because gender discrimination prevented either from winning appointment to a social science department at a coeducational university, both stayed alert for new professional possibilities.

Such options opened when the community of Chicago's female reformers discovered these two discontented academics, and by offering first Breckinridge and then Abbott new professional possibilities, drew them into reform activism. Breckinridge unwittingly slipped into the company between 1905 and 1907 when two articles she had written on the legal aspects of female industrial employment caught the attention of leaders in the female reform community and merited her invitations to live at Hull House and to teach at the Chicago School of Civics and Philanthropy.[21] In 1907, Breckinridge was forty-one. She had reached this age without showing any particular propensity to political activism or public leadership. But when a set of female mentors asked her to direct her research toward their causes and to combine that research with advocacy, offering professional advancement in exchange, Breckinridge agreed.

Breckinridge's conscious motive for joining progressive causes was sincere concern for those exploited by industrial capitalism. Concern, however, did not lead all citizens to political activism; neither did interest itself dictate the sorts of solutions they preferred. The very same attention to social problems might have expressed itself in paralysis or in a commitment to anarchism, in a decision for racist anti-immigration policies or the scientific management of industry. Professional self-interest explains not why Breckinridge worried about the social dislocations of her day but why her concern took the particular form it did: why she became an activist and especially an activist pushing for the expansion of the state into social welfare through bureaucracies filled with professionals.

In fact, Breckinridge became one of Chicago's most prominent reformers, often taking on the most controversial issues. She helped, for example, to found and maintain the Chicago Urban League, the Wendell Phillips Settlement for black Chicagoans, and the Chicago branch of the NAACP. She was a co-founder of Chicago's Immigrants' Protective League and a vice president of the National American Woman Suffrage Association. In 1911 and 1915, the southern lady participated actively in strikes by Chicago's garment workers. These were certainly the actions of a convinced and genuine reformer, but at the same time such enthusiastic conformity to progressive ideals gained

Breckinridge the respect of Julia Lathrop, who consequently facilitated Breckinridge's promotion to director of research at the Chicago School and eventually to dean.[22] For Breckinridge, as for so many women of her generation, professionalism and reform were inseparable.

Abbott proved more resistant to the reformers than Breckinridge. This was due in part to the mentorship of J. Laurence Laughlin.[23] Laughlin, a political conservative, had been involved in the late-nineteenth-century battle between those who wanted to use social science for reforming ends and those who preferred to avoid the appearance of passionate attachment to any particular political or social ideals. A firm supporter of established interests, Laughlin had opposed any hint of liberal political activism in his profession.[24]

Moreover, Abbott represented a new generation of college-educated women who sensed that the days of struggle for female opportunity were over. Ten years younger than Breckinridge and eighteen years Lathrop's junior, she and her cohort believed that they could now burst into their professions on equal footing with men, and, owing no debt to the female community, could ignore its peculiar values, including its dedication to advocacy. Abbott's belief that she could identify herself solely as an economist and dissociate herself from gender-solidarity attested to the degree of success that women had achieved in the public sphere. But Abbott's subsequent career provided evidence for the conundrum that only through continued solidarity could women hope to increase their individual freedom.[25]

Her generational position, her professional heritage, and her personal political beliefs initially steered Abbott away from reform. Despite employment by the National Women's Trade Union League and the Carnegie Institution—both organizations devoted to reform—despite meeting English socialists Sidney and Beatrice Webb, and despite exposure to the poverty of London's East End, Abbott avoided confusing her research with political involvement, and she maintained fairly conservative political opinions.[26] In the summer of 1907, she wrote to her father from London: "I think now if I had a vote I would vote with you against the Progressives." She disapproved "mad experiments out of any body's money," and referred to one English reformer as a man "who began life as mad as our Mr. [Eugene] Debs."[27] On the eve of her job at Wellesley, Abbott saw herself as an economist whose research had no immediate political motive and who was not in special sympathy with America's reform movements.

Only a few months later, when Abbott had begun to chafe under the constraints of her job at Wellesley, she accepted Breckinridge's invitation to serve as assistant director at the Chicago School of Civics and Philanthropy. Taking up that post in 1908, despite misgivings about progressivism, she moved into Hull House.[28]

The settlement and her new job transformed Edith Abbott. Chicago's female reformers so completely changed her mind about the progressives she had disparaged only a year earlier in letters to her father that she joined the same causes as Breckinridge and even modified her view of the social scientist. No longer did she research to hone her academic skills but investigated social conditions with an eye toward changing them. In her own words, she now "rejected the academic theory that social research could only be 'scientific' if it had no regard for the finding of socially useful results and no interest in the human beings whose lives were being studied."[29] Like Alice Hamilton before her, Edith Abbott was a scientist whose female community bent her scientific skills toward reform; Hull House feminized her career.

Although a range of motives congealed to produce Abbott's conversion to activism, the primary incentive for her—as for Breckinridge—was career advancement. If Abbott had received appointment to the social science faculty at a coeducational university, she would not have been ripe for picking by the reformers. After all, she had shown little inclination to reform activism until progressives offered a way around the dead end in her career. For this second generation of educated women, then, commitment to reform opened some of the few avenues to professional growth.

Thus, the peculiarities of the female search for professional opportunities begin to explain the continuity of progressivism among middle-class women. Although America's second generation of college-educated women surely enjoyed wider professional opportunities than its predecessor, some of those possibilities were controlled by the first generation, committed to reform partly by its own search for channels to professionalism. Those narrow streams, vigilantly patrolled by the likes of Jane Addams, Julia Lathrop, Florence Kelley, and Lillian Wald, offered ambitious younger women little choice but to conform to the values and strategies of the old guard. Edith Abbott's conversion experience is only one of the most vivid examples of the power that the first generation had to shape the lives and goals of the next.[30]

Eleventh-hour converts though they were, Breckinridge and Abbott became not only two of the most passionate and wide-ranging reformers of their day but also participants in the creation of a profession that embodied many of the values and methods of their adopted reform culture. In 1908, when Abbott and Breckinridge found themselves running the research department at the Chicago School of Civics and Philanthropy, the profession of social work was as yet undefined, and the two women were in a perfect location from which to influence that definition. Once they had established their own dominant position within the profession of social work, they would imbue still younger women with the ideals of progressive reform.

Their struggle to identify social work with reform involved Breckinridge and Abbott in fascinating conflicts that disclosed not only the different needs of women and men in the early twentieth century but also the diversity within female experience—in this case, among middle-class white women—in the 1910s. Indeed, their own peculiarly female needs for professional standing put the interests of Breckinridge and Abbott at odds with both the School's male administrators and the vast majority of the School's female students. The role of gender in shaping interests on matters such as the mission of professional social work was wonderfully complex.

Graham Taylor, founder of the Chicago School, represented the opposition to the Breckinridge-Abbott definition of social work. Although Taylor held a place of honor among progressive reformers, his work at the Chicago School aimed almost exclusively to transform the nineteenth century's friendly visitors into the twentieth century's caseworkers. He wanted to play out the theme of rationalization in charitable work: in his own words, "to raise and maintain standards of efficiency in public service through the training of capable men and women for professional and volunteer social, civic and philanthropic work."[31]

Crucial to such training, according to Taylor, was the School's intimate relationship with the social service agencies of Chicago. He envisioned his institution as an integral part of both the city and its complex of social service organizations, and he considered this relationship the real strength of his program. "But the distinctive feature of this School is the correlation of the field work, for which we use the entire City of Chicago[,] with the class room work," he explained, "and in the class room work we draw those with us, the regular staff of these various agencies, from the great manufacturing plants, from the play grounds, from the voluntary and official agencies, to tell of the work they are doing. . . . "[32]

Taylor's commitment to practical training and to his school's organic relationship with the city were expressions of a larger philosophy common to his generation of settlement residents. He believed that the only knowledge worth having was knowledge derived from experience. In the foreword to his *Religion in Social Action*, Taylor wrote: "Both the course of thought and the conclusions that follow are the outgrowth of experience. They grew from the ground up. They bear the earth-flavours of each field of endeavor—rural, pastoral and professorial, civic."[33] Like John Dewey and Jane Addams, Taylor believed that education came from doing, experiencing, acting.[34] Just as settlement workers gained much of their authority from actually living among the human beings they hoped to help, so the Chicago School should win its legitimacy from participating directly in the agencies it sought to serve.

For all their organic participation in the life of working-class neighborhoods, settlements nevertheless spawned another, more detached approach to social problems, which became the hallmark of Breckinridge's and Abbott's research department. That more impersonal approach involved researchers in gathering and analyzing statistics that were supposed to reveal the existence, extent, and cause of social problems. Jane Addams and Graham Taylor did not disapprove this statistical data-gathering, but neither settlement founder could completely trust the method if it were cut off from life lived among the problems studied. If statistics replaced rather than supplemented personal, neighborly exchanges with the indigent, outcast, or corrupt, then the method began to look suspicious. As Taylor put it, through friendship "only can be obtained not charity alone, but that justice which, by giving equality of opportunity to the citizen makes possible the progress of the city and the state."[35]

Moreover, without these personal relationships, according to Taylor, researchers would be figuring out solutions to other people's problems without the participation of those other people. "The settlement," he insisted, "exists not to superimpose the ideals or standards of one class or locality upon another, but to help the neighbors develop their own ideals and standards."[36] Taylor's assumption that his neighbors had no ideals or needed his help in devising them and the practical difficulty of distinguishing between "superimposing" and "helping to develop" should not obscure the fact that Taylor viewed his approach to social problems as a cooperative effort between the weak and the strong. Any approach that did not appear to enlist the weak frightened him; by believing in the cooperative effort, Taylor reconciled his approach to reform with his belief in democracy.

In keeping with all his purposes, Taylor prepared his students more knowledgeably to do their jobs in social service agencies. He taught the general survey courses at the school, including "Introduction to Social and Philanthropic Work." True to his vision of the relationship between his school and the city, he relied heavily on outside speakers and field trips. In fact, in a course on institutional administration, Taylor never spoke but instead scheduled representatives from various institutions to speak at every single class meeting.[37]

At least two levels of motivation shaped Taylor's approach to the professionalization of social work. First was his rejection of abstract knowledge. Trying to work out a theoretical base for social work would have been a cop-out for this man who wrote: "In form and substance the Scriptures of both Testaments are biography and genealogy, history and experience, folk lore and personal epistles, songs and sighs of the soul and of peoples."[38] In Taylor's understanding, even religion emerged from human experience; the more practical answers to social problems could hardly come from elsewhere. Given this conviction and his corollary emphasis on personal relationships, no mystery surrounds Taylor's enthusiasm for caseworkers, those women who actually walked through the doors and sat at the tables of the needy.

At another level, the professional opportunities available to Taylor because of gender played an important part in shaping his choice of definitions for social work. This ordained minister, seminary professor, and settlement head resident had no stake in redefining social work so as to gain it prestige and respect among other professions. He had secured his professional identity outside that particular field, and consequently had no incentive to do more than rationalize the status quo in charity work. He was free not even to try to make social work compete with medicine, law, or ministry because he already belonged to those more respected professions.[39]

Breckinridge and Abbott did not have that freedom. As social scientists, largely excluded because of gender from the highest positions in their fields of study, they had different perspectives from Taylor's and very different needs. The combination of gender discrimination, social scientific training, and their desire for success in academe encouraged these two women to define social work in a different way. In contrast to Taylor, they wanted to transform social work into an academic discipline that would underlie a profession equal to law or medicine.

Little interested in caseworkers, Breckinridge and Abbott intended to groom powerful, respected policymakers, and in their department of social investigation, they energetically pursued that construction of social work. Following in Lillian Wald's footsteps, they insisted that their goal was the "collection of a body of authoritative data upon which programs for social reform and recommendations for changes in social legislation may be based." To that end, Abbott and Breckinridge required their students to master statistics and the latest social research methods; to contribute to the expanding body of information on social legislation, social conditions, and reform experiments; to formulate recommendations for change in the conditions they studied; and to become the prime movers in making those changes.[40] As Breckinridge and Abbott insisted on this policymaking emphasis for social work, they employed social scientific techniques. They believed that social problems were "for scientific investigation rather than for emotional generalization from a limited field of observation."[41] No concept — not even reform — ranked above scientific methods, because sound reform depended on them. Emotional and limited were the words they used to describe the dangers of a more personal approach to social problems: whatever might be said for personal experience, it was inevitably narrow and subjective, incapable of encompassing a big enough chunk of reality to justify social policy. To Breckinridge and Abbott, the big picture that abstract statistics could draw was infinitely more reliable than the detail sketched by concrete experience.

Moreover, Breckinridge and Abbott were much more skeptical than Taylor about the ability of personal relationships between caseworkers and clients to be anything but meddling middle-class intrusions. Their experience with friendly visitors had convinced them that many continued to assess applicants' virtue as a condition for aid, and the social scientists did not approve of such moralistic evaluation. They condemned what they called "the older attitude toward relief-giving [which] regards it as the appropriate expression of a favorable moral or social judgment on the part of the donor."[42] And they were more pessimistic than Taylor about the possibilities for genuine inter-class friendship. In Abbott's characteristically straightforward words: "Neighborliness, in the old village sense, has long since disappeared in the metropolitan areas except as the poor assist each other. . . . "[43]

In a fascinating reversal of expected male/female positions, Abbott and Breckinridge were sprinting down the track of science, impersonal power, and self-assertion while Taylor lingered along the lane of belief, personal relationships, and self-sacrifice. Indeed, the two women chided Taylor for being "somewhat romantic about what he calls his 'seventeen years of sacrifice'" for social work education.[44] In the women's view, no amount of sacrifice could compensate for what they called "Mr. Taylor's educational disqualifications" for the job of teaching at the school.[45] Because he eschewed the "scientific method" in the classroom, relying instead on personal experience, the women thought him an incompetent teacher. Moreover, they were impatient with his concern for caseworkers, whom they believed to be technicians instead of professionals. In a statement to the School's Board of Trustees, Breckinridge said: "We have the courses to which Doctor Taylor referred, growing out of the demand for case work agencies, charity organizations, relief societies, children's aid societies and all that group of agencies; but besides that we have been able to develop our department of social investigation, which does turn out young persons who have had one year at least of a very high order of training in this investigational work in a field which had hitherto not been developed and organized." She was especially proud of this work because "there is no question as to its academic prestige or its social value."[46]

This conclusion slapped Taylor's face and also denigrated traditionally female roles in social work. Breckinridge and Abbott had little interest in establishing personal relationships with the poor or in the women whose jobs required such relationships. Thus, their distinctly female need for professional status encouraged Abbott and Breckinridge to devalue conventionally female work. Such friction between women of the same race and class highlights the increasing heterogeneity among American women in the early twentieth century and the consequently complex role of gender in shaping their interests.

During their first decade at the Chicago School, Breckinridge and Abbott gained national recognition for their research. Abbott's investigation, *Women in Industry*, appeared in 1910; *The Delinquent Child and the Home*, co-authored with Breckinridge, came out in 1912; *The Real Jail Problem* was published in 1915; and another book co-authored with Breckinridge, *Truancy and Non-Attendance in the Chicago Schools*, appeared in 1917.[47] To aid in their work, the women employed an elite group of students by providing assistantships from research contracts they made with various agencies, including the Russell Sage Foundation, the federal Department of Labor, and local health authorities and women's clubs. During 1911–12, the department supported thirteen students through such contracts, and throughout the 1910s students were publishing articles from their research.[48]

Their alternate approach to social work set Abbott and Breckinridge on a collision course with Taylor and the female caseworkers whose interests he represented. Anxious to secure a place for themselves and their students within the academic community, Abbott and Breckinridge advocated affiliation of the Chicago School with a local university. They insisted that their students needed the resources of a larger institution—libraries, fellowships, faculty—in order to make their mark on the world. Abbott argued that "the Training Schools [for social work] . . . would never become properly equipped professional schools until they were made University schools."[49] Of course, the caseworkers had no such need, and Taylor defended them. He feared that university administrators would force the school's curriculum to become too theoretical and would never preserve "the democratic spirit and close co-operation with the official and voluntary agencies" in which he took such pride.[50]

Financial difficulties gave Abbott and Breckinridge the leverage they needed to interest the School's trustees in their arguments. With no endowment, the independent Chicago School of Civics began financial floundering in 1912, and by 1915, the burden of funding so oppressed the trustees that they agreed to a suggestion by Breckinridge that the school seek affiliation simultaneously with three local universities—Northwestern, the University of Illinois, and the University of Chicago.[51] Although the University of Chicago nibbled at the bait, negotiations toward a merger broke down when war pulled many of the negotiators out of the city.[52]

War's end and a leave of absence for Taylor allowed Breckinridge to reopen negotiations in 1920. At that point, she submitted to the University of Chicago a plan for a graduate school of social work. The president agreed to this plan, which, despite Taylor's objections, won the trustees' support. In August 1920, the Board of the School of Civics signed a contract for the takeover.[53] The university then appointed Breckinridge and Abbott associate professors of social economy in its new School of Social Service Administration. In 1924, Abbott would become dean of the School; in 1925, Breckinridge would be made full professor and four years later receive an endowed chair. Taylor received no position.[54]

In a painful irony born of their own peculiarly female need for a route to professional advancement, Breckinridge and Abbott deprived the majority of female students at the old Chicago School of Civics and Philanthropy of their opportunity to earn certificates for social work training. When the university agreed to take over the Chicago School's work, it refused to accept the school's programs for recreation specialists or public health nurses. Furthermore, since it was establishing a graduate program, only those college-educated women able to pursue full-time graduate work could follow Breckinridge and Abbott. That omitted the vast majority of students at the Chicago School, who had always been female. Of 193 registrants in 1914–15, for instance, 180 were women. Most of them studied either part-time or took only occasional classes. Of hundreds of students who attended classes between 1906 and 1912, only 96 graduated during that time. In 1918–19, only 27 out of 683 students earned certificates.[55]

The part-timers were often women already working for private social service agencies, and many had no undergraduate degrees. Breckinridge referred to these sisters as "in general persons for whom for some time to come there will be considerable demand by agencies whose funds are limited and whose work has not been raised to a high level of professional efficiency." The program that served their needs, she wrote, "could be abandoned without great social loss."[56]

Breckinridge's perspective obscured what a boon part-time study was for many women. Already in the 1910s, graduate study and professional programs in law, medicine, and ministry were growing increasingly expensive, which disadvantaged women more than men. Families were less likely to pay for their daughters' extended educations than for their sons'; women's jobs, paying lower salaries, made it more difficult for women to stockpile enough savings to carry them through professional schools; and most faculties granted fellowships more readily to male than to female students.[57] Indeed, Breckinridge and Abbott had embarked on their graduate careers when graduate schools were new, experimental, and looking for good students to justify their existence. As those schools gained acceptance and could afford to limit the number of women admitted, they preferred male applicants. Because the Chicago School of Civics allowed part-time study, its certificates and the modest professional advancement they might bring were accessible to many more women than were the older, male-dominated professions. As a consequence, merger with the University of Chicago was a great triumph for a few women.

The ambiguity of Breckinridge's and Abbott's achievement exposes the frame in which these women were working. Despite the relative freedoms that they had in the process of creating their own niche in the professional world, they were nonetheless limited by a culture that was increasingly granting esteem, financial security, and public authority to those who could convince their public that they possessed esoteric knowledge. The proof of such possession was an advanced academic degree unavailable to the many. Worse still, that degree gained value not only by excluding others from possessing it but also by its grant of authority over other people's lives. In the case of doctors, lawyers, ministers, or social workers, professional degree-holders assumed authority over the sick, the criminal, the sinning, or the poor, who were concomitantly reduced to dependence. Thus, the elitism of Breckinridge and Abbott is not so much a reason for castigating them as for lamenting a society in which the wish for personal security, independence, and public influence could be satisfied only at the expense of others.

Predictably, Breckinridge and Abbott displayed no ambivalence toward their coup. In announcing the merger with the University of Chicago, Breckinridge proclaimed a new era. "The experimental, exploratory work has been done," she declared. Education for social work had passed into "the assured stage" of its work.[58] The political scientist and doctor of law meant that the academic community had accepted social work as a profession worthy of graduate training and had put her and Abbott in charge of America's first graduate program in social work. By helping to create a professional discipline with its own specialized skills and knowledge, Breckinridge and Abbott had finally secured for themselves the respected faculty positions they wanted.

Once settled in the academic environment, the two women encountered a new threat to their discipline and therefore to their hard-won status. At the Chicago School, the challenge had been to distinguish their work from that of soft-hearted friendly visitors. With gusto, they had separated themselves by churning out social scientific studies that defined charity cases as expressions of larger, more abstract social and economic relationships. But at the university, social science methods did not distinguish their discipline from sociology, political science, or economics. Indeed, in some places, the close kinship between sociology and social work had resulted in the subordination of social work programs within departments of sociology.[59] For Breckinridge and Abbott that trend posed a problem: if social work were not recognized as a unique discipline but as a sub-field of sociology, then the two women could sink into low-level instructorships in a sociology department directed by men, losing their professional status, their base for reform, and perhaps the ability to open educational and professional opportunities for other women.

To defend the special identity of social work in this academic context, Abbott and Breckinridge had to walk a fine line between the established social sciences and the friendly visitors. To do so, they did what had become ritual for new professions in the Progressive era: they published a series of textbooks and founded a professional journal for social work, the *Social Service Review*. Until it began to receive regular contributions from other sources, the *Review* was not only edited by its creators but also packed full of their own research.[60] The journal continued the tradition of research begun at the Chicago School of Civics and Philanthropy. But in their textbooks, the dons of social work education were reclaiming and re-creating casework. The message of their textbooks was that well-educated caseworkers could transform their door-to-door experiences into scientific data and learn to become the policymakers that Abbott and Breckinridge hoped to produce at their school.[61] This interesting retrieval of the casework heritage may have seemed the best way to prevent their discipline's absorption into sociology and thereby to protect their own status in the academic community; it may have been an attempt simply to reconcile factions within the profession. In any case, it infused Breckinridge's and Abbott's conception of social work with elements of a female heritage they had previously avoided.

Ever anxious to defend the professional standing of social work and yet to distinguish it from related social sciences, they developed a broad and unique curriculum for social work education. Their program offered courses in social research, public administration, the history of social work, economics, sociology, and social psychology. Specific courses addressed issues in immigration law, social welfare legislation, the criminal justice system, and social insurance.[62]

Among the nation's leading educators in social work, Abbott and Breckinridge were in a position to build their own convictions into the profession itself. In relationship to their own students and those reached through textbooks and the *Review*, they now occupied a station analogous to that of the Hull House community: they controlled eagerly sought professional opportunities for younger women and could use that power to socialize aspirants into the culture of progressive reform. Breckinridge and Abbott took full advantage of their authority and helped to professionalize the values and strategies for reform learned at Hull House.

Into every aspect of their curriculum, Abbott and Breckinridge wove the conviction that the social worker's primary purpose was reform. Abbott wrote: "We [social workers] have other friends who are afraid we are not scientific because we wish not only to learn to diagnose the social evils with which society has to deal but we insist on going on to find out what ought to be done about them. But if trying to follow diagnosis by curative treatment is being unscientific then we must be content to be described in some other way."[63] Casework, according to Abbott, was necessary because the economic system was not providing opportunities to all American citizens. If social workers were truly committed to alleviating suffering, then they must work to adjust economic and political relationships so that no one needed a friendly visitor's patronage. Both women believed that government should establish an economic level below which no American family could fall; that employers should be required to pay a living wage; and that if

government took responsibility for those unable to work, then such problems as juvenile delinquency, substandard housing, hunger, and poor health
could be eliminated.[64] In other words, Abbott and Breckinridge charged
their professional education with a commitment to what Americans would
later call the welfare state.

This commitment to public social service, spinning out of female experience at places like Hull House, put Breckinridge and Abbott in a minority
among social work educators in the 1920s. During the 1920s, the prevailing
trend among social workers was toward private agencies and psychiatric
treatment of individuals rather than social change.[65] As a consequence,
Breckinridge and Abbott were bucking the trend in their determination to
dedicate social work to social reform.

They remained undaunted. So long as private, voluntary associations
retained control of ameliorative policies, they argued, the problems of
poverty would remain unsolved. As long as "donors give to ease their own
conscience or to save their souls," Breckinridge insisted, "the distribution of
alms or of services will lack the scientific method that is based on study
of the community's needs, and of the origins of those needs in social or
industrial or political maladjustment." She added: "It is not possible for the
private agency to take a comprehensive view of the needs of the situation.
. . . " Consequently, she concluded: "[T]he preference of the social worker
would probably be for public rather than private service. . . . For the social
worker can be satisfied with nothing less than a universal provision for a
continuous service. And only the state can be both universal and continuous."[66]

To create and staff these public agencies constituted the calling of social
workers. In her *Welfare and Professional Education*, Abbott concluded: "One
reason for the slow progress of some important social reforms in the past
has been that social workers were not trained for research and were not
expected to analyze and interpret their own data. . . . "[67] Elsewhere she
would insist: "The caseworker of today should become later . . . the Secretary of a Commission to redraft the poor laws of a State or organize a new
system of prison labor." "The social worker," she continued, "meets at every
turn questions of social legislation, proposals for social reform, and even the
more immediate problems of inadequate wages, of trade unionism, of insurance, of workmen's compensation. She is called on to recommend revisions
of the poor law, of probation statutes, of the criminal law. The community
wishes to know what ought to be done about old age pensions, blind

pensions, or unemployment—and the social worker should be able to give sound advice."[68] More strongly: "[T]he young workers should . . . realize that the social legislation of the future is to be in their hands."[69]

In the kinds of studies they undertook and assigned to their protégés, Breckinridge and Abbott drew students deeper into reform culture. During the 1920s, Abbott conducted further studies of housing conditions in Chicago and the relationship between crime and punishment. Her students cranked out studies of illegitimacy in Illinois, adoption laws, juvenile detention homes, children of wage-earning mothers, employment of children in street trades, employment of retarded children, immigrant groups, and the institutional care of dependent children.[70] To earn the degrees they sought, graduate students were expected to provide grist for the reform mill.

Moreover, the Hull House graduates made the connection between research and activism central to their profession. They constantly boasted the practical results of their students' investigations. They pointed to the establishment of the Chicago Vocational Guidance Bureau, a Bureau for the Aged, and a Bureau for the Care of Negro Dependent Children to prove the value of their students' work. They listed two groups of model apartments as products of their research. They, with their students, reorganized the administration of the Juvenile Detention Home and convinced the Chicago Orphan Asylum to switch from institutional to foster care.[71]

In addition to educating their students in the tradition of progressive reform, Breckinridge and Abbott found jobs for those who faithfully mirrored that heritage. For instance, when Breckinridge was serving on an Illinois commission on child welfare, she maneuvered one of her school's fellowship students into the commission's secretarial position. Abbott meanwhile tapped the Local Community Research Committee to obtain funding for three students who she wanted to conduct surveys for the commission.[72]

Indeed, the professors' commitment to reform usually dovetailed nicely with obtaining placements for their students. Through an attempt to control civil service requirements, for instance, the two women hoped to make the state welfare system an exclusive preserve for their graduates. Both were dissatisfied with the civil service requirements for applicants to positions in the state's welfare system, because such requirements were often vague enough to allow political appointments or at least to admit applicants without the graduate training offered by the School of Social Service Administration. While Breckinridge served on the executive committee of the Illinois Welfare Commission, the two champions of social work tried to change that. In a letter to her sister, Abbott described their two-pronged attack: "[Sopho]Nisba and I both feel that Miss Zimmerman can be manipulated and made to rewrite some of those civil service requirements. I believe Nisba can get the Executive Committee of the State Welfare Commission to appoint a special State Committee on Civil Service Requirements for the Public Social Services and I think I could get appointed chairman. . . . "[73] Thus, Breckinridge and Abbott sought power simultaneously to place their students and to reform the delivery of social services in Illinois.

Occasionally, however, Breckinridge and Abbott seemed to care less for the future of individual students than for the potential of their work as fuel for change. In a letter to the Children's Bureau in 1926, Abbott referred to a student who was working on a study of employment among children who left the "subnormal" schools of Chicago. Abbott wrote: "[S]he hoped to use this as an M.A. thesis; however, it is quite probable that she will have to leave in June, and working by herself she will never finish it, so the thesis aspect of it is unimportant. We should be glad to have the investigation completed properly and adequately." Abbott then offered the project to the Bureau.[74] In this instance, Abbott was ready to give away a student's thesis topic before the student had decided not to complete it. Sometime later, Abbott discussed another student's illegitimacy study: "This she expected to use for an A.M. thesis. As you know, I am not so concerned about a thesis as I am about possibly losing a chance of pulling something out of the Illinois situation that will be a permanent advantage."[75] Whether or not the student received a degree struck Abbott as inconsequential. What was important was that the state revise its treatment of illegitimate children.

Students thus shaped by Breckinridge and Abbott often filled positions that permitted them to mold others and to affect public policy. Of eleven graduates of the School of Social Service Administration between 1920 and 1924, seven were either teaching at the college level or serving in public agencies devoted to social welfare. Over half of the graduates between 1926 and 1930 went into college teaching and administration of public agencies. Many of those in public agencies were in policymaking positions. Aleta Brownlee, 1930 graduate, became county commissioner of public welfare in Santa Barbara, California; Pauline Thrower, the assistant commissioner of the State Department of Charities and Corrections in Oklahoma. Rhoda Morgan Starr supervised the Home Relief Bureau of the New York State Department of Social Welfare; Alice Channing assisted the President's Commission on Social Trends in the 1930s. Among the graduates who went into private organizations, many took executive positions. Savilla Millis Simons became the legislative secretary of the Illinois League of

Women Voters; Anita Jones served as headworker of a settlement house in San Diego, California; Myrtle Brannon Ferrell was executive secretary of the American Red Cross in the state of Washington; Arlien Johnson became assistant secretary of the Seattle Community Fund.[76]

Although their dedication of social work to reform represented the minority view in their profession during the 1920s, Breckinridge and Abbott were not utterly alone. In addition to the small numbers of women graduating from the School of Social Service Administration, Breckinridge and Abbott affected many more students in their own undergraduate classes, through the textbooks they authored, and through the *Social Service Review*. Indeed, in some other schools of social work, as well as in programs for public health nursing, departments of home economics and public administration, and even a few social science departments, female progressives infused professional training with their values and strategies for reform. In these forums, professionalization and reform remained interdependent and mutually sustaining for women.[77]

All that Breckinridge and Abbott were doing after 1908 had profound implications for the nascent female dominion. As Chief of the Children's Bureau, Julia Lathrop was trying to define the parameters of her field. Even in the 1910s, when the boundaries enclosing areas of expertise were fluid, she had some difficulty locating a territory to call her own. Before undertaking any project, she consulted with the Census Bureau, the Bureau of Education, and the Public Health Service to make sure she was not transgressing their borders. Until she could establish a distinct identity for her field, the statisticians, educators, and doctors threatened to invade the child welfare bailiwick and divide it among themselves. Breckinridge's and Abbott's efforts to distinguish social work from both casework and the other social sciences and to develop specialties within social work provided Lathrop with defenses against intrusions by these other agencies. Furthermore, by providing the Bureau with a claim to a scientific foundation for its authority, Breckinridge and Abbott legitimized its quest for a monopoly over child welfare policy.

Lathrop consequently maintained a very close relationship with the research team. When she left the Chicago School to head the Children's Bureau, she remained a trustee and occasional lecturer. Beginning in 1917, she transformed her personal involvement into an institutional connection between the Children's Bureau and the School's research department. With money from her increasing appropriations, she contracted the department to do specific research projects. In 1918–19, contracts with the Children's Bureau allowed the department to hire a staff assistant and, in the 1919–20 school year, to create two new full-time and two half-time positions.[78] Most important, because of Lathrop's confidence in the Breckinridge-Abbott team, she often hired their students after graduation.[79] These students won responsibility and promotions more quickly than their colleagues.[80] Indeed, Lathrop confessed that "the Children's Bureau had more people from the Chicago School of Civics than from any other school." She explained: "When we held our first civil service examination, we wanted people who could make some scientific inquiry with a statistical basis which the government required. Forty from the school passed the examination for our work triumphantly."[81]

By 1917, the research department had thus become an integral part of the emerging dominion's organizational structure. It occupied a leadership position in part because it acted as an auxiliary staff conducting research that the Bureau's own staff had no time to do. In addition, students of the Chicago School who did not go directly to work for the Bureau scattered into other public and private agencies then receptive to the Bureau's leadership because of shared commitments. Finally, the training ground, which molded an elite crew of professionals to staff the Bureau, assured it a continuing supply of women sworn to the same ideals and methods regarding child welfare. The professionalization process as it progressed under Breckinridge and Abbott made it possible for Lathrop to recruit only women committed to an expansive governmental role in social welfare, to the combination of research and advocacy, to enactment of child labor laws, mothers' pensions, juvenile courts, to the gamut of social justice reforms advocated by Progressive-era female reformers. This reliable stream of ideologically congenial newcomers made Lathrop's patronage machine possible, and in turn Lathrop's ability to preserve jobs at the Bureau for just such women supported Breckinridge and Abbott in their socialization work. Lathrop's position at the Bureau and Breckinridge's and Abbott's at the School were symbiotic: they empowered each other in the common enterprise of sustaining their reform program.

A serious test of Lathrop's ability to resist intrusions by those holding other views came with the election of Warren G. Harding in 1920. Lathrop herself had survived the turnover from Taft's Republican administration to Wilson's Democratic one by arguing that the Bureau was an investigative agency staffed by experts whose political affiliations would in no way affect the Bureau's scientific work.[82] After eight years of Democratic ascendancy, however, she feared that the new Republican President would reward a party loyalist with the Children's Bureau.

Longing to retire in 1920, Lathrop had reason to fear. Mrs. Harry A. Kleugel of San Francisco wanted to head the Bureau and organized a constituency to support her nomination. During World War I, Kleugel had administered the Pacific Coast Junior Red Cross and, more important, had contributed to Harding's presidential campaign. Based on those qualifications, she believed herself fit for the Children's Bureau job.[83] If Kleugel had won her bid for the position, the dominion's history might well have ended right there. Kleugel's appointment would have branded the Children's Bureau a patronage agency for the political parties, open to new appointments with every new President. Discontinuity among the Bureau's top officials would have meant a loss of purpose and focus for the reforming organizations that looked to the Bureau for leadership. And, given Kleugel's lack of connection with any segment of the professional social work community, her appointment would have meant the temporary victory of the belief that the essential quality for policymakers in child welfare was femininity, not professional training or reform commitments.

Lathrop determined not to see her work destroyed. She identified a reliable successor and then shifted the lower echelons of the dominion into high gear. Kelley, Addams, Wald, and Breckinridge not only hauled in the usual organizations but also went to the women serving on the Republican National Committee, arguing that Kleugel had no expertise in social work, much less child welfare. They easily won over the well-connected female Republicans, who advised the President that they preferred "a specialist" to Kleugel.[84] Together with the broader reforming organizations, they lobbied Republican congressmen and convinced the Secretary of Labor, who was, according to Lathrop, "singularly unacquainted with any modern social theory or practice."[85] The President accepted his secretary's recommendation.[86]

Lathrop's victory set the Bureau outside the party patronage system, a location that had advantages and disadvantages. While in office, Lathrop and her successors had to remain outside the intimate circles of any one presidential administration, for to become too closely identified with one administration would risk ouster at the election of another. This meant that the women had no special pull with any President and were on the fringes of every administration. They could not count on the disciplined support of a political party but had to rely on the lobbying of their female network to win concessions from Presidents and congressmen. The advantage of standing outside the party system was that female reformers in the Bureau maintained control of their own system of patronage.

Thanks to that control, Lathrop passed on the leadership of the Children's Bureau not to Mrs. Harry A. Kleugel but to Grace Abbott, yet another woman whose career depended on her Hull House connections. Two years younger than her sister, Grace in some ways followed in Edith's footsteps during her early career. In 1898, Grace graduated from Grand Island College and the following year taught at Grand Island High School, where she stayed until 1907. In 1904, she had imitated her sister by spending a summer at the University of Chicago and, inspired by that experience, moved to Chicago in 1907. The following year, she moved into Hull House; the year after that, she earned a master's degree in political science from the University of Chicago.[87]

Although their interests were very similar, Grace and Edith Abbott differed in ways that made them perfect complements to each other. Edith was a thin, very intense smoker, who suffered from "sick headaches," and once admitted that she had gotten so mad at a meeting that she "would have tried to take a few scalps . . . if the chairman and the present president of the Conference had been within reach, which fortunately, they were not."[88] Edith, like her colleague Breckinridge, loved struggle. One of her favorite quotations was by Justice Oliver Wendell Holmes: "The joy of life is . . . to ride boldly at what is in front of you, be it fence or enemy; to pray not for comfort but for combat."[89] Referring to Abbott's preference for combat, a friend once said, "I am exceedingly skeptical of Miss Edith Abbott's ability to loaf."[90] Edith Abbott belonged behind the scenes, where she threatened no one's scalp but could put her prodigious intellect and commitment to use.

Grace was more relaxed, though no less hard-working. She was a buoyant theater-lover, whose incredible energy seemed to flow from some sort of inner contentment. One colleague wrote to her: "You are a regular old brick and I am all for you. I wish you were quintuplets!"[91] Grace Abbott had a gift for administration and was, like Lathrop, a born diplomat. She could not have been suited better for public life and planned throughout her career to run for office.[92]

In recognition of the younger Abbott's talents, Breckinridge and other Chicago activists hired her to head a new agency, the Immigrant's Protective League, when they founded it in 1908. From this position, Grace Abbott established herself as an authority on immigration. Her articles appeared in the *Survey*, the *American Journal of Sociology*, and the *Chicago Evening Post*.

In 1917, her first book rolled off the presses, titled *The Immigrant and the Community*. In all of her activities on behalf of immigrants, Grace proved herself an able lobbyist and administrator, abilities that won Lathrop's admiration before she moved to Washington. Repeatedly, the Chief tried to persuade Abbott to join her Bureau.[93]

In 1917, she succeeded. Grace Abbott then left Chicago to head the Child Labor Division of the Children's Bureau, created to administer the first federal child labor law. A considerable victory for child welfare activists, the law prohibited shipping across state lines "any products of a mill, factory, or manufacturing establishment that employed children less than fourteen years of age."[94] For children above fourteen, the law regulated hours. In her administration of the law, Grace Abbott cooperated with state agencies that were already overseeing state child labor laws. In fact, she integrated them into the administrative apparatus for the federal law—an approach to federal-state relations that aggravated some male members of the National Child Labor Committee.[95] But the difficulties between Abbott and her male antagonists had no time to grow, because in June 1918, the Supreme Court ruled the Child Labor Law unconstitutional, and Abbott, after dismantling much of the bureaucracy she had assembled, returned to Chicago as director of the new Illinois State Immigrants' Commission. The young commission soon disappeared, however, because Abbott refused to cooperate with a new governor's patronage plans, and she rebounded from the loss by reestablishing the private Immigrants' Protective League. At this point, Abbott decided she wanted to return to Nebraska to run for Congress.[96]

Lathrop and company had other ideas. Abbott was their choice for chief of the Children's Bureau, and they would not take no for an answer. Grace Abbott wrote: "I was I quite confess altogether unhappy when Mrs. Kelley and Miss Lathrop began to close in on me and insist *whether I wanted to or not* it was up to me to take the job" (emphasis added).[97] Kelley and Lathrop argued that Abbott had unique qualifications and that the Bureau would almost certainly be politicized should Abbott refuse. Given that Lathrop, Kelley, and the Hull House community had made her career possible, Abbott suppressed her own preferences and agreed to head the Bureau if Lathrop could engineer her appointment. The first generation of female reformers thus opened marvelous opportunities for professional women, but they came at the cost of submission to a hierarchy's will for one's career. Here again was the pressure to conform to the "settlement spirit": each woman was expected to subordinate individual ambition to the interests of the reforming, policymaking dominion.

Grace Abbott fulfilled Lathrop's every hope for an heir. She continued Lathrop's traditions and even tightened certain institutional ties with the Bureau. Because she was Edith Abbott's sister, Grace pushed the relationship with the School of Social Service Administration even farther than Lathrop had. She so continually sought advice from the Abbott-Breckinridge team that a close associate wrote: "[I]t would be a mistake to think that either she [Grace] or the others worked in complete independence or that the contributions of any one of the three would have been quite what they were without the help of the other two." The writer continued: "[T]he flood of letters that went back and forth, the long-distance telephone calls, the frequent trips to Chicago from Washington or to Washington from Chicago, attest to the close contact that was maintained and the extent to which advice was both sought and given on her [Grace's] problems and on theirs."[98]

Furthermore, the School of Social Service Administration remained the Bureau's most valued training ground. Every year in the early 1920s, at least one graduate of the School went to work for the Bureau.[99] Usually, that occurred because of special negotiations between the Abbott sisters. In 1929, for instance, Edith identified one of her students as just the person Grace needed as a juvenile delinquency expert and suggested that Grace should require applicants for the position to have a degree from an accredited college, six years of graduate study in juvenile delinquency, four years of administrative experience in an institution dealing with delinquents, and a thesis of not less than 10,000 words on the public care of children. To qualify her favorite student, Edith said, these specifications "are perfectly safe."[100] With such precise requirements, Edith's student was probably the only person in the country who qualified for this civil service position.

Even for entry-level jobs, Grace Abbott relied heavily on recommendations from her contacts at the School of Social Service Administration. In 1926, the Bureau needed field agents to supervise a study of children in home work and street trades. Applicants for the positions had to take a two-part assembled exam that consisted of educational and experiential qualifications in the first half and a written test in the second. Unlike so many later civil service exams, these did not offer an applicant several hundred multiple choice questions but instead required an outline of statistical tables from raw data, a thesis on one of several sociological subjects, and a plan for investigating a social problem. Before Grace announced these positions, she asked Breckinridge to suggest qualified candidates, and, once her friend had sold her on two students, she instructed Breckinridge to ask them to take the Junior Agent exam for which she would mail an announcement as soon as it was printed.[101] Both parts of the exam coincided perfectly with the curriculum at the School of Social Service Administration, and Abbott and Breckinridge screened for convictions before suggesting applicants. Patronage based on gender and culture thus extended into the lower levels of the Bureau.

Grace Abbott also continued Lathrop's tradition of contracting for studies by students of Breckinridge and the elder Abbott. The Bureau published the first dissertation to come out of the School, and throughout the 1920s, the School had students working on projects for the Bureau. So regularly did this sort of cooperation go on that Edith could write of one unusual male student: "We want to keep him next year to go on for the work for his Doctor's degree and I have been wondering whether we might not use him to do a contract study which he could use as his Doctor's thesis."[102]

Graduates of Hull House thus manipulated the civil service merit system to protect and increase their own power and to advance the careers of like-minded women. Because the Children's Bureau and other public agencies offered more positions than the School of Social Service Administration could fill, the system remained open to applicants unknown to the old girls, but in order to progress through the ranks in the child welfare network, a woman needed to win the sponsorship of someone already established within the hierarchy. To win that sponsorship, she had to show commitment to the reform program blocked out by an earlier generation.

Because Lathrop and her volunteer lobbyists protected the Children's Bureau from political turnover, the leaders within the dominion remained remarkably constant into the mid-1930s. Grace Abbott did not resign from the Children's Bureau until 1934—when she was replaced by a woman who had been in the agency since 1914—and Edith Abbott continued to rule the School of Social Service Administration with Breckinridge until long after. Through the 1920s and into the 1930s, this professional and institutional network continued to socialize aspiring professional women into the reform culture of the pre–World War I generation by controlling the educational process at an important school and some of the most prestigious jobs available to women in the first half of the twentieth century. Just as Lathrop and Addams had won the Abbots and Breckinridge to reform by opening professional opportunities, so these women attracted younger females. Among such women, professional interests preserved reforming aspirations and provided continuity between the Progressive era and the New Deal.

CHAPTER 4

Consolidation and Expansion of the Dominion: The Sheppard-Towner Maternity and Infancy Act, 1918–1924

Only a few months after the United States officially entered World War I, a newspaper in New York reported on Julia Lathrop's leadership at the Children's Bureau. "Out through the south and west," the article began, "her army of trained women is moving on the households of the poor, attacking the city and village that does not insure its babies pure milk. . . . " The report continued: "Miss Lathrop has a brigade of home education workers in the field. Armed with working models of outdoor cribs, fireless cookers and iceless ice boxes, they are invading homes having babies, teaching mothers to make and use these baby-saving devices."[1]

In very few words, this article dramatized the character of the child welfare dominion in its maturity. Before handing the Children's Bureau over to Grace Abbott, Julia Lathrop had solidified its affiliations with female voluntary organizations and expanded its monopoly over child welfare policy especially by directing wartime organization and patriotic fervor toward child welfare reforms. The farthest reaching of those reforms came with congressional approval of the Sheppard-Towner Maternity and Infancy Act in 1921. Embodying the country's first federal program for social welfare, this legislation expressed, consolidated, and broadened the dominion's authority. Indeed, during the implementation of the Maternity and Infancy Act, the Children's Bureau and its subordinate organizations achieved their greatest power.

For American women, that power had multiple meanings. As the New York reporter indicated in 1917, an expanded dominion opened opportunities for "trained women," whose career needs continued to support reform commitments. But, as the reporter inadvertently revealed, these opportunities for professional women potentially threatened the autonomy of other women, most especially those mothers whose homes were "invaded" by Lathrop's troops. While some women certainly welcomed the intervention of child welfare workers — in fact, begged for their help — others resisted and resented the intrusions. Resistance was located particularly in communities of African-American, Native American, and foreign-born women. A study of the dominion between 1917 and 1924, with an emphasis on its implementation of the Sheppard-Towner Act, exposes then not only the persistent interrelationship between reform and professional opportunities for women but also the race and class identities that divided American women and moreover empowered some at the expense of others.

In 1914, war in Europe began rearranging the political alliances responsible for child welfare reform in the United States. Activists who united in 1912 on behalf of child labor laws and mother's pensions soon divided over military preparedness. Along with all other residents of the United States, they asked whether their country should arm itself just in case the European conflict should demand an American response. For members of a culture that had long defined itself over against European decadence, whose most revered statesman had warned against "entangling alliances" with Europe, and yet whose most essential blood, economic, and cultural ties remained with that continent and moreover with countries on both sides of the current conflict, the prospect of participation in this war proved agonizing. From 1914 to 1917, some progressives dribbled into the camp of Theodore Roosevelt — and ultimately Woodrow Wilson — who believed that the United States must prepare for war. Others, out of pacifist convictions or practical judgments, agitated against military build-up. Others, finally believing American involvement inevitable, backed preparedness and soothed their souls with the hope that the war might actually strengthen the country's commitment to reform.

Alliances split yet again when the United States finally declared war on April 6, 1917. Most of the progressives who had continued to oppose preparedness now resigned themselves to war and, responding to Wilson's insistence that this was a war to make the world safe for democracy, threw themselves into the effort with characteristic passion. Those who, like Jane

Addams, remained publicly opposed to American belligerence, found themselves isolated and accused of disloyalty.[2]

In some ways, experience during the war seemed to bear out the hope that belligerence would promote reform. To the extent that progressivism urged the federal government into the economy, for example, World War I counted as an ally of reform because it shoved the central government into partnerships with industry to assure military production.[3] So hopeful did some progressives find this trend that one could proclaim: "Laissez-faire is dead! Long live social control! Social control not only to enable us to meet the rigorous demands of war, but also as a foundation for the peace and brotherhood that is to come."[4] Moreover, the support of moderate suffragists for the war effort helped to win the woman suffrage amendment, and public health concerns enjoyed such vital popularity that one journalist concluded with regard to public health problems: "Into a year there has been packed the progress of a decade."[5] Finally, both the flow of young men into the military and the near end to immigration temporarily opened new jobs for African-Americans and for white women, especially in transportation and industry.[6] Indeed, Julia Lathrop thought that the situation for women looked so bright during the war that she announced: "Equal suffrage, equal pay for equal work, equal business and professional opportunity, and equal authority over the family and the family purse are rights almost attained—their justice is recognized and their realization within sight."[7]

As it turned out, Lathrop was overly optimistic: most of the gains born of the war died with the armistice. Euro-American men returned to their jobs, leaving African-American women and men and Euro-American women demoted if not unemployed. Moreover, the central government abandoned even the degree of economic planning it had finally achieved during the last months of the war. And public concern for most social justice issues not only petered out but actually found itself under attack. As pacific progressives had feared, American participation in World War I whipped up a patriotic frenzy that ultimately doomed many of their progressive projects. Assaults came, for instance, from the Postmaster Albert Burleson, who used the extraordinary prerogatives granted him under the Espionage Act (1917) to cripple the Socialist party, the left wing of the labor movement, and numerous ethnic organizations. The Committee on Public Information, an agency meant to manufacture support for the war, read its mandate as permission to attempt eradication of ethnic diversity both to ensure the loyalty of German-Americans and to create a citizenry uniformly enthusiastic for war.⁸ Settlements and other progressive organizations that had opposed preparedness and that fought the trend toward homogenizing ethnic cultures lost public approval and funding, a loss that deepened after the Bolshevik Revolution in Russia, which allowed self-styled American patriots to brand any suggestion for change in America as an egregious lack of patriotism.⁹ Such accusations of un-Americanism carried increasingly serious consequences in the growing virulence of official and vigilante repression that swept across the United States during and immediately after the war. In fact, the legacy of this narrowest intolerance would haunt the entire postwar decade, and especially in the second half of the 1920s, the forces of intolerance would prove strong enough to re-route the political mainstream to the right.

Nevertheless, child welfare reform was one of the progressive beneficiaries of World War I, and one of the very few whose benefits did not end with demobilization. This surprising relationship between child welfare reform and war developed in large part because female progressives had professionalized their movement for child welfare and given it an institutional home in the federal government, a location of which Julia Lathrop made shrewd use. Lathrop was one of the progressives who opposed American involvement in the war, but in order to keep her job and retain her effectiveness in the public arena, decided to keep her opposition quiet.¹⁰ As important, Lathrop had come into her own as a national leader: her authority, no longer filtered through the leadership of the settlements, rested on her own reputation. Had Lathrop's influence continued to flow from her association with the settlements, her program for child welfare reform might easily have been identified with unpopular radicalism and lost favor among the nation's women. But because Lathrop was perceived as an independent, professional leader, entrenched in the very government prosecuting the war, her patriotism remained untarnished, and from her unique position, she was able to save child welfare reform from decline during the war years.

Indeed, Lathrop chose to milk the war for all it was worth to the cause of child welfare reform, and it turned out to be worth a lot. One way that it bolstered the cause was by interesting middle-class women in patriotic service. Women were just as anxious as men to contribute to America's military venture, but constraints imposed by the contemporary construction of gender largely forbade them to express their support through military or managerial participation. As they fished around for other ways to feed the effort, Lathrop provided a satisfying catch: she billed her child-saving drives as manifestations of the highest patriotism. She proclaimed that "saving babies is a vital part of fighting the war," and even convinced President Wilson to announce: "Next to the duty of doing everything possible for the soldiers at the front, there could be, it seems to me, no more patriotic duty than that of protecting the children, who constitute one-third of our population."[11]

In fact, the war riveted attention to child welfare by revealing, through military physicals, the prevalence of ill-health among American boys. "One reason for unusual attention to the health of children at the present time," wrote one of the Bureau's staff, "is, of course, the large number of draft rejections because of inability to pass the physical examination."[12] Lathrop herself argued: "The fact that one-third of the men in the first draft were rejected for physical defects which, we are told, in large part might have been removed if recognized and treated in infancy, certainly justifies us" in maintaining that children are a vital resource of the nation for which the community as a whole must take responsibility.[13]

Adding power to this appeal was one more resource offered up by the war: the unification of female volunteers into a single organization. This consolidation of female voluntary organizations occurred under the auspices of the Woman's Committee of the Council of National Defense. As a move toward military preparedness in 1916, Congress had created the Council to begin studying the country's economic capacity for war. Seven appointees formed an advisory commission, and, eventually, each adviser headed a committee responsible for some aspect of the war effort. After America's declaration of war, the Council added a State Councils Section and a Woman's Committee to coordinate the voluntary, war-related activities of men and women in the states. The Woman's Committee, chaired by one of the country's leading suffragists, Dr. Anna Howard Shaw, established ten departments. Each had a national chair as well as chairs in every state so that women from all voluntary organizations could join together under one department for a particular kind of work.[14]

Julia Lathrop, serving as the executive chair of the Child Welfare Department, used this wartime organization of women to broaden the popular base for child welfare reform and to solidify the ties between that base and the Bureau. All the state chairs of child welfare she made special agents of the Children's Bureau and gave them responsibility for implementing the Bureau's wartime program, which amounted to an ingenious publicity campaign called Children's Year.[15] In an announcement of Children's Year, Lathrop urged American citizens "to make the second year of the war beginning April 6 a year in which, after all has been done for our men at the front which we know how to do, the civil population shall do all in its power to protect the children of this nation as a patriotic duty."[16] The purpose of Children's Year, she explained, was "to save the lives of at least 100,000 children under 5 years of age and to make life safer for all children."[17]

In her more specific outline of goals for Children's Year, Lathrop listed measures long advocated by female reformers and which, when federalized, would constitute major provisions of the American welfare state. She did not back away from insisting that ultimately the welfare of children required the outright abolition of poverty. "If we decide that the abolition of poverty is a necessity of the democratic State, and not an unattainable luxury," she argued, "then it can be accomplished in our own day, even in the throes of war."[18] And to that end, the hopes of Children's Year included mother's pensions, a family wage for fathers, maternity health care for all women, well-baby clinics for infants, a safe milk supply, decent education for all children, enforcement of child labor laws, adequate birth registration in every state, and the creation of state and municipal bureaucracies to make these things possible.[19] Thus, Lathrop's professional position allowed her to keep alive and even broaden support for the female progressives' child welfare agenda, and in turn, that reform agenda—by consistently including the demand for public agencies staffed by professionals—promised expanding professional options for women.

Especially important for the consolidation and expansion of the child welfare dominion was the crusade for child health. America's unhealthy boys were not news to women in the Children's Bureau. While pushing for birth registration and child labor laws, the Bureau had also been researching infant health and more specifically infant and maternal mortality rates since 1913. Comparisons showed that America's rates were among the highest in the industrialized world, and studies suggested that informed prenatal and infant care might have prevented half of those deaths.[20] Moreover, Lathrop perceived a special need for health care in rural areas. Among the thousands of letters that the Children's Bureau received each year were many that attested to the isolation of rural women and what one correspondent called her "perfect horror at the prospects" of delivering a baby alone.[21] Statistics collected by the Children's Bureau corroborated these individual testimonies, showing even before 1920 that America's maternal mortality rate was higher in the country than in the city, and that by 1921, the infant mortality rate would be greater for farms than cities.[22]

During Children's Year, Lathrop's response was twofold. With $150,000 from President Wilson's wartime emergency fund, she expanded educational and promotional activities that the Bureau had already pioneered to improve prenatal and infant care.[23] She oversaw, for instance, the increasing distribution of pamphlets on prenatal and infant care; she continued to send workers to national gatherings of women to demonstrate hygienic techniques; and she worked through local women's groups to sponsor child health conferences where volunteer doctors and nurses measured, weighed, and examined babies and then taught parents how to keep their children healthy. Lathrop hoped that these conferences would inspire localities to establish permanent public health nursing services and well-baby clinics.[24]

The drive for these conferences proved phenomenally effective. An estimated eleven million female volunteers participated in them. As a result of their work, six and a half million children received medical examinations; 24 states permanently employed new public health nurses; 143 new health centers opened; and ten states established new milk stations.[25] Here was evidence for the conclusion of one historian who claimed that during World War I the Department of Child Welfare was "the most spectacularly successful of the departments of the Woman's Committee."[26]

But because these activities reached mostly urban women and children, Lathrop also wove into her program for Children's Year a proposal for federal aid permanently to support such programs in rural areas. As Lathrop's recommendation responded directly to the needs of many farm women who faced incredible hardships in childbirth, it would also, if implemented, open new professional opportunities for women and strengthen the Bureau's authority over child welfare policy by requiring participating states to appoint new agencies to administer the federal funds under the direction of the Children's Bureau. According to Lathrop, the new agencies would comprise a physician from the state board of health, a teacher from a state university, and a public health nurse. The public health nurse, keystone of the program, would lead a cadre of subordinate nurses in visiting local communities to demonstrate the value of maternal and infant health programs and help local communities to establish permanent health centers for children and pregnant women.[27]

Especially because federal legislative energies were absorbed by the war, this proposal received minimal attention in 1918, but its suggestion for the creation of state agencies devoted to child health received an enormous push, and the success of this drive built a new level of authority into the child welfare dominion as it increased career opportunities for women. Although the Bureau had treated voluntary groups as respected partners in its projects, Lathrop had begun early on to promote the establishment of public agencies devoted to maternal and infant care at the state and local levels. The urge to create these public agencies was in keeping with the preference for public rather than private services which had developed in female communities during the 1890s and was receiving formalization at the Chicago School of Civics and Philanthropy. Female leaders believed that public agencies in the states would better protect children by providing care that did not depend on the unreliable charity of almsgivers, and the proposed child welfare divisions might enhance the research capabilities of the Children's Bureau by providing a bureaucratic partner in the states. In addition, leaders in the Bureau were explicit about the potential of these public agencies to employ ever more women. "I feel that women physicians are particularly fitted for these positions [as directors of Child Hygiene Divisions]," insisted one policymaker in the Bureau. "I am also quite certain that there will soon be a very large increase in the number of municipal Child Hygiene Divisions, thus affording additional opportunities for medical women."[28]

During Children's Year, women under the Bureau's direction staged an effective campaign for the creation of these public agencies. While Lathrop persuaded directors of state boards of health to join the movement, volunteers lobbied governors and legislators. And whereas the Bureau had previously succeeded in convincing only seven states and about 40 cities to establish these divisions, by November 1920, 35 states had created child hygiene divisions, and four years later only one state would lack such an agency.[29]

Personnel in these agencies fulfilled hopes for the continued interdependence of child welfare reform and professional opportunity for women. In 1921, 42 of 45 directors of the state divisions were female, just as women in the Bureau had predicted. Moreover, the agencies employed hundreds of female public health nurses, and the vast majority of each division's staff was female.[30]

The relationship between the Children's Bureau and these new state agencies illuminated not only the unexpected and unpredictable power of a small federal bureau but also the degree of authority that the Children's Bureau had established over child welfare policy. In law, the state divisions owed no allegiance to the Children's Bureau. In fact, they acted as the Bureau's subsidiaries: they asked the Bureau to provide organizational blueprints; the boards of health often asked the Bureau to recommend directors for their new child hygiene divisions; and without fail, the new agencies offered their cooperation in the Bureau's work.[31] As soon as Ohio formed its Division of Child Hygiene, the new director expressed her desire to work closely with the Bureau and later conducted her programs exactly according to the Bureau's dictates.[32] Pennsylvania's Chief of Child Hygiene insisted that she needed the Bureau's help in her work and would do all she could "to be of help to" the Bureau.[33] The director of the Kansas Division of Child Hygiene offered to cooperate in studies the Bureau might do in her state.[34] The head of California's Child Hygiene Division was "specially anxious to help [the Bureau] in every way possible."[35] And these were just a few of the numerous pledges of fealty to the Bureau's leadership.[36]

In keeping with their subordinate status, the state agencies went so far as to submit regular reports to their superior. By 1920, the Bureau received quarterly reports on budgets, legislation, and programs from the state divisions. The Bureau in turn summarized the reports and published them in a quarterly newsletter sent out to each agency.[37] Even without a legal mandate, the state agencies accepted their place under the Bureau in the world of child welfare policy, a testimony to the Bureau's role in creating the agencies and an acknowledgment of the Bureau's pre-eminence in the field.

Coming out of the war, then, Lathrop's Bureau stood at the head of a consolidated female dominion devoted to child welfare. The Children's Bureau dominated the states' child hygiene divisions and the female voluntary organizations that had united under the Woman's Committee of the Council of National Defense. As yet, the relative authority of the state agencies and the voluntary groups remained undetermined, but both groups were unswervingly devoted to the Bureau's leadership. As the government was dismantling much of its emergency organization, Lathrop's corps was scrambling to find ways to sustain its work. Whenever possible, the state chairs of the Woman's Committee transferred their work either to a permanent organization of women or to one of the newly created public agencies.[38] Indeed, while male volunteers saw the armistice as ending their wartime work, according to one historian, "many of the women in the state divisions felt that it was just beginning."[39] The Bureau intended to retain that loyalty. As one journalist reported: "According to those in charge of the nationwide movement to reduce infant mortality, the year set apart as Children's Year is only the inception of a vast organization which it is hoped to make a permanent institution."[40] To serve that end, although the war

ended in November 1918, the Bureau maintained the wartime organization
of women first by continuing Children's Year until April 1919 and then by
gathering all the chairs of the states' child welfare committees into a permanent advisory committee for the Bureau.[41]

As middle-class women emerged from the war better organized than
ever before, they carried their clearest agenda for child welfare reform.
Their wish list, duplicating Lathrop's goals for Children's Year, demanded
activism at both the local and national levels.[42] The two issues that required
national attention were child labor and child health, and it was child health
that occupied pride of place. This was in part because of the wartime and
postwar history of federal child labor measures. During the war, the Supreme Court struck down the child labor law that Grace Abbott was
administering, and when a new law took effect in 1919, its administration
rested not with the Children's Bureau but with the Treasury Department.
When in 1922 the Court declared that law too unconstitutional, the Children's Bureau and all of its forces joined to pass a constitutional amendment
that would permit Congress to legislate on child labor. The amendment
received congressional approval in 1924 and went on to the states for
ratification.[43] Though many female voluntary organizations continued to
work for ratification in their states, child labor was temporarily off the
national agenda at the same time that the Children's Bureau and its organizational partners were deep in the administration of a maternal and child
health program that had become their top priority.

The campaign for maternal and infant health care helped to draw the
political parameters of postwar America. Several alternative visions of the
state, all representing some compromise between laissez-faire liberalism and
state socialism, were competing for resources and expression in the early
1920s, and until mid-decade they competed fairly evenly. Herbert Hoover,
the new Secretary of Commerce in 1921, energetically promoted one of
the most popular options, which historian Ellis Hawley has called the
"associative state." Believing in the ability and willingness of American business to make socially responsible decisions, Hoover opposed governmental
involvement in economic planning or the provision of social services. He
saw the federal government rather as a "catalyzer and coordinator of cooperative endeavors" among private decisionmakers in the business community.[44]
In many ways, Hoover's activities in the Department of Commerce mirrored Lathrop's earlier tactics in the Children's Bureau, with their emphasis
on the central government as a clearinghouse of information for and an
organizer of associations in the private sector as well as a publicity agent for
expert advice.[45]

Women in the child welfare dominion advocated a stronger state than the Hooverites. While their opinions varied on the proper degree of governmental control over economic decisionmaking, these women uniformly supported federal involvement in social welfare programs.[46] This preference carried forward the values that had developed in female communities during the 1890s, that had created the Children's Bureau in the 1910s, that the Bureau had institutionalized in its work, and that women like Abbott and Breckinridge professionalized in theirs. After World War I, these values expressed themselves not only in approval for federal limitation of child labor but also in support for Lathrop's plan to provide maternal and infant health care through federal grants-in-aid to the states. When, in 1919, a modified version of Lathrop's proposal was introduced in the Senate by Morris Sheppard and in the House by Horace Towner, the state chairs of child welfare for the Woman's Committee met to organize their plan of attack on the bills' behalf, and they agreed to begin by publicizing the accomplishments of Children's Year with the expectation that this good press would surely rouse support for the Sheppard-Towner Maternity and Infancy Bill.[47]

This movement toward a more active state proved viable in the early 1920s for several reasons. First, despite conservative men in the White House, Congress harbored a coalition of progressive southern Democrats and western Republicans who made common cause in support of a more powerful central government than the executive branch preferred.[48] Moreover, disastrous economic conditions for both farmers and workers forged a farm-labor link in the Congress that was inclined toward a more active state.[49]

Second, legislators feared the censure of women finally enfranchised by the Nineteenth Amendment. Passed through Congress in 1919 and ratified by the states in 1920, the amendment sent politicians scrambling for the votes of this new, untested constituency. Perceiving Lathrop's Maternity and Infancy Bill as a measure cherished by the women's bloc, Democrats supported the goals of the bill in their national platform during the 1920 election, and Warren Harding endorsed the measure despite its exclusion from the Republican platform.[50]

Finally, the women's dream of a state responsible for social welfare was given substance in the early 1920s by the institutionalization and professionalization of female lobbying activity. Organized in 1920, the Women's Joint Congressional Committee (WJCC) formalized the lobbying network that Wald, Addams, and finally Lathrop had built. Initially representing ten national women's organizations, it provided them a common conduit for information on federal legislation, and it organized lobbies on their behalf. Female voluntary organizations could now rely on a single professional staff to keep them abreast of legislative maneuvers and to coordinate their responses. Procedure held that whenever three of the WJCC's organizations voted to support or oppose a piece of legislation, they formed a subcommittee to do their lobbying. Charter members—the General Federation of Women's Clubs, the National Consumers' League, the National League of Women Voters, the National Women's Trade Union League, the National Congress of Mothers and Parent-Teacher Associations, the American Association of University Women, the Women's Christian Temperance Union, the National Federation of Business and Professional Women's Clubs, the National Council of Jewish Women, and the American Home Economics Association—voted unanimously in 1920 to make the Sheppard-Towner Maternity and Infancy Bill the WJCC's top priority.[51]

That vote rested on groundwork that Julia Lathrop had laid even before the WJCC formed. In 1918, she had asked the General Federation of Women's Clubs to endorse her bill, which they had agreed to do at their biennial convention in 1920.[52] While the League of Women Voters was forming as the successor to the National American Woman Suffrage Association in 1919, Lathrop convinced its leadership to create a Child Welfare Committee specifically to lobby for her bill.[53] Through personal friends, Lathrop had already won the approval of the National Board of the Young Women's Christian Association and the National Women's Trade Union League.[54]

True to Lillian Wald's conception of an agency that would stir up public support for its own recommendations, Lathrop orchestrated the movement on behalf of her legislation and then claimed that her legislation simply responded to demands of the nation's women. She wrote, for instance, to one highly placed woman in the General Federation: "You will understand it is very difficult for a government bureau to push legislation which would seem to increase its power and responsibility."[55] She needed for women's organizations to lead the movement, Lathrop explained, so that the Bureau itself could hang back and allow the nation's women to demand an increase in the Bureau's power. Later she wrote: "I should, of course, be very glad indeed to see the matter so urged that it ceased to be in any sense a Bureau measure."[56]

The WJCC made that possible, and though the most active lobbyists represented the General Federation, the WCTU, the League of Women Voters, and the National Consumer's League, all organizations contributed to the effort.[57] As the bill flowed in and out of congressional committees in 1920 and 1921, the WJCC scheduled representatives from its constituent organizations to testify at hearings.[58] It arranged the arrival of thousands of letters in support of the bill on specific days during the hearings and voting process, which prompted one inundated aide on Capitol Hill to exclaim: "I think every woman in my state has written to the Senator."[59] The staff of the WJCC also conducted personal interviews with legislators and, during the last weeks before passage in 1921, they interviewed fifty congressmen per day.[60]

With the WJCC thus serving as the lobbying arm of the child welfare dominion, Lathrop had time to rouse support outside her usual network. To gain support for her bill, she negotiated long and hard with the heads of the American Child Hygiene Association and the American Public Health Association.[61] She persuaded the executive secretary of the National Organization for Public Health Nursing to rally nurses to the cause.[62] Moreover, she convinced the American Federation of Labor and the National Council of Catholic Women to lobby for the bill. Women's committees from both the Democratic and Republican parties offered critical support. Smaller groups such as the National Association of Deans of Women, the National Women's Association of Commerce, the Women's Press Club, the Service Star Legion, and the Women's Foundation for Health joined the chorus of advocates.[63] One observer in Washington called it "the most widespread and popular lobby that probably has ever visited this city."[64] A disgruntled opponent accused Lathrop of having built up "a political machine."[65]

While lobbying, this machine made public not only its altruistic motive for supporting the bill but also its interest in increasing possibilities for female professionals. Female journalists praised the bill for its potential to provide new jobs for women.[66] Advocates roused women at large to the cause by pointing out the program's power to employ female professionals.[67] Female doctors and nurses anxiously asked how they might find employment under the program.[68] And Jeannette Rankin, the first woman to serve in Congress and the first to introduce Lathrop's bill in the House, tried to add a provision to the bill requiring that only women be hired to implement it.[69] In this drive, middle-class white women self-consciously wove together the causes of child welfare reform and professional opportunity for women.

To attain victory, lobbyists had to compromise with the larger authority vested in the male Congress. For instance, legislators from urban states forbade discrimination against cities. Penny-pinchers in Congress allotted less money than the women preferred, and skeptics limited the first appropriation to a period of five years, after which Congress would reconsider the program. Opponents who feared the nationalization of children won a provision to prevent any public employee from entering a home without the permission of parents.[70] And in negotiations with the American Child Hygiene Association and the American Public Health Association, Lathrop agreed not to require the creation of new state agencies to administer the act: the final legislation said that if a participating state had a child hygiene division within its department of health, that division would administer the funds. If no such division existed, the state had either to create one or to designate some other agency to cooperate with the Bureau.[71] Although the Children's Bureau retained administration of the act and $50,000 per year to cover its costs, the act created a Board of Maternity and Infant Hygiene comprising the chief of the Children's Bureau, the Surgeon-General of the United States Public Health Service, and the United States Commissioner of Education. That board ultimately approved all state plans for use of Sheppard-Towner funds before the federal Treasury released money to the states.[72]

With these concessions, the child welfare dominion won the farthest reaching federal welfare program to precede the New Deal. And it won by a landslide: the Senate passed the bill 63 to 7; the House by 279 to 39. Without argument, President Harding signed the bill into law on November 23, 1921.[73] The victory was especially remarkable because the policy embodied in the Maternity and Infancy Act was not the Congress's preference. "If the members [of the House and Senate] could have voted on that measure secretly . . . it would have been killed as emphatically as it was finally passed in the open under the pressure of the Joint Congressional Committee of Women," admitted one of the bill's senatorial supporters.[74] Passage of the Sheppard-Towner Maternity and Infancy Act, then, expressed women's power at this unique juncture to determine federal child welfare policy even despite the legal ability of a male Congress to prevent it, and success was due in large part to the professionalization and institutionalization of the female movement for child welfare reform.

The question now was whether female activists could gain tighter control over policies in the states. The Sheppard-Towner Act required state legislatures to vote acceptance of the act. For those states in which legislatures were not meeting right away, the governors could conditionally accept, and the legislature could later uphold or revoke the governor's decision. Along with acceptance, the legislature had to set the state's contribution for the work. If the state accepted federal funds but appropriated no state monies, the act provided an outright grant of $5000. Each state also qualified for up to $5000 in matching funds and a second matching grant based on the state's population. Once a state accepted and designated a state agency to administer its programs, that agency had to present the Children's Bureau with a program proposal. If the Bureau approved a proposal, it went to the federal Board of Maternity and Infancy to receive final okay.[75]

To push their victory to completion, Sheppard-Towner advocates shifted their focus to the states. Lathrop, who retired from the Children's Bureau in 1921, agitated in her home state of Illinois.[76] Her successor, Grace Abbott, urged all governors to take advantage of the new funds.[77] Most decisive, the Federation of Women's Clubs, League of Women Voters, and other women's groups led lobbies in state capitols. In some states, several women's groups united under a special umbrella organization formed specifically to lobby for acceptance of the act. In New York for example, 21 organizations organized in this way.[78]

An overwhelming majority of states jumped at the chance to receive federal money, and even in recalcitrant states advocates won strong support. By June 30, 1922, 42 of 48 states had accepted the Sheppard-Towner Act, 11 by legislative enactment and 31 by gubernatorial decree.[79] One year later, when all the state legislatures had met, 40 states accepted funds. Not accepting for fiscal 1923–24 were Connecticut, Illinois, Kansas, Louisiana, Maine, Massachusetts, Rhode Island, and Vermont. In Maine, the governor vetoed the legislature's acceptance. In Connecticut, Illinois, Kansas, and Vermont, the legislatures had not upheld the governor's provisional acceptance. In Illinois, Kansas, and Louisiana, the acceptance passed the Senate but failed in the House.[80] By June 1927, only three states remained outside the Sheppard-Towner fold: Illinois, Connecticut, and Massachusetts.[81]

Child welfare programs in 45 of the 48 states were now officially under the Children's Bureau's supervision. The interposition of a special board to approve proposals in no way diluted the Bureau's control because at its first meeting on April 18, 1922, the members of the board elected Grace Abbott as chair, and thereafter simply rubber-stamped the Bureau's decisions on states' programs.[82] The Maternity and Infancy Act thus legalized the previously unofficial relationship between the Children's Bureau and analogous agencies in the states.

Indeed, the women in the Bureau circumvented even the influence that Congress had attempted to exert on child welfare policy. For instance, administrators of the act decided to reject any proposal that did not aim especially to provide services to rural mothers and children. Despite congressional refusal to restrict funds to rural areas, female policymakers in the Bureau insisted that because drafters of the legislation had intended the funds for rural work they should reject any proposal that did not favor the countryside.[83] Furthermore, they decided that federal funds could not be used to support the work of any voluntary organization. When, for instance, one state proposed to take over the salary of a Red Cross nurse and another to expand the work of a clinic sponsored by a Parent-Teacher Association, the Bureau rejected those proposals.[84] In these ways, the women in the Children's Bureau used their interpretive powers to restrict the state's programs in ways that Congress had not intended and especially to express their preference for professional, public social services over private ones.

This use of federal power to build up public social services at the expense of private agencies clearly distinguished the goals of the Children's Bureau from those at the Commerce Department. At precisely the time that Hoover and his men were using federal influence to empower private trade associations, women in the Children's Bureau were swinging their resources into public institutions even where that choice directly affronted private groups in their own network. Nowhere were the competing views of the state more obvious or more apparently gender-related. Following the logic of the female professional ethos as it had evolved in formal bureaucratic and professional contexts, women in the Bureau stood as leading proponents of an American welfare state in the 1920s.

As expected, the professionals employed by the new public agencies were female. At the federal level, the Bureau created a new division to administer the Sheppard-Towner Act. In the beginning, it employed two physicians who served as director and associate director, a public health nurse, an accountant, a secretary, and a stenographer, all of them women. Later, the Bureau hired three more female doctors and a female social worker to help with the work.[85] In the states, women also ran the show. At least 75 percent of the states' directors of the maternity and infancy programs were female.[86] In 1927, the states employed a total of 812 public health nurses with Sheppard-Towner funds, which number did not include the nurses paid by local units or voluntary organizations cooperating with the state agencies. All of the nurses were women.[87] Almost half of the states' full-time doctors were women, despite the fact that only 5 percent of all doctors were female.[88] Of 52 staff members in New York, 47 were women. The director and associate director were both female M.D.s.[89] Women from professions as diverse as social work, accounting, home economics, public relations, community organizing, and dietetics also found jobs under the act.[90]

Within the web of organizations and agencies that implemented the Sheppard-Towner Act, women from very different professions thus united to improve the lot of mothers and children. In some cases during the 1920s, professionalization built barriers between middle-class women because instead of identifying themselves first as women united by sex with other women, professionals identified themselves primarily as doctors, social workers, or teachers whose interests were confined to advancement within their professions.[91] In the child welfare establishment, this was not true. Doctors, nurses, social workers, teachers, stenographers, clerks, dieticians, writers, administrators, lobbyists, and home economists—women from very different professions—united in a common project and identified themselves more with a mission than with their professions. Professionalization no doubt complicated the loyalties even of women who held fast to this vision—after all, female doctors at the Bureau belonged to the American Medical Association and social workers to the National Conference of Social Work—but in their lives, professional loyalties did not overwhelm their primary commitment to child welfare reform, which as it developed under the Children's Bureau committed them to struggle with other women across professional boundaries.

Working in the states' child hygiene divisions, these women expanded the child welfare dominion's monopoly over child welfare policy. With techniques recommended by the Children's Bureau, state agencies reached into the most isolated areas of the country to influence policies of local governments and the child care practices of more mothers than ever before. Just as Lathrop had specified in her original proposal, public health nurses scattered into remote towns to conduct child-health conferences, to offer classes on infant care, and to advise individual mothers whose children had specific problems.[92]

These meetings between rural women and Sheppard-Towner nurses represented complicated transactions within and across classes, cultures, and races. In the tradition of social control theory, they can easily be interpreted as attempts by the white, professional middle classes to establish their cultural as well as political hegemony, in response to which women from some ethnic groups formed pockets of resistance, while others capitulated. But such an analysis captures only part of the situation. It misses the undeniable fact that women and children of all classes and races were actually suffering from conditions surrounding childbirth, and that women from all sectors of the population welcomed some of the help they received from itinerant nurses. Indeed, some lower-class women invited intervention by middle-class professionals. In this instance, working- and middle-class values were not utterly different, and such similarity, as historians Linda Gordon and Judith Trolander have argued, requires qualification of social control theories that see social welfare programs simply as attempts by one class to control another. Unmodified social control analyses also overlook the changes in childrearing that professionals were advocating for women of their own class.[93]

The enormous complexity of these relationships, then, makes generalization nearly impossible. But analysis can certainly flag some of the dynamics at work in these meetings. First, the encounters between professionals and the women they hoped to help were prompted by real risks and suffering that mothers shared; second, professionals—in addition to sincerely wanting to help their clients—were involved in a project aimed at establishing their own authority and the dominance of their class and culture; finally, this project pushed professionals into relationships with women who actively participated and jointly determined the outcome of their meetings. Clients were not passive victims in these relationships but less powerful partners whose interests sometimes meshed with those of their privileged associates and sometimes did not. Especially because most programs funded by the Sheppard-Towner Act were voluntary, those who were objects of the programs usually remained subjects as well, and subjects who were able to negotiate their own fate.[94]

Between 1922 and 1929, the Sheppard-Towner initiative reached hundreds of thousands of women through child health and prenatal conferences as well as through mothers' classes. For the fiscal year ending June 30, 1924, alone, the states reported 15,547 child health conferences during which 303,546 children received examinations. They reported 6,088 separate prenatal conferences at which 38,662 women were examined. That same year, 95,500 mothers attended 3,000 mothers' classes taught by employees of the act. Furthermore, these activities convinced local governments to join the crusade for prenatal and infant care: the year's activities resulted in the establishment of 1,084 new, permanent children's health centers and 188 prenatal clinics.[95]

Because the ultimate goal of the Maternity and Infancy Act was to establish these permanent, public clinics, a nurse's success depended on her ability to rouse local interest in her work. Just as women in the Children's

Bureau had drawn national female voluntary groups into their work, so the nurses organized local associations. Just as the Bureau had lobbied state governments for the implementation of its child welfare policies, so the nurses lobbied local governments. Methods and policies that had become common among a national elite of women through the Bureau's work now moved into locally elite groups through Sheppard-Towner nurses.

Although the routine varied from state to state, Kentucky's procedure contained elements common to most programs. In Kentucky, a public health nurse traveled from one county to the next, organizing health conferences. Once arrived at a central town in the county, she wrote to all local doctors, explained her purpose, and asked their cooperation. A second set of letters went to female organizations, schools, elected officials, and churches. Then the nurse met with these groups to detail her program and to enlist volunteers for specific tasks. Doctors she recruited to examine children on the days of the conference. From other groups, she formed a committee of canvassers to approach every local family with pre-school children and ask them to attend the conference. For those without transportation, the committee established a motor corps to deliver mothers and children to the conferences. On the days of the conference, several volunteers weighed and measured children, kept records, explained procedures, and helped screaming children in and out of their clothes. If any examination revealed abnormalities, examiners explained the problem and advised the parents to consult a physician. Those families then received visits from the nurse before she moved on to the next county. She considered her work successful if, when she drove out of town, the local committee had promised to remain united until it had established a permanent health center for children.[96]

This procedure reverberated with possibilities for both the oppression and empowerment of mothers. In fact, it perfectly illustrates the inevitably double character of a program designed by one group of people to help a different group: even when such a program has something genuinely important to offer, outreach on its behalf is intrusive. In the case of Sheppard-Towner programs, though no woman or child had to participate in the prenatal or child health conferences, representatives of the national child health establishment were, wherever possible, sending local elites to mothers' doors to invite them to the conferences and even to provide them with transportation. While these visitations could and often demonstrably did embody warm, community interest resulting in real gains for a family's health, they also represented surveillance by elites—a sort of motherhood patrol, visits from which potentially pressured women to attend conferences and to open their homes to uninvited evaluators.

More intrusive were home visits by nurses themselves. If a mother attended a conference and seemed to need any sort of follow-up or if someone reported that an absent woman needed help, she might well receive a home visit by a Sheppard-Towner nurse. According to Grace Abbott: "Home visits give to the nurse an opportunity to observe the living conditions of the patient."[97] They were times when a nurse "inspects the children, advises the mother, and frequently gives a demonstration of preparation of a feeding, or of bathing, or of other care of the infant."[98] Although the law said that no person had to allow a nurse into her home, nurses did not have to read mothers their right to resist, so probably few women knew the law. Certainly, few reports indicate that a nurse was ever turned away at the door, but the meaning of cooperation is impossible to determine. No doubt many women welcomed the nurses, but indifference, resentment, and hostility also seem possible responses. Whatever the feeling of clients, in fiscal 1927, states reported 587,673 visits to homes of pregnant women and young children.[99]

Demonstrations and advice given during these home visits and in all aspects of the Sheppard-Towner programs came straight out of the publications of the Children's Bureau, and some of the advice genuinely aimed at improving health. All pregnant women were advised to see a nurse or physician as early in their pregnancies as possible, to eat a balanced diet, to exercise, and to sleep at least eight hours a day. Nurses explained the value of sterilizing all items used during delivery and guided local women's groups in preparing packets of sterilized necessities to distribute to pregnant women. Child welfare workers—having discovered that breastfed babies were less likely to die than their artificially fed counterparts—were staunch advocates of breastfeeding "up to about the eighth or ninth month" and made it one of the central concerns of all their work. This struck a blow especially against white, middle-class mothers, who were the least likely to breastfeed in the 1920s. If breastfeeding was impossible, child welfare authorities recommended whole milk or some appropriate formula including as much whole milk as a baby could stomach. Condensed milk was anathema to them. As babies grew older, the going wisdom counseled play with other children in order to teach fairness and cooperation. And nurses emphasized the value of immunization against typhoid, diphtheria, and smallpox.[100]

Other parts of the child care canon, however, could be seen only as an attempt to order all homes according to the standards of middle-class professionals and to routinize them in the same way as offices and factories. Referring to babies as "wonderful little mechanisms," representatives of the child welfare corps insisted that babies should eat, sleep, and breathe on a strictly controlled, regular schedule.[101] They even distributed time cards outlining "a schedule for the baby's daily routine," which were especially to help mothers "guide their children in habit formation," a goal that women in the Children's Bureau considered of utmost importance to the creation of a self-controlled, disciplined citizenry.[102] Repeatedly, leaders in the child welfare elite condemned parents who kept "disorganized homes" or whose home life was "confused," for these were the families that inevitably produced delinquents.[103] Leaders in child welfare were thus extending their bureaucratic ideals, their need for rationalized standard operating procedures to human relationships, and specifically to parent child relations. Their goal was to "standardize the care of babies," to eradicate diversity and spontaneity in childrearing.[104] Mothers who fed babies whenever they were hungry or cuddled them whenever they cried were simply rearing little tyrants, according to the professionals' understanding. "The rule that parents should not play with the baby may seem hard," acknowledged one member of the Children's Bureau staff, "but it is without doubt a safe one."[105] Safe perhaps if one hoped to transform a living human being into a "little mechanism."

Child welfare workers spared no mother the duty to change her child-rearing ways. In a direct critique of middle-class childrearing, the nurses insisted that mothers should raise their own children without recourse to outside help, and advice to all new mothers included prohibitions against rocking their babies or sleeping with them. Rocking, they declared, interfered with babies' digestion, and sleeping with babies not only risked their safety but also encouraged immorality. Reformers had long protested over-crowded homes because they believed that cramped quarters bred promiscuity, and, while worries about physical abuse of children were well-founded, the prohibitions against sleeping with children were often impossible for poor families to uphold. Moreover, mothers' napping with their children hardly posed a threat to babies but only offended the professionals' sense of propriety and stance against physical affection.[106]

Legitimate concerns with housekeeping practices also opened the door to superfluous advice. In their home visits, nurses demonstrated how to clean houses and prepare food.[107] In some cases, these demonstrations touched domestic conditions that truly threatened a family's health—especially problems with the disposal of garbage and excrement and with the storage of food.[108] One nurse, for example, saved a baby's life by showing his mother how to protect milk from heat and flies.[109] But entrance to a home was by nature invasive, and it tempted visitors to suggest material alterations that had nothing to do with health. One state actually sent a team through black communities "to show families how to remodel, arrange, and improve their homes," and another devised a traveling "exhibit that showed a sanitary home and surroundings."[110] These initiatives emphasized the need for properly built toilets, screens on windows to deter flies, and equipment needed to store food that would maintain a family's health.[111] But even the furnishings that honestly sanitized living conditions were often beyond the means of lower-class families, and many parts of these model dwellings were nothing more than indicators of middle-class taste and fashion.

There is no question but that the needs and values of many mothers dovetailed perfectly with those of Sheppard-Towner nurses. The nurses themselves, their state divisions of child hygiene, and even the Children's Bureau received letters from women grateful for their help.[112] In places like Kentucky, the director of the Bureau of Maternal and Child Health reported in 1924: "We are beginning to receive . . . letters from mothers wanting advice about the care of their children."[113] In some cases, mothers endured terrible traveling conditions to attend child health conferences at considerable expense of time. One woman in the West, for example, had to cross a river "in a basket swung on an overhead cable" to attend a conference.[114] Another woman drove fourteen miles in a horse-drawn buggy to have her children examined. And many less heroic sacrifices were made by thousands of women who were worried about their own health and that of their children.[115]

At the same time, there were resisters. These were especially among older women who were foreign-born, Native American, or African-American. In some instances, these women rejected the notion that any but traditional healers should preside over childbirth.[116] Others simply did not feel the need to change their customary practices. "Very many of the people in the district," reported a nurse from St. Louis County, Minnesota, "are foreign, mostly Finnish, some Polish and Austrian. Of course, the older women who have raised families of five to fifteen children care not what nurses teach about prenatal attention, as they have been delivered at home without assistance, or maybe interference, of doctors. . . . " She also reported that these women insisted on feeding their babies whenever they were hungry and on rocking whenever they cried. No amount of advising by nurses would change those habits. Some of these mothers, who attributed authority to personal experience rather than professional training, asked their visiting nurses the devastating question, "What do you know about babies? You have never had any, have you?"[117] The assertiveness of such women showed that, though mothers might find it increasingly difficult to avoid the advice of America's child welfare establishment, they remained free to reject it and turned a deaf ear when their own values did not support the recommendations given by professionals.

But of course the professionals never said die. To reach families in which mothers rejected their intervention, nurses taught "little mothers" classes. These short courses usually enrolled junior high girls who had younger siblings at home. One justification for these classes was that oldest daughters often cared for younger children, but administrators of the Sheppard-Towner Act also hoped that some mothers would absorb prescriptions for child care from their daughters.[118] As one writer explained: "In these [little mother] leagues the children, who often have the care of younger brothers and sisters, are instructed in approved methods of child care, and by demonstrating what they have learned at home they can do much to convince their mothers of its value." The author went on to say that this approach was for "foreign born mothers" who "were perpetuating in their small groups the superstitions and old country ideas with which they had come to the United States."[119] Surreptitious as their methods could be, professionals could not force their ideals on women who did not share them, and so diversity in childrearing prevailed: "Superstitions" and "old country ideas" continued to thrive in immigrant communities.

The professional arrogance and cultural chauvinism inherent in accusations of superstition also manifested themselves in campaigns to discipline midwives. Attempts to control midwives were certainly not new in the 1920s. In the United States, the movement was as old as the country, and it had originally been led by the male medical profession. By the Progressive era, it had just about succeeded in wiping out midwifery among white, native-born communities, but a new group of midwives rode in on the waves of immigration from southern and eastern Europe, and midwifery had never diminished among native-born African-American communities. By the 1920s, then, the movement to control midwifery was fraught with cultural and racial tension: white, native-born professionals versus foreign-born women and women of color.

Another change in the movement was that its leaders were no longer only male doctors but also female professionals in medicine, social work, and a host of related vocations. Because of her work in immigrant communities, Grace Abbott had conducted her own research on the subject, as had several other female reformers, and unlike the male doctors, these women conceded the economic and cultural necessity of midwives. Although they hoped ultimately to see midwifery disappear, they sought more immediately to standardize the practice through education and licensing laws.[120] In other words, leaders wanted to pull midwives into the child welfare dominion where the professional hierarchy could supervise them.

To achieve that goal, policymakers in the Children's Bureau made the training, licensing, and supervision of midwives one of Sheppard-Towner's central concerns. By 1921, only six states had no regulations at all for midwives, but the Bureau insisted that the country's 45,000 midwives were practicing without proper—that is, professional—training or supervision. In states where midwives attended a high proportion of births, Sheppard-Towner funds consequently helped to pay for surveys of midwives' practices, classes for untrained midwives, and inspections of licensed midwives. To support that effort, the Bureau hired an African-American doctor, Ionia Whipper, especially to work among southern black midwives, and in the fiscal year ending June 30, 1924, for example, 24,899 midwives enrolled for 2,300 courses from Sheppard-Towner nurses.[121]

Like the advice given to new mothers, some of the requirements imposed on midwives seem justified. They included, for instance, the necessity of sterilizing everything used during deliveries; they required midwives, like physicians and nurses, to register births; they demanded drops of silver nitrate in babies' eyes to prevent ophthalmia neonatorum.[122] If the testimony of white nurses is to be believed, some midwives needed this instruction: when one nurse asked all the student-midwives to bring to class the tools they used in deliveries, most reportedly arrived with only a pair of rusty scissors for cutting the umbilical cord.[123]

But supervision of midwives went so far beyond these legitimate requirements that it proved the most intrusive of Sheppard-Towner initiatives and the one that pushed hardest toward professional cultural hegemony. The director of Michigan's child health work reported, for instance, that in 1926 her inspector of midwives had started her regular duties, which were "to visit the midwives in their homes, inspect their homes and equipment, and investigate their moral character and standing in the neighborhood."[124] In some places—especially in the South—midwives were routinely tested for syphilis.[125] Pennsylvania reported that its midwife campaign included the intent "to oversee the midwife's personal cleanliness and to inspect her home and her equipment."[126] Moreover, supervisors of midwives believed it completely within their rights to set standards for midwives' *appearance*. North Carolina announced after giving "intensive instruction" to 2,000 of the state's 6,000 midwives: "The women have improved in appearance and in their practice, have a standardized equipment, are cleaner, interfere less during labor, and call a physician in complicated cases."[127] The Children's Bureau itself supported the attention to appearance. In 1927, it proudly reported that in all states where midwife programs were under way, "improvement is being made in the midwives' appearance, equipment, and procedures. . . . "[128]

Women in the child welfare network claimed that their concern with midwives responded to the very high infant and maternal mortality rates in ethnic communities, but in fact they intended to supervise these caregivers whether or not they contributed to those mortality rates. No hard evidence could possibly hang the high infant or maternal mortality rates on minority midwives, and indeed historian Molly Ladd-Taylor has concluded that mortality rates would surely have been higher in ethnic communities without the attendance of midwives.[129] Moreover, some contemporary research explicitly concluded that mortality rates were not attributable to midwife practice. In California, for instance, the director of Sheppard-Towner work reported that in her search for ways to justify training programs for the midwives in her state, she tried "to decide whether we might lay any of our maternal or infant deaths at their door." To her disappointment, investigation showed "that we cannot blame the midwives, even though uninstructed, for our maternal or infant deaths." She remained determined, however, to see the midwives "educated and improved."[130] If lowering maternal and infant mortality had really been the goal, then this director would have had absolutely no interest in "educating and improving" the midwives in her state after her research ended. Professional control over and standardization of midwife practice were more fundamental issues.

Cultural chauvinism largely accounted for the character of the midwife campaign. Child welfare professionals made no attempt to disguise their contempt for the "nonscientific" birthing practices especially of African-American and Native American midwives. "Racial groups such as Negroes and Indians still have primitive ways of dealing with childbirth," explained Grace Abbott in 1927. "The high maternal mortality rate among negroes may be correlated with the large number and the prevailing ignorance of negro midwives."[131] Especially in her consistent contrasts between African-American midwives and their foreign-born counterparts, the Bureau's chief revealed professional chauvinism as the crux of her disdain for black midwives. "The task which confronts the Southern States with their enormous numbers of illiterate, aged negro midwives, untrained except by observation," she argued, "is scarcely comparable to the undertaking which has been successfully carried out by New Jersey in obtaining the cooperation of well-trained foreign midwives."[132] Women of any race or nationality who had received formal education in midwifery, whose clothing satisfied middle-class professional standards, whose level of general education permitted them to read and write, and whose demeanor conformed to middle-class professional ideals received Abbott's highest regard. She effusively praised European- and Japanese-born midwives whom she insisted were far more trustworthy in the delivery room than many, if not most, male American doctors.[133] Moreover, she encouraged directors in the states to hire nurses from their largest ethnic groups. These were women who, regardless of race or ethnicity, shared the values and methods of the female professionalism that formed the core of the culture that Abbott and her colleagues so uncritically assumed superior and felt free to impose.[134]

At the state level, more explicit racism shaped the midwife campaign. According to a white nurse in Mississippi: "The negro women, although illiterate and ignorant, are natural nurses and are tractable, teachable, and for the most part, eager to learn the 'white folks way.'"[135] A director from Tennessee reported that her work among black midwives was "doing away with superstitions," and African-American women on staffs in the states often found themselves with lower salaries and fewer resources than their white counterparts.[136]

To the credit of the leadership among child welfare reformers, their chauvinism did not result in indifference to the suffering of women and children in the country's ethnic minorities. In states with a significant non-English-speaking population, Sheppard-Towner funds paid for translations of *Prenatal Care, Infant Care*, and *Child Care*.[137] These states also employed nurses and midwives from their largest ethnic communities. In the southwest, child health divisions sent Mexican nurses into Mexican counties and Native American nurses onto reservations; in the northeast, French-speaking nurses visited the French-Canadian immigrants; and in Minnesota, Native American nurses conducted all conferences for the Chippewas.[138] In the South, African-American nurses and doctors carried out programs in black communities, and the Children's Bureau itself hired in addition to a black physician an African-American social worker, Vinita Lewis.[139] Thus, though its leadership was white, the child welfare dominion was minimally integrated at lower levels of authority, and policymakers did intend—for good or ill—to include all women irrespective of race in what they saw as the benefits of the Sheppard-Towner Act. In the decade of the Ku Klux Klan's vigorous re-emergence and appalling acceptance among mainstream white Americans, even this degree of commitment to racial justice was noteworthy.

And even with the coercive power of the state on their side, professional midwife supervisors could not determine the conduct of a midwife once she was in a delivery room. Like mothers who refused to bow to the will of itinerant nurses, midwives retained much of their autonomy and decided for themselves what parts of the new birthing canon to use and which parts to ignore. Although some were denied licenses and even threatened with arrest, they continued in many places to practice. Where regulations required midwives regularly to produce their black bags filled according to specification, they did so, and then left the bags at home during a delivery. While many midwives apparently began to use sterile procedures and drops of silver nitrate, they combined those techniques with their customary rituals, especially the use of herbs, massage, and traditional birthing positions.[140] Midwives' practice certainly changed in response to brushes with the child welfare establishment but not without the active mediation of midwives themselves.

Sheppard-Towner practices probably left the least room for resistance when nurses involved themselves in local politics. In one southern town, for instance, a nurse discovered a tent village along the banks of a river. Her informal study showed that the villagers suffered a very high infant mortality rate. So shocked was she to find the conditions in which the villagers lived that she mounted a campaign to clean up the site and, if possible, abolish it. To this end, she spoke before religious congregations, women's groups, and men's organizations. By the time she left town, the women's organizations had taken steps to provide pure milk and to organize public health services for the residents. The men's clubs had determined to pass an ordinance prohibiting tent colonies in the city limits.[141]

Although the Sheppard-Towner Act contained provisions meant to protect the rights of parents and to assure that each beneficiary of its programs participated voluntarily, it failed to protect families from local initiatives inspired by the act's employees. In many ways, the act thus fulfilled Lathrop's hope that federal funds would spur not only medical work but also measures to ameliorate social problems that contributed to infant deaths. But by doing so, it permitted campaigns against conditions unacceptable to middle-class Americans without consultation with or acquiescence of those most affected: apparently without thought as to where the villagers might live after their tents were outlawed or to why they might be living on the river, a Sheppard-Towner nurse prompted local elites to try to forbid life in tents. Records indicated no conferences with the villagers themselves except to establish mortality rates. One day, they might simply awake to find their community outlawed.

Sheppard-Towner nurses alone could hardly shoulder the blame for this sort of tyranny. Indeed, the greatest value of studying their work subsists in its expression of overarching social and cultural relationships. The one nurse's work vis-à-vis a tent village exposed a stratified society that provided few channels through which those in need could speak to their larger community, could define their own problems in the context of that larger community, or design their own solutions with the expectation of resources from the broader group. Even when an outsider—the nurse—had identified unconscionably high maternal and infant mortality rates in the village, she felt no compulsion to call meetings of the villagers themselves to discuss her findings and seek their responses, ideas, analyses, and prescriptions. She expected instead that local elites would enact her agenda for change on a subordinate community. The power relations of American society were thus stamped on activities pursued under the Maternity and Infancy Act.

In addition to affecting women as mothers, the Sheppard-Towner Act reshaped the role and re-evaluated the status of women as community leaders and volunteers. Here too, the act had ambiguous meanings. On the one hand, it offered female voluntary organizations an active role in its implementation. Volunteers lobbied for state and local funding, publicized child health conferences, provided transportation and lodging for public health nurses, rented facilities for clinics, aided doctors and nurses during the conferences and canvassed their communities to find children and expectant mothers who might use the services. In some states, local women assembled sterilized obstetrical packages to send to pregnant women and helped with local surveys on infant health.[142] Sometimes, the voluntary organizations themselves funded local health programs when public officials refused to shoulder the burden. Almost all states reported cooperative work with some state women's organization, and many invited those groups to serve on state advisory boards overseeing maternal and infant health work. In 1927, 31 states reported actively cooperating with their parent-teacher associations; 25 with the state's women's clubs. At least 12 cooperated with Red Cross chapters, and the same number involved state tuberculosis societies. Eight listed the Women's Christian Temperance Union, and two cited the American Association of University Women among the societies offering aid.[143]

But this deep involvement carried with it no power for women's organizations, which found their roles less authoritative than during the birth registration campaign or Children's Year. In those instances, the Children's Bureau had dealt directly with the executives of the women's associations. No other public body had stood between the volunteers and their professional leadership in the Children's Bureau. This was not so in the implementation of the Sheppard-Towner Act. Through the legislation itself and the guidelines later added, the Bureau set up state and local public agencies that then enlisted the voluntary organizations. The act fixed a new echelon within the dominion's hierarchy, which distanced the leadership from the volunteers. In this way, the act demoted the voluntary associations.

Policymakers underscored this demotion when they decided that federal funds could not be used to expand the maternity and infancy work that voluntary organizations had initiated before passage of the act. In Oregon, for example, the state's director proposed to provide staff for a clinic created in Portland by the local Parent-Teacher Association. The Bureau rejected the proposal on the grounds that it would use federal funds to support a private organization. It would be all right for the PTA to provide space and equipment and to recruit the clientele, but the clinic must be billed as a public center aided by the PTA rather than a PTA clinic subsidized by the government.[144] The actual work and organization of the clinic would have been similar in either case, but the Bureau's directive meant that the state's public agency must be in charge and the voluntary organization a sidekick, not vice versa. This set the record straight on the lines of command within the dominion: though voluntary organizations were no less active during the 1920s, their authority distinctly diminished.

Just as the professionalization of social work demoted masses of female caseworkers, the creation of state child hygiene divisions and the formation of the Women's Joint Congressional Committee demoted masses of female volunteers. Now that leaders of the child welfare corps could turn to professionals in the states to help with programs and studies, they no longer had to rely directly on their non-professional sisters in the voluntary organizations. The role of the volunteers reverted to the locale, where many of them aided migratory Sheppard-Towner nurses and sought county funds for the local clinics that leaders recommended.

While implementing the Sheppard-Towner Act in the 1920s, the child welfare dominion reached its peak of power. The Children's Bureau headed the whole operation and supervised the activities of two lower echelons of authority: the analogous public agencies it had helped to create in the states, and the women's organizations, which continued throughout the 1920s to help implement programs at the local level. Attached to this organizational trunk were an educational branch that provided younger professionals who shared the goals and values of an older generation of reformers and a lobbying branch that united female voluntary organizations in efforts to expand the dominion. This child welfare establishment kept child welfare reform alive in the 1920s. It successfully passed America's first federal program for social welfare. It improved prenatal and infant health care for thousands of American women and children. It opened new professional opportunities for women at a time when women were making few strides in professional life, and it united those women in reforming campaigns. Indeed, as women professionalized and institutionalized the reform spirit in such national agencies as the Children's Bureau and the Women's Joint Congressional Committee, they increasingly disciplined their efforts toward reform and won greater authority.

But these accomplishments contained ambiguities. Prescriptions for mothers, for instance, tended to encourage the reproduction of domestic roles for most women. Indeed, one of the cruel ironies of this history is that professional women used their hard-won positions of public authority to advocate the limitation of opportunities for the majority of women, who *were* mothers. In an era when constructions of gender would certainly not allow women any authority over men, those women who did gain authority wielded it over other women, and in many cases, used it not to liberate but to restrict their sisters. Insistence that all mothers should breastfeed their children and rear them without recourse to outside help meant that working-class mothers, forced to work by financial need, could not hope to fulfill expectations for proper motherhood and that a professional woman who chose to have children should forgo her career while her children were young. Advice to mothers did not provide flexibility or offer alternative child-care techniques for varying familial circumstances but instead insisted that there was one good way to rear children. Apparently professionals never considered the possibility that many different approaches might well have produced happy, healthy children, and consequently their admonitions would allow only women without children to participate fully in public life.

Moreover, the conviction that only one set of rules could rear thriving children prompted child welfare professionals to attempt to impose their preferences on every family. Despite their unusual sensitivity to cultural diversity in other arenas, women in the child welfare establishment saw only danger in permitting diverse childrearing practices or birthing techniques. This narrow view imbued their campaigns with cultural chauvinism that pitted them against many foreign-born mothers and midwives of color. The implementation of the Sheppard-Towner Act, then, revealed some of the class, race, and ethnic identities that divided American women in the 1920s.

Perhaps these divisions contributed to the demise of the female dominion in child welfare policy. Surely many of the political and cultural trends that had favored the dominion in the early 1920s came to an end in mid-decade, and permanently diminished female public authority. The next chapter investigates this decline.

CHAPTER 5

Contraction and Dissolution of the Female Dominion: Federal Child Welfare Policy, 1924–1935

In 1930, President Herbert Hoover convened a White House Conference on Child Health and Protection. Despite the chief executive's long experience in producing such events, he lost control of this one, which built toward an intensely dramatic showdown between women in the child welfare dominion and men in medicine. "Not since the days of the suffrage fight have so many trained, able women been so full of wrath about anything," reported one national newspaper, "as specialists in child welfare, health, education, medicine and social work became at the recommendation to transfer the [Children's] bureau's child health work to the U.S. Public Health Service." The reporter continued: "Only after the unfortunate males who had tried to jam the proposal through had been badly rattled and had decided to eliminate it from the conference findings did the meeting conclude in peace and harmony."[1]

By 1930 the Children's Bureau was under severe attack by men who — not nearly so "unfortunate" as this journalist would have his readers believe — succeeded in constricting the Bureau's monopoly over child welfare policy. Constriction came during the second half of the 1920s, as male opponents of the Bureau put an end to the Sheppard-Towner Maternity and Infancy Act and refused to ratify the Child Labor Amendment. Not until the 1930s, however, did female control over child welfare policy dissolve, and that dissolution resulted not from opposition to the women's policies but ironically from the success of their agenda: the New Deal, embodying many of the women's ideals, represented the movement of social welfare from the banks to the mainstream of public policy, and that triumph created new programs for mothers and children that offered professional opportunities and authority attractive to men. Women thus lost control of child welfare policy.

This chapter seeks to explain the decline of the female dominion in the late 1920s by studying opposition to the Sheppard-Towner Maternity and Infancy Act. The act had proved controversial as soon as Lathrop proposed it, but opposition had not been strong enough to prevent passage. After 1924, opponents gained strength from a variety of sources, not the least of which were a Congress committed to budget-cutting and an administration as devoted to the interests and values of business as any administration in U.S. history. As these commitments achieved ascendancy in the mid-1920s, they privileged an understanding of professionalism antithetical to that of the women in the child welfare dominion. And the triumph of that brand of professionalism had important implications for public policy, including the repeal of Sheppard-Towner and the consequent shrinking of the female monopoly over child welfare policy. Despite this contraction, however, the female child welfare establishment remained intact until 1935, and it continued with such vitality that it helped to shape the foundation of the American welfare state as laid in New Deal legislation such as the Social Security Act (1935) and the Fair Labor Standards Act (1938).

Decline was certainly the last thing on Grace Abbott's mind as she led her organizational network into its campaign for a new appropriation to support maternal and infant health work.[2] The Sheppard-Towner Act had funded maternal and infant health programs for five years ending June 30, 1927, with the understanding that Congress would consider extending the appropriation after evaluating actual projects in the states. With absolute confidence, Abbott initiated proceedings for this extension in 1926. The result, a bill that funded the work for two additional years and allowed Congress to renew the appropriation yet again thereafter, sailed through the House by a vote of 218 to 44.[3]

In the Senate, the bill hit a brick wall. One committee countered with a bill to repeal the act after one additional year of funding. Bargaining ensued. By the time the Senate recessed for the summer, no vote had occurred, and when the Senate reconvened, opposition was so strong that supporters of the act had to compromise: they agreed to a two-year extension of the appropriation and repeal of the act on June 30, 1929.[4]

Remarkably, Grace Abbott and Florence Kelley remained undaunted. Both believed that by 1929 they could woo enough senators simply to pass a new law containing the same provisions as the Sheppard-Towner Act, and, in fact, Abbott insisted that a new law would be no harder to win than a new appropriations bill. In her characteristically buoyant and assured spirit, she concluded: "It requires exactly the same legislative procedure for the extension as it does for a new bill, and so under the circumstances we yielded very little."[5] She was wrong. Between 1928 and 1932, congressmen introduced fourteen bills to stop the repeal of the Sheppard-Towner Act, and none passed.[6] The federal government's first foray into social welfare programs consequently ended in June 1929.

The explanation for congressional refusal to renew maternal and infant health programs did not lie in diminished female enthusiasm for the work. From 1926 until 1932, the Women's Joint Congressional Committee mounted the same sort of drive as it had to pass the original act, and its constituent organizations responded with their full support. Again, thousands of letters arrived at crucial times; again, women testified before congressional committees; again, women's groups outside the WJCC joined the lobby.[7] Defeat of the Maternity and Infancy Act and the resulting contraction of the female monopoly over child welfare policy did not result, then, from flagging energy among women themselves. Rather, after 1924, that energy no longer sufficed to persuade lawmakers.

One reason for the diminished force of the women's lobby was the impossibility after 1924 of threatening congressmen with reprisals from a female voting bloc. In the elections of 1924, women did not vote as a cohesive group. In fact, both male and female observers lamented the low registration rates among eligible women and the low turnout among those who did register. Moreover, the women who cast ballots apparently split their votes in much the same way that men did: most flocked to the Democratic and Republican parties, while some backed candidates from the Progressive and Prohibition parties.[8]

Disunity at the polls reflected economic and social diversity among female voters. Although women shared many economic, political, and social disabilities, their interests remained as divided by class, race, and ethnicity as men's were. Such divisions were bound to express themselves at the polls. Indeed, even among white professional women, whose interests might have seemed similar, deep fissures opened especially between those who wanted to follow the suffrage victory with an equal rights amendment for women and those who feared that an equal rights amendment would threaten protective legislation that in some places shortened the hours and eased the conditions of female labor. Activists in the child welfare dominion opposed the Equal Rights Amendment, first introduced to Congress in 1923, which drove a political wedge between them and many of their professional sisters.[9]

Furthermore, though American women had a long tradition of participation in the political processes that occurred outside of elections — massive publicity campaigns, rallies, lobbying — they had little experience in partisan politics. Many suffragists and most of the women active in other Progressive-era legislative drives had prided themselves on being unsullied by what they saw as the low-down, dirty deals inevitable in partisan politics. Female activists often argued that it was precisely because they operated outside the corrupt arena of political parties that they should be granted authority in public life; they could claim the high moral ground of disinterestedness specifically because of their exclusion from the smoke-filled backrooms where party bosses purportedly exchanged public influence for private gain. Once women won suffrage, men in the political parties were surely not eager to share power with such recent detractors, and much of the explanation for women's absence from partisan politics during the 1920s lay in blatant discrimination by these men.[10]

As important as discrimination, however, was the continued ambivalence that many female reformers felt about participating in the political world that they had painted as immoral. They were unsure whether they wanted to step down from their moral high ground into the gullies of what one historian has called "ward-level vote hustling."[11] After her retirement from the Children's Bureau, Lathrop herself considered running for Congress, but in the end she — like so many of her sisters — decided to stick with the political methods she knew well and trusted more. "The more I think things over," she confided in Grace Abbott, "the more I feel sure that I ought not to run for anything. This makes me all the more eager to see what can be done to influence platforms and get good candidates."[12] Operating from outside the political parties, a location familiar to female activists, Lathrop hoped to pressure both parties on the issues she cherished.

It might have seemed that long female experience in lobbying would have set women in fine stead during the 1920s when much political power actually seeped out of the political parties and into organized interest groups such as the Farm Bureau Federation, the National Farmers' Union, the National Association of Manufacturers, and the Joint Committee of National Utility Associations.[13] But this was not the case. Much of the power of these pressure groups subsisted in their ability and willingness to affect political campaigns especially through huge monetary contributions. Lacking funds of the necessary magnitude, the women's lobby depended on the possibility of grassroots political organizing. When such organizing failed to materialize, the women's lobby could not compete.[14]

Moreover, even women who were willing to descend into the precincts usually achieved little on behalf of a peculiarly female agenda. As Nancy Cott has so perfectly defined the dilemma: if postsuffrage activists committed themselves to a party in order to gain political power, they could not give primary loyalty to a women's agenda; but if they eschewed partisan politics in order to remain loyal to their own female agenda, they denied themselves the political power that only full participation in partisan politics could bring.[15] Expectations of a female voting bloc were groundless.

Patriotic women's groups that burst onto the political scene in the 1920s embodied striking evidence for the impossibility of a women's voting bloc and for other political trends that would weaken the female dominion. Virulently attacking the Sheppard-Towner Act and other initiatives by the Children's Bureau, some of these associations—like the Daughters of the American Revolution—had participated in the Bureau's early work and only later joined the chorus of reaction that crescendoed in the mid-1920s.[16] Other groups continued a female tradition of opposition to increased public power for women. The Women Patriot Publishing Company, for instance, carried on the work of the Association Opposed to Woman Suffrage. Through its newspaper, *The Woman Patriot*, it voiced the opinions of right-wing women who called the Children's Bureau a "radical federal bureau of social workers," insisted that the Sheppard-Towner Act was communistic, and accused the Children's Bureau of taking orders from Russia's Bolsheviks.[17]

The extrusion of American politics through the die of World War I made these fanatical harangues possible. During the war, the Wilson administration had stirred up a patriotism that defined loyalty as unquestioning support for America's military participation in the European conflict. And democracy's enemy, the cause of the war, was identified as "Prussianism" or an over-strong state that oppressed its own people and aimed to rule others. After the Bolshevik Revolution took Russia out of the war and especially after Germany was defeated, some Americans shifted their hatred and fear from Prussianism to communism. In either case, U.S. patriots were defining Americanism over against European polities that they saw as hostile to the principles of freedom and self-determination so dear to their idea of America.[18] Although the Red Scare of 1919 quickly subsided, anti-radicalism remained very much in evidence during the 1920s, and its female contingent proved particularly committed to identifying the legislative agenda of the child welfare dominion with Russian communism.

In fact, the superpatriots placed all female reformers and their organizations under suspicion of Russian domination. The notorious Spider Web Charts, which began circulating widely in 1924 and probably originated with a librarian in the federal War Department, drew connections between individual reformers and voluntary organizations to show that they were all in the service of international socialism. Most leaders of the child welfare establishment both past and present appeared on one or more versions of the chart, as did the National Congress of Parents and Teachers, the Girls Friendly Society, and the American Home Economics Association.[19] Grace Abbott, considered a central figure in the communist conspiracy, did not take the female patriots one bit seriously. Describing one of their appearances before Congress she wrote, "Today's [hearings on the child labor amendment] were amusing for a wild anti suffragist performed who embarrassed her supporters in the Committee and added to the gaiety of the morning. She is one who describes Miss Lathrop, Mrs. Kelley and Miss Addams as bolsheviks . . . and takes a whirl at me from time to time."[20]

Some of Abbott's contemporaries and many later analysts would give the patriots more respect. One historian, for instance, argued that "the very presence" of the patriotic groups "tended both to polarize political opinion and to shift the whole spectrum to the right."[21] According to this analysis, Grace Abbott's cavalier attitude, on the one hand refreshing, missed on the other hand the power that the "wild anti-suffragists" exerted in helping to reroute the political mainstream, such that female reformers who had swum in the middle of that stream during the 1910s found themselves stranded on the left bank in the 1920s. Even though women in the child welfare dominion had changed their own minds about nothing, their position on the political landscape changed significantly in the mid-1920s because the landscape itself shifted around them. And other women—those in patriotic organizations—actively participated in the reconstruction that left reforming women high and dry.

Other actors in that reconstruction were men in Congress. Unable to threaten legislators at the polls, female reformers needed congressional allies amenable to notions of an active state responsible for social welfare. Consequently, prospects for the reforming women's legislative agenda dimmed when the elections of 1924 returned a Congress much warier of an expanded federal government than its recent predecessors. This plenary wariness resulted less from the conservatism of individual congressmen than from the inability of progressive individuals to unite. Indeed, if representatives of farmers, organized labor, urban Democrats, and independent radicals generally stood under the progressive umbrella, then progressives continued to predominate in Congress until 1927.[22] But problems like the McNary-Haugen bill, which suggested price supports for western (Republican) farmers and nothing for southern (Democratic) farmers, temporarily split the usually progressive farm bloc during the mid-1920s. And the connection between farmers and organized labor also weakened as congressional representatives of large commercial farmers replaced those of small, struggling cultivators.[23] Thus, once-powerful coalitions in favor of an active federal government blew apart and left maternal and infant health programs in the lurch.

Another dynamic which moved Congress away from activism after 1924 was the way Democrats apparently read the landslide victory of Republican presidential candidate Calvin Coolidge. Fearful that their own party might be withering away, congressional Democrats saw the Coolidge triumph as a mandate for the generally inactive federal government that Coolidge advocated, for a government devoted to big business, and for such specific measures as tax cuts for the wealthy. Democrats had successfully opposed those revisions of the tax code throughout the Harding presidency, but after 1924, they capitulated so completely that they were accused of out-Republicaning the Republicans.[24]

Democrats need not have translated the presidential election as a mandate of any sort. In 1924, Silent Cal—as the excruciatingly reserved President was known—ran against two opponents, who split his opposition: Battlin' Bob La Follette, age-old reformer from Wisconsin who represented the Progressive party, and John W. Davis, a compromise candidate who finally won the Democratic nomination on the 103rd ballot, who represented the Democratic party. Davis proved to be a pale imitation of Coolidge, but this certainly did not mean that the constituencies of the Democratic party now supported the pro-business platform drafted by Republicans. Quite the contrary. In the 1924 Democratic Convention, racists loyal to the Ku Klux Klan had joined rural southerners in fighting immigrant-stock urbanites to an absolute stalemate. Ballot after ballot failed to settle the score between the countryside's candidate, William McAdoo, and the city's Alfred E. Smith.[25] Neither of their constituencies supported the business interests that Coolidge represented, but neither could they agree with each other on a candidate to oppose the quiet Republican.

Especially given the low voter turnout in 1924, observers need not, therefore, have seen Coolidge as representing some broad new consensus among the electorate. Rather, among many competing visions of the body politic in 1924 — which included that of the racist/nativist Klan, that of the urban, immigrant machines, and that of the Progressive party — the one represented by Coolidge simply mustered more enthusiasm among those actually voting than any *one* of its competitors.

Largely because of the way that congressional Democrats interpreted the presidential election, this advantage was enough to determine a temporary winner in the contest among the various visions of the state that the Progressive era had bequeathed to the 1920s. Throughout the first decades of the twentieth century, female and male reformers had defined their positions along a spectrum that stretched between classical liberalism and state socialism. The early 1920s allowed them all to battle fairly evenly for legislative enactment. But the election of Coolidge declared a victor in that match, and the decision went to Herbert Hoover's associative state. Staying on as Secretary of Commerce under Coolidge, Hoover and his colleagues continued to insist that their commitment to governmental economy and efficiency stood in the way of their support for public social services. The federal government, they argued, best served the common good by encouraging businesses to regulate themselves through voluntary pacts aimed at stabilizing the economy.[26]

The triumph of this particular position along the *via media*, of course, meant trouble for women in the child welfare dominion. Since early in the Progressive era, these women had championed an ideal that held the state directly responsible for social services and economic welfare. Although they did not advocate profligacy or inefficiency, they interpreted "economy" and "efficiency" differently from the men in the Department of Commerce. In one of her textbooks, for instance, Sophonisba Breckinridge wrote that economy and efficiency must have different meanings "in their application to public welfare and to domestic welfare as contrasted with their significance in the field of industrial and business organization." She explained: "In the latter fields the profit-seeking impulse makes the balance sheet the final criterion. In political and domestic organization, human well-being under conditions of justice, freedom, and equality, are the objects sought, and business administration can never be the guide to truly successful organization."[27]

But Hooverites temporarily succeeded precisely in making the balance sheet the final criterion for decisions on public policy. As early as 1923,

Julia Lathrop recognized the trend at lower levels of government. While an activist in the Illinois League of Women Voters, she noted: "It is plain that no more sob stuff or high ideals afloat will give us solid votes and aid to clean up Illinois." If the League were to win votes for Sheppard-Towner and other female initiatives in Illinois, it "must go to work lower down and find some women able and willing to study the finances of Illinois." In fact, Lathrop suggested that the League must organize for its members "an elementary course in Illinois taxation and expenditure."[28] By the mid-1920s, then, the way to a legislator's heart was through the budget, and though the appropriation for maternal and infant health work was a pittance even in the context of the federal budget in the 1920s, still the new congressional consensus on economy spelled doom for such unconventional line items as maternal and infant health programs, particularly vulnerable because their constituencies now held no fear for elected officials.[29]

Indicative of these changes was the increasing resonance of diatribes by Senator James Reed. Representing a rural America hostile toward urban intrusions embodied in advertising, automobiles, movies, school curricula, and even maternal and infant health conferences, Reed lashed out at the Sheppard-Towner Act for its invasion of private life and for its promotion of female professionals. Delivering the most offensive speeches against the Maternity and Infancy Act both in 1921 and 1926, Reed's sentiments sounded extreme and out of fashion in early debates but more compelling in the later years. The apotheosis of budget-cutting gave new stature to almost any opposition to federal spending, and the perceived failure of the women's vote created safe space for the open expression of sexism.

Because male politicians no longer worried about women as voters or opposing candidates, they felt free on the public record to deride professional women, to demean them as policymakers, and certainly to vote down their prized projects. They gave increasing attention, then, to Reed, who since 1921 had blasted the "female celibates" who ran the Children's Bureau. He railed against the absurdity of childless women instructing mothers on the details of childrearing. He thought it more appropriate for the Senate to "provide for a committee of mothers to take charge of the old maids and teach them how to acquire a husband and have babies of their own." He wondered "whether one out of ten of these delightful reformers could make a bowl of buttermilk gruel that would not give a baby the colic," and offered sympathy to "the office-holding spinster" who administered maternal and infant health programs rather than mothering "the dream children she does not possess." Reed was, he claimed, trying to save America's motherhood from visitations by the "bespectacled lady, nose sharpened by curiosity, official chin pointed and keen" who "sails majestically and authoritatively to the home of the prospective mother and demands admission in the name of the law."[30]

By 1926, such monologues should have carried no weight. In its final version, the Sheppard-Towner Act, of course, did not require parents to admit its employees to their homes but in fact specifically stated the right of parents to turn public workers away. Experience showed that innumerable parents welcomed help with childrearing precisely because uneducated maternal affection did not necessarily rear healthy babies: although America's infant mortality rate had declined since passage of the Maternity and Infancy Act, it remained one of the highest among industrialized countries. More poignant, in 1929 a larger proportion of mothers died in childbirth than in 1921 except in rural areas.[31] To preserve the mothers that Reed extolled, evidence argued for an expanded Sheppard-Towner program, not its repeal.

Nevertheless, almost despite himself, Reed spoke eloquently for those whose lives were disrupted by the interventions of uninvited professionals. As sexist and abusive as he was, his objections to Sheppard-Towner echoed those of immigrant mothers who could not imagine accepting advice from women who had never given birth; his victory would have prevented nurses from urging local elites to abolish tent communities; and he expressed the chill that should have tingled anyone's spine at the reference to babies as "wonderful little mechanisms" or at the description of representatives of the Children's Bureau "moving on the households of the poor" or "invading homes having babies."[32] For all the wrong reasons, Reed raised some concerns that female policymakers would have done well to hear.

Like Reed, states' rights theorists had consistently opposed national initiatives by the child welfare establishment, and though states' rights theory itself gained few new adherents after 1924, the victory of economy and sexism supported a states' rights agenda. During the Progressive era, those who believed that each state should freely formulate its own policies without any interference from the federal government had lost ground to a growing acceptance of cooperative efforts between the national and state governments. In 1914, for example, the Smith-Lever Act had offered federal money to the states for agricultural extension programs. The federal Good Roads Act of 1916 had provided federal grants-in-aid to the states for improving their highway systems; the Forest Fire Prevention Act of 1911 distributed federal monies for forest conservation; and in 1917, the Smith-Hughes Act did the same for vocational education.[33] In these areas and even more in social welfare, federal programs did not seem so much to threaten the power or restrict the prerogatives of the states as to expand their capacities by making possible new programs that the state governments could not otherwise afford. But U.S. participation in World War I and more especially the Bolshevik Revolution reinvigorated states' righters who argued that increased federal power was un-American and threatening to the individual liberties that Americans treasured. Empowered by the acceptance of federal budget cuts and by the new dangers associated with federal authority, states' righters chastised the states for refusing their responsibilities in the case of maternal and infant health programs. President Coolidge wrote, for instance: "To relieve the States of their just obligations . . . is hurtful rather than helpful to the States. . . . "[34] An angry senator accused the Sheppard-Towner Act of educating "the state to place upon the Federal Government duties which it should perform."[35] And in addition to making state governments lazy, federal intervention, according to states' righters, made individual citizens indolent. One argued that Sheppard-Towner would "enervate the people" and "destroy the individual sense of responsibility."[36]

Experience refuted these predictions. Because of its emphasis on involving local communities in the provision of maternal and infant health programs, the Sheppard-Towner Act energized rather than enervated local elites. Voluntary groups never before interested in maternal and infant health were roused to action by peripatetic nurses and, by the thousands, committed themselves to the new cause. That the federal government here took the initiative was unquestionable, but the cooperative scheme of funding and administration ignited state and local officials as well as individual volunteers. What states' rights theorists missed were the very real intrusions into individual lives that the national program supported. But congressmen on the whole cared no more—and often much less—than women in the child welfare dominion about the autonomy of poor households or ethnic communities. Their opposition did not aim to protect the people truly at risk under Sheppard-Towner.

Exposing the weakness of states' rights theory outside the context of budget-cutting and business values were inconsistencies in objections to federal aid to the states. When Massachusetts, for instance, challenged the constitutionality of the Maternity and Infancy Act on the grounds that it interfered with the states' police powers and violated property rights by failing to allocate funds to each state according to the state's proportion of federal taxes, Massachusetts itself was concurrently enjoying federal grants-in-aid to build its highways, to fight white pine rust, and to build up vocational education. These programs would have transgressed the same rights that Sheppard-Towner did, but the Commonwealth objected to none of them. Even Massachusetts was fortunate, then, when the Supreme Court threw out the case for lack of jurisdiction and forestalled any further constitutional challenges by announcing that the act did not violate the states' constitutional rights because it did not force any state to participate.[37]

Ultimately then, although states' rights theorists opposed federal sponsorship of social welfare programs and this sponsorship died in the late 1920s, it was not states' rights theory that actually triumphed. Rather, changes in the perceived political power of women, in the coalitions ruling Congress, and in the value placed on economy coalesced after 1924 to give victory to Hoover's associative state.

Contained within this success was an element often obscured but crucial for comprehending the defeat of Sheppard-Towner, namely that a particular understanding of professionalism rose on the same wave that elevated the Hooverite state over its competitors. In fact, Grace Abbott and her colleagues, who could laugh off the testimony of superpatriots or dismiss the abuse of James Reed, considered in deadly earnest their professional competition and bureaucratic foes because they believed that the federal government's child welfare policy would be decided by professional and bureaucratic in-fighting.

Just as the Progressive era left to the 1920s a spectrum of opinions on the proper role of the state, so it handed down a variety of professional codes. And just as the various visions of the state competed fairly evenly during the early 1920s, so did the range of professional creeds. Indeed, precisely because each understanding of professionalism carried implications for the formation of public policy, the victory of one approach to policy meant the victory of a particular form of professionalism. And the specific professional code that received political power after 1924 was not that of women in the child welfare dominion; it was that of the men in the Public Health Service. The defeat of the women's understanding of professionalism simultaneously brought down their approach to public policy, which killed the Maternity and Infancy Act and shrank the dominion's monopoly over child welfare.

The public imbroglio between women in the child welfare establishment and men in the medical profession began as early as 1914 but intensified in 1922, when the American Medical Association's House of Delegates voted to oppose the Sheppard-Towner Act at the state level. In Massachusetts and Illinois, where the AMA was strong, it successfully blocked attempts to accept federal funds for maternal and infant health programs, and by 1926, the Association was ready to fight at the national level.[38]

For women in the child welfare corps, the medical profession represented an opposition especially formidable. On the one hand, it was like the women's dominion: its authority rested on claims to non-partisan, scientific knowledge; it mobilized a voluntary organizational network to lobby on behalf of special issues; it was a professional group trying to establish a monopoly. But on the other hand, the AMA was antithetical to the women's policymaking structure: it was male rather than female; it was profit-seeking instead of service-oriented; it aimed to hoard rather than to popularize its expert knowledge; its monopoly competed against non-medical professionals while the women depended on cooperation among professions. When medical men fought women in the child welfare establishment, different understandings of professionalism collided.

Even among male doctors, a range of professional codes existed, and the group of doctors who controlled the AMA represented one extreme end of the continuum. In the battle over Sheppard-Towner, only men operated according to this uncompromisingly exclusive, profit-seeking, elitist professional code. At the AMA conventions where doctors renounced the Sheppard-Towner Act, no female doctor spoke. The House of Delegates, which actually voted to oppose the act, had no female members. Men authored every editorial that denounced public maternal and infant health programs in the *Journal of the American Medical Association*.[39] Although women belonged to the AMA, they had been formally admitted to membership only in 1915 and had never yet found their way into positions of influence. Silenced in the AMA, the voice of female doctors spoke through other organs, as for instance the Medical Women's National Association, which supported the Sheppard-Towner Act. Indeed, all of the women's medical associations publicly advocated the act, and female physicians who belonged to the AMA nonetheless welcomed the employment opportunities offered by Sheppard-Towner and served on state staffs in numbers well over their proportion in the medical profession.[40]

At the same time, not all male doctors opposed the act. Several male physicians testified on its behalf during congressional hearings, among them Professors John A. Foot from Georgetown University and Philip Van Ingen from Cornell.[41] The renegade Pediatrics Section of the AMA endorsed the act in 1922, and among the innumerable doctors who volunteered their services to Sheppard-Towner programs in the states—at least 2,276 in 1927, for example—a goodly number must have been male. Furthermore, the heads of state boards of health, usually male physicians, overwhelmingly supported the act, and a few male doctors found paid positions in the child hygiene divisions administering the states' programs.[42] In sum, not all male doctors opposed Sheppard-Towner, but the medical opposition was entirely male.

Following a professional code less exclusive and elitist than the leadership of the AMA, male doctors who supported the act were either in small-town practices or not in private practice at all. Many were employed by government agencies or universities. Others, especially those scattered individuals who volunteered in child health clinics and prenatal conferences, were probably small-town general practitioners. These were men who did not find their way into the AMA's House of Delegates or onto the pages of the *Journal of the American Medical Association* and who, during the 1920s, complained that the AMA's House of Delegates under-represented them.[43] Members of the decisionmaking body of the AMA were elected either by their state medical societies or by national committees representing each medical specialty. In order to vote in those committees, a doctor had to be a fellow of the AMA, which required payment of a fellow's fee, and had to attend the annual conference of the AMA wherever in the country it might be held. Small-town general practitioners, rarely able to justify the expense of fellowship or travel to the conference, complained that only physicians wealthy enough to foot those bills received double representation in the House of Delegates by voting in their states' medical societies and again in their national committees. Throughout the 1920s, those grievances fell on deaf ears, and the small-town practitioners remained outside the decision-making body of the AMA.[44]

Thus, although the AMA contained competing groups, its hierarchical structure permitted the organization to bring its full weight to bear on the side of an issue dear only to the upper echelons of authority. And in the 1920s, those leaders comprised an elite group of ambitious men in private practice. Between 1922 and 1927, all except one of the officers of the AMA engaged in private practice, as did the entire Board of Trustees. Most were specialists rather than general practitioners: of 27 officers and trustees about whom information was located, only three listed no specialty, and the experts represented only five of the 18 specialties recognized by the AMA. The leadership counted eight surgeons, eight eye, ear, nose, and throat specialists, five internists, two neurologists/psychiatrists, and one dermatologist. No officer practiced obstetrics, gynecology, pediatrics, public health, urology, orthopedics, proctology, or any of the specialties in research. With one exception, these officers and trustees practiced in large cities, half in the Midwest.[45]

The professional culture of this elite group of male doctors rested on the very values underpinning Hoover's associative state. For these men, medicine was a business, and they thought that as private practitioners of medicine they should organize and regulate themselves without interference from the government. The doctors who so severely castigated the Sheppard-Towner Act were socialized into a professional culture that promised greater financial rewards to those who established the largest practices, an ethos that depended on the fee-paying client, a customer, who paid the doctor for his services, a commodity. The exchange between doctor and client mimicked any business transaction, and these doctors, like any businessmen, were in the enterprise to make money. This professional attitude produced such best-selling books as *Dollars to Doctors* by Nathan E. Wood, *Large Fees and How to Get Them* by Albert V. Horman, and J. J. Taylor's *The Physician as Businessman or How to Obtain the Best Financial Result in the Practice of Medicine*.[46]

Although these doctors often employed states' rights arguments against the Sheppard-Towner Act—ranting, for instance, at the "prussianization" of American doctors—the real foundation of their opposition to public health programs lay in a perceived threat to their incomes. One physician from Alabama ridiculed his fellows for pretending that their hostility had anything to do with the protection of states' rights. Pointing out that his colleagues had not earlier fought against federal grants-in-aid for roads, vocational education, and forest-fire prevention and angry that medical opposition stemmed especially from the North, he went on to insist that the South, impoverished and consequently in need of federal funds for maternal and infant health, "needs the money [from the Sheppard-Towner Act] to help furnish the nation with stronger men and women. If Massachusetts does not need it," he continued, "very well; but let her keep her hands off of Alabama's share."[47] Another doctor more carefully scolded his associates: "I want to apologize for our profession in its efforts to refute the activities that this bill makes possible. Of course, the economic condition of the medical profession is endangered by a further extension of public health activities. Yet the medical profession must know that it has to get in line with the changing conditions."[48]

Further admission that doctors opposed the Maternity and Infancy Act out of fear for their incomes came during a debate between one defensive doctor and a group of women in Chicago. Exasperated with his audience, the doctor exploded: "There can be absolutely no objection to any public health center which teaches personal or public hygiene, and which provides medical fare for the poor. But the minute a public health center provides medical service for those who can afford to buy it from their physician, it is ultimately doing much damage, incidentally to the medical profession and ultimately to the whole country." The doctor went on to say that public health centers had become "a competitor" with private doctors. State hospitals surely could handle those unable to pay, according to the speaker, but all fee-paying clients must be referred to private practitioners. Otherwise, "it will ruin the private practice of medicine."[49]

A great irony ran through the doctors' fears of the Sheppard-Towner Act: if anything, the immediate result of the act must have increased the prestige of and demand for private physicians. Prenatal and infant health conferences examined clients and gave advice about how to stay healthy. Though nurses and physicians here did offer advice to those who were sick, their major goal was to prevent illness, and in most cases, examiners advised clients to see their own physician if tests revealed any abnormality. Administrators of the act repeatedly emphasized that their aim was to educate parents so that they would demand of private physicians the best care possible, and nurses were advising pregnant women—who otherwise *never* used a doctor—to see a physician early in their pregnancy and to avoid midwives. Obstetricians and pediatricians in particular had much to gain from this advertising, and physicians in these specialties often did support the act.[50]

Nevertheless, leaders in the AMA understood rightly that the professional code embodied in the Sheppard-Towner Act clashed utterly with their own: while public service values were central to the professionalism of women in the child welfare dominion, profits were central to that of the AMA leadership. Indeed, the fee-paying element was so central to the AMA's conception of the medical profession that its members often referred to female doctors engaged in Sheppard-Towner activities as social workers.[51] Though female doctors held credentials identical to those of the private practitioners who headed the AMA, their rejection of the profit motive made them seem first social workers and only secondarily doctors. Private practitioners apparently believed they had little in common with those of their own profession who did not charge their clients.

Although medical women received the same degrees as their male counterparts, the two groups certainly did operate according to different professional creeds. Female physicians entered public service out of all proportion to their numbers in the medical profession. In some part, this resulted from discrimination by private patients and hospitals.[52] But in addition, female physicians were socialized into a different ethos from their male colleagues. Unable to avoid the Victorian emphasis on self-sacrificing female service, women in medicine brought a different set of values into their professional lives and sought a different set of rewards. Historian Regina Morantz-Sanchez has shown that women physicians had always been more likely than their male counterparts to popularize medical knowledge, especially on the public health circuits which male doctors distinctly avoided. Indeed, even when they ran private practices, female doctors often taught hygiene as well, and in 1909, when women convinced the AMA to organize a public health education committee, women ran it because men were simply not interested. In general, female physicians participated much more actively in health reform movements than male doctors.[53] Moreover, and perhaps most important, female doctors refused to focus their attention exclusively on the medical aspects of disease. More than men, they explored the effects of poverty, sanitation, housing conditions, industrial processes, and nutrition on health.[54] They admitted that doctors alone could not guarantee the population's health but had to work with experts in other fields to change the environmental conditions that contributed to disease. Many activist female physicians, then, did not guard the boundaries of their profession so jealously as men. They were much more likely to acknowledge the limitations of their expertise and consequently to cooperate with other sorts of professionals in their crusades to improve America's health.

Women in the medical profession itself thus embraced a different professional culture from the male leadership of the AMA. The professionalism of female physicians was service-oriented, devoted to popularizing scientific knowledge, and cooperative with other professions. That of the AMA was profit-seeking, devoted to hoarding scientific knowledge, and jealous of its professional territory.

If the values of female physicians clashed this sharply with those of the men in the upper reaches of the AMA, then the professional code of other women in the child welfare dominion clashed even more dramatically. Public health nursing, developed by Lillian Wald in New York, and social work, arising from settlement houses and charity societies, shared none of the profit motive. Nurses and social workers were trained specifically to serve clients who could not pay, and in the early days of these professions, practitioners had received incomes from wealthy contributors who supported their work among the dispossessed. Later, their incomes came increasingly from local, state, and federal governments, but never did these nurses and social workers expect fees from those they served.[55]

Moreover, the peculiar history of these professions had prevented their practitioners from hoarding their knowledge and from inventing an esoteric language that excluded lay people. Always and everywhere, their success depended on popularizing, on drawing as many non-professionals as possible into their work. And they required cooperation with other kinds of specialists as well. Even in their energetic attempts to give social work a unique identity, for instance, Sophonisba Breckinridge and Edith Abbott insisted on their profession's connection to others. Breckinridge explained that social workers operated at the center of a complicated web of professions and were inextricably bound to practitioners of law, medicine, and education. In her collection of medical casework records, she wrote: "The medical case-worker is only one of an increasing number of social workers whose services are conditioned by their association with another highly developed professional group."[56]

These interprofessional associations were necessary, according to the women who forged them, because the object of social work, public health nursing, and even *female* medicine was not one small aspect of an individual's well-being but the individual's entire well-being, and no single specialty could secure that object alone. During the height of the debate on the extension of funds for the Sheppard-Towner Act, Lathrop reported to Abbott that a friend of theirs had overheard someone saying that "the Children's Bureau is an anomaly cutting straight across learned professions especially medicine & education." Lathrop commented: "That is of course the precise reason why others of us believe it should exist."[57] The Children's Bureau along with many of the state agencies and private organizations in its network took the child as their focus and involved experts from many fields in attempts to improve the welfare of the whole child.

No wonder then what the battle between leaders of the AMA and the child welfare dominion was so violent. On the one side were profit-seeking men aiming to increase their fees by hoarding their expert knowledge, while on the other side were service-oriented women trying to increase their professional opportunities through public programs that popularized the specialists' knowledge. Both sides fought from professional self-interest. Each was trying to promote a particular understanding of professionalism itself, an understanding that would open jobs for practitioners of either the service or profit-seeking bent. If either understanding should prevail among legislators or the general public, it would undermine the foundation of the other.

Male doctors in the Public Health Service occupied an intermediate position between the two extremes. These men argued not that Congress should end federal involvement in maternal and infant health programs but that the Public Health Service should administer those programs. Many AMA members finally allied with the Public Health Service in the fight over the Sheppard-Towner Act, because, even though administration by the Public Health Service would not stave off governmental forays into medical strongholds, it did answer some of the problems that the AMA had with the act. First, men would run the program, which would prevent the dilution of prestige that inevitably followed women's entrance to any professional activity. Second, AMA members could rest assured that the Public Health Service would protect the medical monopoly rather than contaminate it by association with, for instance, social work, education, or home economics. Although the profession of public health had originated as a broad field devoted to public sanitation projects, decent housing, a host of environmental issues, and nutrition education, it had narrowed during the 1910s to focus on bacteriology. Medical men came to dominate the field, and as historian Elizabeth Fee has argued: "Only the minority continued to relate the problems of ill health and disease to the larger social environment. As most bacteriologists and epidemiologists concentrated on specific disease-causing organisms and the individuals who harbored them, the larger social environment became almost irrelevant."[58] That trend brought men in public health closer to the male leadership of the AMA. Third, as contrary as it seemed to the enterprise of public health, those who led the field resisted popular education. Like their counterparts in private practice, men in the public health field usually preferred to protect their expert knowledge rather than to disseminate it.[59]

On the professional spectrum, then, the Public Health Service sat between the AMA and the child welfare dominion. Because it did not practice medicine for profit, it avoided the extreme advocated by the leaders of the AMA. But its resistance to popularizing knowledge and refusal to involve other professions in the study and solution to health problems edged it closer to the professionalism of the AMA than to that of the child welfare establishment.

The bureaucratic system of the federal government shaped the expression of conflict between the different professional cultures of men in public health and women in the Children's Bureau. Male and female bureaucrats came into chronic conflict, because, guided by their peculiar professional values, they defined public problems differently. The problem of maternal and infant mortality provided a case in point. Male doctors in the Public Health Service insisted that mortality was strictly a medical problem subject to medical solutions. As a consequence, as soon as the Children's Bureau began to study the causes of maternal and infant mortality during the 1910s, the Public Health Service (PHS) insisted that the chief of the Children's Bureau should be a doctor.[60] Women in the child welfare corps, immersed in a professional culture that encouraged cooperation among professions and with the laity, defined maternal and infant mortality as a multi-faceted social problem requiring the attention of specialists in medicine, social economics, sanitation, nutrition, education, industrial safety, city planning, home economics, and law. Lathrop and her network of female supporters argued that they were not studying a strictly medical problem, and that no single profession should be allowed to establish jurisdiction over it. An agency filled with social workers, doctors, nurses, teachers, home economists, and nutritionists would better address maternal and infant mortality than a bureau of doctors, who would take too narrow a view of the issue to study its fullest causes.

The Children's Bureau won the first round against the PHS: it retained the right to conduct maternal and infant mortality studies and resisted the demand that the Bureau's chief be an M.D. The female understanding of professionalism, with its broad definitions of public problems, thus proved a viable alternative to the narrower male approach. But the two understandings regularly collided. In the end, Lathrop's maternity and infancy bill brought the conflict to a head.

This dispute over the maternity and infancy bill pitted against each other male and female bureaucracies seeking to expand into the same territory. For the Surgeon General's part, he had shown not one bit of interest in maternity and infancy work until the Children's Bureau had won increased appropriations and prestige based on such work. Only after the Bureau's pamphlets on prenatal and child care proved popular did the PHS begin to issue similar pamphlets.[61] When Lathrop initiated studies on maternal and infant mortality, the Surgeon General assured her that his agency intended no such studies, but as soon as Lathrop attracted widespread publicity for the work, the PHS objected that only doctors should conduct these studies.[62] By 1919, the Bureau had demonstrated how maternity and infancy programs might expand the domain of a government agency, and at that point, the Surgeon General began to lobby for their removal to the PHS.[63] In fact, he was at the time agitating for the creation of a Department of Health and threatening to subsume the entire Bureau in his new department.[64]

Similar motives inspired Lathrop. She had since the day she took office expected the Children's Bureau to become a Department of Public Welfare, with the chief of the Children's Bureau at its head.[65] Aware by the time of her maternity and infancy bill that the PHS was her most dangerous competition, she carefully drew up her bill to avoid direct confrontation. Her original draft sidestepped the states' boards of health, for instance, because she feared that ensconcing the states' administration in the boards of health would encourage the PHS to claim federal administration of the program.[66] Only because she needed support from the American Public Health Association and the American Child Hygiene Association had she compromised on that issue.[67] In conference with the Surgeon General, she had also decided that she could brook a federal board that included the nation's chief medical officer, but that was as far as she would go in sharing power with another agency. When asked in congressional hearings whether she would support her own bill if legislators granted its administration to the PHS, she said no.[68]

As might have been expected, each institutional network in this struggle, embodying a peculiar professional culture, produced a unique definition of the policy issue at hand. Women in the Children's Bureau took an expansive and wholistic view of maternal and infant health, insisting that high mortality rates represented more than a medical problem. Though they admitted that a small federal program could not begin to speak to the myriad elements that combined to produce high rates of mortality among women and children, women in the Bureau believed that education in its broadest sense should lie at the center of the federal response. As a result, the programs funded by the Maternity and Infancy Act were more educational than medical. After all, public health nurses, aiming to keep mothers and babies healthy, taught nutrition, the importance of basic hygiene, sterilization techniques, methods to prolong breastfeeding, and the warning signs of complications during pregnancy. This sort of popularizing, integral to the female professional culture of the Children's Bureau, no one expected the PHS to do.[69]

Moreover, women in the Bureau opposed dividing a child into medical, social, and educational parts. Each child, they insisted, must be treated as a whole. "Prenatal and maternity care means more than good obstetrics," one of the Bureau's pamphlets argued, "it means normal family life, freedom of the mother from industrial labor before and after childbirth, ability to nurse the child," and other things completely unrelated to medicine.[70] Lathrop elaborated that "the first essentials [of health] are social: good and wise parents, decent housing, decent living in surroundings of civic cleanliness. . . . The child cannot be partitioned among the sciences. Social science must invite and secure increasing cooperation of teacher, doctor, and other specialists. . . . "[71] The Pubic Health Service, she argued, was in no position to coordinate all of those specialties and as a result would take much too narrow a view of problems surrounding maternity and infancy. Only the Children's Bureau, commanded to investigate and report on all conditions related to child life, could provide the comprehensive kind of work required to lower maternal and infant mortality rates.

Rank and file workers in the child welfare dominion agreed. Before a congressional committee, one woman explained: "We do not regard maternity and infancy exactly in the light of a disease. We believe it is a normal experience of human life and an experience of paramount concern to women, we in whose hands the first responsibility for the conservation of human life has been placed."[72] This woman objected to the implication by the Public Health Service that pregnancy was an illness and therefore a medical problem. If anything, pregnancy and childhood were social conditions that warranted special public consideration but could not be made safe by medicine alone.

Furthermore, women in the lower echelons of the child welfare dominion agreed that education and publicity were central to the task of lowering maternal and child mortality. And they believed that the Children's Bureau had the skills to conduct the necessary campaigns. A flier produced by the League of Women Voters read: "The work done under this bill will be a success in so far as local community interest and responsibility are aroused to make it so." Only the Children's Bureau had proven itself capable of exciting such interest: "Everywhere it is trusted. Women have faith in its high standards of public service, in the disinterestedness of its officials, in the capacity and quality of its workers."[73] Another leaflet put the issue ironically when it stated that the Children's Bureau was the only agency "manned by women," and most agreed with the lobbyist who argued: "[T]his is a task which I believe will be better done by women than by men."[74]

Despite the differences between the professional cultures represented by the female dominion and the male medical establishment, both defined public problems in dangerous ways. Men construed the mortality problem, for instance, so narrowly that they could never hope to solve it because they refused to admit the array of issues that congealed to produce maternal and infant deaths. But women defined the problem so broadly as to allow professionals to interfere with aspects of citizens' lives that had no bearing on the problem at all. How to define, for instance, "normal family life"? Who was to set the standards for "good and wise parents"? No amount of training or cross-professional consultation enabled a specialist to make these judgments, which would always be bound by a particular class and culture. Both approaches, then, were shot through with professional arrogance, and both inadvertently represented a social control project that empowered professionals at the expense of clients.

It was, however, the apotheosis of male professionalism and rejection of female professionalism that, after 1924, made it impossible for women in the child welfare dominion to win a new appropriation for maternity and infancy programs. Had the women been willing to relinquish even parts of the program to the Public Health Service, Congress probably would have enacted a new law. Between 1928 and 1932, many of the bills for renewal of the work would have involved the PHS. One bill proposed to extend the work under the Children's Bureau for five years and then to transfer it to the PHS. Another would have split the work between the two agencies. None of these suited the women in the child welfare dominion, who decidedly rejected each proposal that did not vest all authority in the Children's Bureau.[75]

This competition between the Public Health Service and the Children's Bureau reached its zenith during the White House Conference on Child Health and Protection in 1930. Herbert Hoover, having won the presidency in 1928, had to take a stand on the issue of maternal and infant health programs. Penny-pincher that he was and hostile as he was to federal involvement in social welfare programs, President Hoover nonetheless supported passage of a maternal and infant health bill *provided it was administered by the Public Health Service*. Befitting his reputation as a consummate publicist, Hoover determined to settle the issue once and for all by staging a conference at which all authority would come down on the side of the PHS. With a mandate from this conference, he and his party would be free to pass a bill that would hand maternal and infant health programs to the men in the Public Health Service, finally ending the controversy that had dragged on for years.[76]

From the start, Hoover obviously intended to control the recommendations of the conference. His self-revelation began with appointment of Ray

Lyman Wilbur as chair of the conference. Wilbur, a medical doctor who served as Hoover's Secretary of the Interior, had served as president of the AMA during the early 1920s when the organization was roundly condemning the Sheppard-Towner Act. Clearly, the chair would succor no movement on behalf of women in the Children's Bureau. Indeed, Grace Abbott believed that Wilbur's intention was to transfer most of the Children's Bureau into the Public Health Service and then the PHS into his own Department of the Interior. She believed furthermore that he was chairing the conference to that end.[77]

After appointing Wilbur to chair the conference, Hoover appointed Surgeon General Hugh S. Cumming as chair of the Committee on Public Health Service and Administration, which was charged with making recommendations about the appropriate agency to administer maternal and infant health programs. In the end, Grace Abbott won appointment to the subcommittee that actually drafted this recommendation, but it was headed by male M.D. Haven Emerson and stacked against the Children's Bureau. By the time that the conference opened to the public, Abbott had been outvoted, and the committee had recommended that all maternal and infant health work—including the studies then being conducted by the Bureau—be administered by the PHS. Grace Abbott's dissenting opinion did not even appear in the packet of reports that all conferees received upon their arrival in Washington.[78]

Female attendees to the conference were so furious that they created what Haven Emerson would call "the Children's Bureau fracas."[79] With the Emerson recommendation already printed even before the conference opened, Hoover expected that the subcommittee would simply meet on the opening day of the conference and officially accept the report. He was surprised. Women who supported Grace Abbott crowded into the room scheduled to hold this final hearing, and in fact spilled out into a large lobby because the room could not contain them. The august crowd included Florence Kelley, Alice Hamilton, Edith Abbott, Sophonisba Breckinridge, and Lillian Wald. As an astute reporter noted, the female group represented women from a wide variety of professions: child welfare, education, social work, medicine, and health.[80] Here again was evidence of the inclusivity of female professionalism, which encouraged women to reach across professional boundaries in their efforts to improve the lives of children.

Although Emerson did not intend to read Abbott's minority report, women in the audience forced him to, and as he read, Emerson repeatedly interrupted to mount what one attendee called "an attack upon Grace

Abbott and the Bureau."[81] Despite the crowd's insistence that Emerson allow a vote on the minority report and the perception by most that the minority report received the majority vote, Emerson announced to the plenary session of the conference the next day that the committee had approved his original recommendation to put maternal and infant health work in the PHS.

Angry yet again, female conferees would not let either Surgeon General Cumming or Chairman Wilbur get away with such dishonesty. During the plenary session, a nearly endless stream of delegates spoke on behalf of the Children's Bureau and insisted that the united conference be allowed to vote on the proper agency to administer maternal and infant health work. Finally the chair restored peace by agreeing to omit from the final report any recommendation on the issue, and to refer it to a continuing committee of the conference.[82]

The issue was now pretty much dead. Although the female child welfare dominion could not find the votes in Congress to renew the Sheppard-Towner Act, it retained enough power to keep such work out of the Public Health Service. The women's monopoly thus shrank, but no outsider took over a piece of it.

Hoover's support for maternal and infant health programs *in the Public Health Service* revealed that competition between professional cultures was truly central in the fight over Sheppard-Towner. Herbert Hoover was, after all, the draftsman of the associative state. If commitment to budget-cutting, anti-communism, states' rights theory, and such business values as competition, economy, efficiency, and the profit motive could suffice to explain the downfall of Sheppard-Towner, then Hoover would have opposed maternal and infant health programs *in any agency*. But he did not. What Herbert Hoover—the embodiment of all significant political shifts during the 1920s—opposed was administration of those programs by the Children's Bureau. And the differences between the approach of the Children's Bureau and the Public Health Service to maternal and infant health had everything to do with their contrasting professional cultures and the very different sorts of public policies that those cultures encouraged. Male professionalism had now won political empowerment.

Julia Lathrop sensed the trend. In 1929 she wrote to Grace Abbott: "Perhaps we must be more old-fashioned and insist on a 'woman's program' Peace Home Children."[83] In that suggestion, Lathrop seemed to understand that if women continued to battle men on the grounds of professional expertise, women would surely lose. Better then to shift ground and argue that women had special interests and gifts by virtue of being female. Lathrop's insight — if vague — was shrewd, but her alternative was not. She failed to see that the female cause was damned in any case. Falling back on arguments of female peculiarity would simply have confirmed cultural expectations that women could not be scientific experts at all, that their abilities were confined to the emotional and spiritual realm. And in a culture that had come to rely on expertise — in part because of activities led by women in the Children's Bureau — female intuition or sensitivity could not support a monopoly in public policy.

Moreover, Lathrop's earlier observation that women could no longer shame a vote out of a representative by citing infant or maternal death rates captured a shift in the dominant culture that further undermined the authority of female professionalism. Nearly complete by 1925, this shift had moved power away from evangelical Protestantism and toward such nonsectarian sources of authority as business and science. Women in the child welfare corps had participated actively in the drive to replace religion with science: although most grew up in Protestant homes, the leaders either rejected religion altogether in their adult lives or subordinated it to other sources of authority. Nevertheless, for them, to drop religion from public discourse was not simultaneously to let go of moral arguments. But in the 1920s, the receding wave of evangelical religion seemed to be towing away the power of explicitly moral argumentation as well.[84] Perhaps the ever-increasing cultural/religious diversity of the citizenry destroyed the foundation for agreement on moral issues, and the shift to business and science represented an unconscious attempt to find some basis for public policy that a culturally diverse population could share. Whatever its cause, the declining power of explicitly moral discussions in the formation of public policy diluted the effectiveness of female policymakers and lobbyists because they had staked their claim to public authority partly on their moral superiority to men. Even female professionalism, rooted as it was in the ethic of self-sacrificing service and a reforming political agenda, needed respect as much for its moral values as for its scientific expertise if it were to retain public authority. The clear-eyed Lathrop recognized the problem in her insistence that no more "sob stuff or high ideals" would sway legislators but that women would now have to learn the ways of accountants if they expected to influence public policy.

In sum, as business values such as economy, efficiency, competition, and the profit motive increased their authority in the mid-1920s, they empowered a professional culture that shared those values. The female professionalism of women in the child welfare corps with its emphasis on service, selflessness, and cooperation lost authority. And that loss of authority had implications for public policy, including defeat of Sheppard-Towner.

After the Maternity and Infancy Act lapsed in 1929, the Children's Bureau and its subordinate groups carried on in their constricted area. As the Great Depression deepened, the Bureau studied the disaster's effect on children and recommended programs, which were, of course, not forthcoming from the Hoover administration, but the Bureau counted itself lucky to retain appropriations for research and publication.[85] When the federal government turned down their ideas, leaders in the dominion peddled their wares to state governments, insisting in 1930 for instance that lower levels of government "might meet the emergency by extension of mothers' aid pensions."[86] By the time of the presidential campaign in 1932, the Depression had destroyed Herbert Hoover and had so decisively bent the electorate back toward reform that two years later Katharine Lenroot could proclaim: "What ten years ago would have been an advanced position [vis-à-vis social welfare programs] now is well toward the center."[87] Once again, the political tides had turned, and women in the child welfare establishment this time found that the waters favored their agenda.

As Franklin Roosevelt's new administration searched for responses to the emergency raised by the depression, women in the child welfare corps were ready with the suggestions they had carried across the hostile terrain of the 1920s. And, as important, they were in positions to be heard. For instance, having come through the ranks of social work via Hull House, the Consumers' League, and the New York State Factory Investigating Commission, Frances Perkins became Secretary of Labor in 1933.[88] In part a product of a female dominion, Perkins was the first woman appointed to head a governmental department, and it was no accident that the first female cabinet member occupied this particular post. Both the Children's and the Women's bureaus stood in the Department of Labor, where women had thus established their expertise and earned acceptance as policymakers and administrators. Under the Hoover administration, a coterie of activists had launched a nearly successful campaign to have Grace Abbott appointed Secretary of Labor even despite Hoover's personal antipathy toward her.[89] Frances Perkins's appointment rested on that history, largely the history of a network of female institutions and organizations devoted to child welfare since the Progressive era.

Mary Dewson was another woman whose political power in the 1930s grew out of earlier experience and support from the child welfare corps. After she had served the Red Cross in France during World War I, Dewson returned to New York to become the research secretary of the National Consumers' League under Florence Kelley. In that position, Dewson so impressed leaders in the child welfare establishment that in 1921 Grace Abbott asked her to become assistant chief of the Children's Bureau. Dewson preferred to remain in New York, however, and from 1925 to 1931 she presided over the New York Consumers' League. In 1932, Dewson took over the women's division of the Democratic National Committee and transformed it into an important engine of Franklin Roosevelt's campaign for President. Political victory earned Dewson several appointments during the 1930s. She was a member of the Consumers' Advisory Board of the National Recovery Administration from 1933 to 1935, served as vice president of the Democratic National Committee from 1936 to 1937, and accepted appointment to the Social Security Board in 1937 [90]

Other women could tell similar stories. Clara Beyer served as part-time executive secretary of the National Consumers' League during the early 1920s. In 1928, she moved to the Children's Bureau, where she directed the industrial department from 1931 to 1934. The New Deal opened new opportunities for Beyer: in 1934, she was appointed associate director of the division of labor standards in the Department of Labor, a position she held until 1957.[91] Josephine Roche, who was editorial director for the Children's Bureau between 1924 and 1927, returned to Washington to become Assistant Secretary of the Treasury in 1934. Ironically, she was in charge of health service and welfare work in her department, which meant that she oversaw the Public Health Service. In the early 1940s, when the government appointed an independent committee to coordinate health and welfare activities, Josephine Roche chaired the committee.[92]

And, of course, there were the women in the Children's Bureau itself. Although Grace Abbott retired from her position as chief of the Children's Bureau in 1934, she sat on the President's advisory council to the Committee on Economic Security. The council suggested programs for a federal social security system and was supposed to provide publicity for the scheme that Roosevelt would ultimately support.[93] Abbott was replaced at the Bureau by Katharine Lenroot, who had worked in the agency since 1914, and Lenroot's closest assistant was Dr. Martha May Eliot, who had been on the Children's Bureau staff since 1924.[94]

These three women—Abbott, Lenroot, and Eliot—drafted several proposals for the social security bill. At the behest of the President and his nearest aides, they proposed federal grants-in-aid for maternal and child health programs, services for crippled children, resources for dependent and neglected children, and federal subsidies for the states' mothers' pension programs.[95] Once the Committee on Economic Security had drafted its final suggestions for legislation on social security and submitted them to Congress, Abbott and representatives from the usual women's organizations testified repeatedly on behalf of the sections affecting children.[96]

And the lobbying network of the child welfare dominion remained so renowned in 1935 that when the social security bill bogged down in the House Ways and Means Committee, an anxious aide to the President approached Grace Abbott for advice on how to pry the bill out of committee. Abbott, he later reported, "took the lead in organizing a small committee to contact leaders of public opinion in all walks of life, who joined in a statement presented to Congress urging action upon the pending social security bill and expressing the idea that it was necessary to make a start if social security was ever to be improved."[97] Indeed, she did more than to organize a small committee. As always, she pulled into play her vast web of women's organizations, which bombarded Congress with letters and telegrams of support for the social security bill in general and the children's programs in particular. Although congressmen themselves showed the least interest in the sections on children, their staffs received more mail in support of those programs than in support of any other section of the social security bill.[98] At least one player in the bargaining for the bill, Edwin Witte, credited Abbott and her associates with bumping the bill out of committee.[99]

When the Social Security Act finally passed in 1935, it included each of the programs suggested by the Abbott-Lenroot team and much of their broader agenda. Title V of the Social Security Act restored the Children's Bureau's maternity and infancy health work and allowed the Bureau to expand through programs for crippled children and those neglected by their parents. Further, the act nationalized mothers' pensions in its Aid to Dependent Children program, and in its other titles, it made overtures toward providing a level of income below which no family could fall. Old-age pensions and unemployment insurance, which constituted the most publicized and controversial aspects of the Social Security Act, had been on the child welfare dominion's broadest agenda since before World War I.[100]

Furthermore, members of the child welfare establishment drafted parts of the Fair Labor Standards Act, passed in 1938. Grace Abbott argued for the abolition of child labor, which the act prohibited; Katharine Lenroot wrote several sections of the draft legislation; and Frances Perkins put together a complete version.[101] When the legislation passed, women in the dominion recognized it as an imperfect culmination to their efforts on behalf of a child labor amendment to the constitution, for which they had worked tirelessly in the 1920s, and to their campaigns for minimum wages and maximum hours for working women.[102]

Female progressivism thus culminated in the New Deal. Although Julia Lathrop and Florence Kelley died in 1932 and Jane Addams in 1935, Edith Abbott and Sophonisba Breckinridge hailed the Social Security Act and the Fair Labor Standards Act as legislation toward their ideals. Grace Abbott, of course, helped to draft the laws as did her colleagues at the Children's Bureau and Frances Perkins. Students of Abbott and Breckinridge, carrying on the tradition of their teachers, applauded the legislation and found that their peculiar training at the School of Social Service Administration prepared them to fill new positions opened to social workers by the landmark legislation.[103]

Nevertheless, for all the progress that these women saw in New Deal legislation, they were not nearly satisfied with it. In the course of negotiations in the Cabinet, in the White House, and in Congress, the ideas and interests of women in the child welfare establishment ground against those of many other groups. Furthermore, in the cases of old-age pensions and unemployment insurance, women other than Frances Perkins were only tangentially consulted, and leaders like the Abbott sisters were disgusted that the programs depended so heavily on contributions by employees, provided such meager benefits, omitted so many of the neediest groups, and failed to redistribute income. Both Abbotts believed that the federal government should have exerted more control over the employment practices of private businesses in order to end what Edith Abbott called the "tidal waves of unemployment."[104] She also came to believe that the only equitable way to assure citizens' health was through "a universal health service."[105]

Even more significant for the child welfare dominion, the Social Security Act put its largest children's program, Aid to Dependent Children, under the administrative auspices of the new Social Security Board rather than the Children's Bureau. Throughout the drafting of the bill, various interests had laid claim to the program, especially the Federal Emergency Relief Administration—which was trying to establish itself as a permanent agency—and of course the Department of Labor. Until the very end of the legislative process, many truly believed that the Children's Bureau would ultimately win the program because, after all, the Bureau had been the only federal advocate of mothers' pensions since 1912 and had designed the program for the social security bill. In the end, however, legislators argued that Aid to Dependent Children aimed not so much at children as at income mainte-nance for families and therefore belonged in the same category as old-age pensions and unemployment insurance. As such, it should be administered by the same agency.[106]

With the Children's Bureau's loss of this major program for children, the child welfare dominion crumbled. Architects of the female policymak-ing structure had established and maintained some semblance of control over public policy affecting children. When the Social Security Act put the largest children's program under the supervision of the Social Security Board, the female monopoly over children's policy dissolved.

Women certainly did not at this point disappear from the child welfare bureaucracy, but neither did they exercise sole responsibility any longer. The Social Security Board, which supervised most of the programs created by the Social Security Act, had three members. Throughout the Board's life, one of the three was female. When Mary Dewson retired from the Board, Roosevelt replaced her with Ellen Sullivan Woodward.[107] To admin-ister its programs, the Board established three bureaus: the Bureau of Un-employment Compensation, the Bureau of Old Age Benefits, and the Bureau of Public Assistance. The last supervised Aid to Dependent Chil-dren, and its director was Jane Hoey, trained in social work at the New York School of Philanthropy before World War I and pushed through the ranks of New York's child welfare agencies.[108] Hoey's two associate directors, however, were men, which signified male infiltration of the child welfare field.[109]

Even within the Children's Bureau, changes signaled the end of the dominion. Because the new maternity and infancy programs were ear-marked for those suffering from severe economic distress, the Bureau was now slated to give service strictly to the needy instead of to the entire population of women and children. More jolting, the Children's Bureau began to hire male doctors to administer its child hygiene programs in the mid-1930s. Indeed, male doctors directed the Bureau's Division of Maternal and Child Health as well as its Division of Crippled Children.[110] Perhaps this was because medical schools had begun to admit fewer women after the turn of the century so that the Bureau simply could not find enough female doctors to staff its divisions. Maybe by hiring men, the Bureau hoped to diffuse sexist attacks on its operations; or maybe, as the Bureau expanded its purview, it could no longer resist regular political appointments. Certainly with the proliferation of public social service agencies during the 1930s, Katharine Lenroot continually complained that she had trouble finding qualified people to fill openings in her agency and even went so far as to "abandon the separate examinations for the Children's Bureau," for which Lathrop had fought so hard only twenty years before.[111]

In this instance, trends at the Children's Bureau reflected more general changes in the structure of employment: throughout the 1930s, men increased their presence in female-dominated professions and further decreased the female presence in male-dominated ones. For example, in 1930 women accounted for 80 percent of social workers but by 1940 only 65 percent.[112] Men, who represented 19 percent of teachers in 1930, accounted for 24 percent by 1940, and they had almost doubled their proportion among librarians.[113] Although women did not—indeed, could not—leave the work force in the 1930s, a gender system that favored male breadwinners used the opportunity of depression to force women back into the lowest-paid, least dependable, and lowest-status positions in the economy.[114]

Moreover, even if women had maintained exclusive control over child welfare programs, the dominion could no longer have been said to exist after 1935 because so many women themselves won their highest positions in the federal bureaucracy through patronage appointments by Franklin Roosevelt. Prior to Roosevelt's presidency, female leaders had exercised tight control over jobs within the child welfare network. Because these women had held themselves aloof from partisan politics and convinced successive Presidents that patronage should not dictate their hiring, female leaders had been able to draw through their own institutions younger women who mirrored their values and strategies for public policy. During the 1930s, this changed: most of the women who achieved high office did so especially because they had campaigned for Roosevelt's election.[115] Even if they were women trained and tested in the child welfare establishment, they reached the apex of their careers through connections outside that network. Thus, these women divided their loyalties and knew that they had to please not just the leadership of the dominion but also the Democratic Party. Female leaders in child welfare in this way lost control over jobs and consequently one of their tools for socializing recruits into their peculiar reform culture.

Years later, President Dwight Eisenhower underscored this trend when he replaced Jane Hoey with a political ally. Hoey pitched a fit throughout the ordeal and raised precisely the same objections that Julia Lathrop had marshaled successfully between 1912 and 1921. The Bureau of Public Assistance was not a political agency, Hoey insisted, and so should not suffer the corruption of political appointments. So adamant were her convictions that she refused to resign and had to be fired by the Secretary of Health, Education and Welfare.[116] Because women had, in the 1930s, begun to compete with men for patronage appointments, their claims to non-partisanship no longer seemed credible.

Moreover, with the proliferation of agencies devoted to child welfare, it would have been impossible to identify any entity so centered or disciplined as the dominion had been between 1912 and 1930. Already in the mid-1930s, the Children's Bureau shared programs with the Bureau of Public Assistance. As time wore on, authority scattered farther. In July 1946, for example, the government transferred most of the Children's Bureau to the new Federal Security Agency, but it left the Bureau's industrial division in the Department of Labor to continue enforcing the prohibition of child labor.[117]

This administrative juggling destroyed one of the dominion's dearest accomplishments, which was its refusal to divide the child. Lathrop and her colleagues had insisted that governments should not attempt to split children into medical, educational, and sociological parts. In order most effectively to minister to children's needs, they insisted, every program must be flexible enough to respond to the whole range of problems affecting a child's life. As professional exclusivity hardened, however, and bureaucratic responsibilities increased, Lathrop's arguments appeared antiquated. Agencies charged with much narrower responsibilities became a sign of the times, because, even with more focused responsibilities, the workload increased. It became virtually impossible for a caseworker who delivered checks to a family from Aid to Dependent Children also to offer medical advice or to deal with a child's alleged delinquency. Those problems required the skills of other experts, supervised by different agencies.

Nevertheless, the dominion's demise resulted largely from its success. When women first moved into the federal government to chart child welfare policy, they did not integrate an area formerly occupied by men. They created a whole, new field of policymaking for themselves. Once they had won acceptance for their field, however, men grew interested and began to compete for pieces of it. Moreover, since early in the Progressive era, female reformers had insisted that the welfare of children could be assured only by establishing the economic security of all families. Child welfare they viewed as only a part of the larger puzzle of general social welfare. The Social Security Act formally recognized that tenet. But the recognition did not redound to the benefit of female policymakers: rather than expanding the Children's Bureau to include wider social programs that incidentally benefited children, legislators created the new Social Security Board and then used the women's argument against them, saying that, although children were affected by such programs as Aid to Dependent Children, their real goal was economic stability, the province not of the Children's Bureau but of the Social Security Board. Male policymakers simply would not relinquish such a wide field, full of opportunity, to women. Child welfare thus ceased to be the preserve of women alone. With the New Deal, then, the sun rose on the women's agenda but set over the dominion itself.

Conclusion

In the earliest months of my research for this project, I read the following diatribe, written in 1926 by one group of superpatriotic women:

> It is of the utmost significance that practically all the radicalism started among women in the United States centers about Hull-House, Chicago, and the Children's Bureau at Washington, with a dynasty of Hull-House graduates in charge of it since its creation.
>
> It has been shown that both the legislative program and the economic program—"social-welfare" legislation and "bread and peace" propaganda . . . —find their chief expression in persons, organizations, and bureaus connected with Hull-House.[1]

On first reading this passage, I smiled and shook my head at what I believed to be a wildly paranoid conspiracy theory. Over the course of the following months, however, I began to acknowledge an element of truth in the superpatriots' vision. Emerging from the documents I studied was the image of a very well-integrated network of persons, organizations, and bureaus devoted to various reform causes, especially to the social welfare legislation that superpatriots so hated. And I could not deny that many of the leaders in this network had indeed graduated from Hull House. To some degree then, the superpatriots recognized in 1926 what I have decided these sixty-five years later to call the child welfare dominion.

At the height of its power in the 1920s, this institutional nexus had several interlocking levels of authority. At its head was the Children's Bureau in the federal Department of Labor, which oversaw the operation of analogous state agencies that served as the second rung of authority within the dominion. Both of these echelons rested on a broad base of support provided by female voluntary organizations. These three layers of authority were aided by two auxiliaries: the Women's Joint Congressional Committee helped with the lobbying, while the School of Social Service Administration at the University of Chicago trained workers to serve in the network. A number of other organizations also educated women in the values and strategies for reform that dominion-builders sought in the women they hired. Hull House and other settlements, the Consumers' League, the New York School of Social Work, and the graduate faculty in some social science departments at Columbia University and the University of Wisconsin each for a time steered appropriately trained students into the child welfare corps.

While my predecessors, the superpatriots, railed against the radicalism of this policymaking corps, I have found in it an explanation for the continuing reform activity of white, middle-class women between the Progressive era and the decade of the New Deal. Documents produced by the residents of Hull House, the heads of the School of Social Service Administration, and the workers in the Children's Bureau reveal that during the Progressive era female reformers professionalized and institutionalized their reform culture, and that they were, as a result, able to socialize younger women into that culture by offering education and employment. Both the old female guard and the new, then, continued to push for reform legislation because their professional and institutional interests encouraged them to do so.

The current study of relationships among governmental, educational, and voluntary agencies has helped to expose some of the connections among public and private authority during the Progressive era. Indeed, it suggests that Daniel Rodgers was right to believe that an understanding of progressivism required the unmasking of these connections. One result, after all, has been to dispel the impression that progressives were naive in their confidence that small, data-gathering agencies could in any way ameliorate the suffering generated by industrialism. From this investigation, we have seen that women and men in the social justice wing of progressivism did not view those small, data-gathering bodies as secluded islands of information but as specialized members of busy, closely connected archipelagos and that progressives had faith in the transformative power of those agencies only as they participated in larger complexes of organizations devoted to reform.

The history of the child welfare dominion suggests that the foundation for this faith was surprisingly solid, for this reforming body accomplished remarkable feats. It designed and implemented the United States' first federal social welfare program, which improved prenatal and infant health care for thousands of women and children. The particular design of that program, with its emphasis on federal-state cooperation and its demotion of private agencies in the provision of social services, provided a model for subsequent social programs that formed the U.S. welfare state in the 1930s, and the institutional affiliations that the dominion afforded a few women allowed them directly to affect the character of those New Deal programs. Furthermore, the female policymaking body opened new professional opportunities for women even in the 1920s, when women were making little headway in professional life, and it united many women in reforming campaigns when reform was decreasingly popular. Indeed, as women institutionalized their reform culture in national agencies such as the Children's Bureau and the Women's Joint Congressional Committee, they increasingly disciplined their efforts toward reform and were emboldened to shift their focus from states and locales to the nation. Through this process, some women married their own professional advancement to the cause of social welfare reform in such a way that professionalization strengthened their commitment to reform.

Professionalization and reform did not, therefore, stand in necessary opposition to each other during the Progressive era. While some people—especially men in male-dominated professions—were fashioning a professional culture that opposed the tenets of social justice reform, this study has identified another version of the professional creed that grew out of female experience and actually sustained the values of reform. By calling it a female professionalism, I have not intended to suggest that all women upheld this particular creed or that no men did. Rather, I have shown that a specific group of women developed this code and that it emerged from gender-specific experiences. Other groups of women, operating in different circumstances, created other sorts of professional creeds, and some men may well have cultivated a similar code, but theirs would have had to emerge from a context different from that of the women in this study.

Indeed, one of the great lessons taught by this investigation is that we cannot hope to understand our past until we commit ourselves to studying the experiences of women as well as men. Even when women and men appear to have been engaged in the same struggle, to have been advocating the same programs, to have been employing the same tactics, their motives, their understanding of the mission, the results of their work have varied according to gender.

In fact, I have argued that part of the explanation for Progressive reform itself and the particular shape of the welfare state in the U.S. lay in the peculiar experiences of white, middle-class women in the 1890s. Finally having broken into higher education but still barred from conventional male routes to independence and authority, college-educated women in the late nineteenth century began to carve out wholly new areas of professional expertise for themselves. Victorian ideals of womanhood and the U.S. social structure shaped this process, which ultimately encouraged ambitious women to gear their professional aspirations toward the service of indigent clients. Consequently searching for sources of funding other than fees paid by clients, these women became part of a movement to expand various levels of government into social welfare. They thus stood at the center of the social justice wing of Progressive reform, and the values and strategies they formed as members of this movement eventually found legislative expression in the Sheppard-Towner Maternity and Infancy Act and in female suggestions for New Deal legislation.

With regard to the New Deal and its origins—on welfare states across the industrialized world—a new body of literature is shaping up. Some of it is attending to issues of gender and focuses especially on the ways that welfare policies have defined gender. To use the phraseology of one of these works, they have looked especially at the ways that welfare policy has *regulated* the lives of women and men, at the ways that social policies have assumed and consequently reproduced the roles of women as economic dependents and men as wage-earners.[2] My own study argues that the relationship between gender and the U.S. welfare state has operated at other levels as well, specifically that gender has itself shaped social policy.[3] As the history of the dominion shows, female policymakers took into policy-making processes assumptions and professional values different from men so that, even when they worked with men on policy aimed at the same problems, women created very different sorts of programs. They did so because of the specific historical context in which they had been professionalizing and building institutions since 1890. Thus, gender, especially by shaping various professional creeds, molded social policy in the U.S. during the 1920s and 1930s.

For all of its successes in the past and its explanatory power in the present, the female child welfare dominion suffered severe limitations. Although the network offered younger women professional opportunities and public authority, the pressure to conform to the leadership's values was

intense and sometimes oppressive. Even Grace Abbott, one of the dominion's stars, had not enjoyed the freedom to decide her own future in 1921.
Instead, she felt forced to obey her mentors' will for her career. Moreover,
because there was very little room at the top, only a few women could hope
for much mobility within the network, and that depended as much on
personal acquaintance with the leadership as on ability.

More disturbing was the refusal of professional women to use their
position in any way to liberate the mass of women who were mothers.
Indeed, the dominion's prescriptions for mothers were singularly restrictive.
They insisted that all mothers breastfeed their children and that all mothers
should rear their own children without relying on outside help or on
fathers. Working mothers, the experts insisted, were more likely to rear
unhealthy children. This meant that working-class mothers, forced to work
by financial need, could not hope to fulfill the experts' prescriptions for
proper motherhood and that a professional woman who chose to have
children should forgo her career while her children were young. Even in
1919, when Lathrop cheered the advances of single women in the labor
force, she advised the National Conference of Social Work: "Let us not
deceive ourselves: the power to maintain a decent family living standard is
the primary essential of child welfare. This means a living wage and whole-
some working life for the man, a good and skillful mother at home to keep
the house and comfort all within it."[4] Even though younger middle-class
women in the 1920s publicly struggled to find ways to combine careers and
motherhood, the dominion's leadership continued to assume that women
had to choose between motherhood and careers.[5]

Here we can see the danger inherent in the relatively closed system built
by female reformers in the Progressive era. Apparently the leadership within
the dominion was so intent on keeping alive the values of the founders that
it could not hear the new concerns of women that were surfacing in the
1920s and that would have required innovations in their program of child
welfare policy. During the 1920s, the Children's Bureau did not, for instance, publicly advocate birth control or a re-creation of the family in
which mothers worked outside their homes and relinquished childrearing to
professional day-care centers. Their ideal of family life continued to include
a working father and stay-at-home mother, a failure of imagination encouraged by the Victorian origins of the dominion, the political conservatism of the 1920s, and the direction of mass culture as embodied in advertising. Thus, although superpatriots and penny-pinchers in Congress often

accused the leaders of the child welfare corps of radicalism in the 1920s, many trends actually restricted the women's vision during that decade and made it conservative of the values developed during the first decades of the twentieth century.

Class and race were part of that restriction as well. Activists in the dominion were relentlessly native-born and middle-class. As shown earlier, Sheppard-Towner nurses invaded working-class homes to order them according to middle-class preferences, and every bit of advice to parents meant to instill a sort of industrial discipline in newborns: regular feedings, regular nap times, no play-time with parents, no baby talk, no rocking, no cuddling, no fun! Whatever variety existed in childrearing practices, the dominion-builders aimed to wipe out. Their advice to mothers did not provide flexibility or offer alternative child-care techniques for varying familial circumstances but instead insisted that there was one good way to rear children. Thus, the child welfare corps showed a distinct prejudice against pluralism in childrearing. Its driving force aimed to abolish cultural variety even in relationships between parents and children, in diet, in birthing techniques. Evidently the experts never considered the possibility that many different approaches might well have produced happy, healthy children.

The leadership of the dominion was caught, then, in the familiar progressive contradiction between commitments to democracy and expertise. On the one hand, they operated very democratically: into their work, they drew thousands of non-professional women and could not hope for success unless their programs met with the approval of those multitudes. Moreover, the policies designed by these women encouraged local participation in funding and implementation and even depended on the cooperation of local elites. Compared with the work of other professionals and policymakers at the time, this inclusion of lay people was remarkably democratic. On the other hand, the active multitudes within the dominion were themselves usually white, native-born, middle-class, and often enamored of expertise. They were more than willing to join their professional sisters in campaigns to impose middle-class practices on those whom they believed in need of expert intervention. Such hard lines against cultural pluralism were hardly democratic, and they set the policies of the dominion within a larger cultural project wherein middle-class professionals were attempting to establish their own authority over all aspects of American life.

This conclusion highlights several issues with which current professionals and policymakers must wrestle. For one, given the class and cultural divisions in U.S. society, which if anything have increased in number and deepened in quality since the 1930s, is it possible to design and implement a truly democratic social policy? For another, is there any way to create a democratic professionalism, or do professionalism and democracy stand in eternal opposition?

Unfortunately, nothing in the past can answer those questions for us, but the experience of the women in the child welfare dominion opens paths of analysis. Their experience suggests, for instance, that, regardless of intent, when one group in society designs policy *for* another, the result will prove intrusive and to some degree authoritarian. No policy can hope to fulfill the requirements of democracy unless it is made by the people it affects. This means that the sources of social welfare policy, for instance, should be the recipients of aid: the elderly, unemployed, parents with dependent children, and those with varying physical abilities. The real empowerment of such folk in the policymaking arena would, of course, require a radical transformation of our tax system, educational institutions, political parties, and the policymaking structures that include the official institutions of government as well as the unofficial pressure groups, think tanks, and bureaucracies that bear down on those operating in the official institutions. If we cannot effect this complete transformation in one fell swoop, perhaps we could begin by creating institutional channels through which policymakers and professionals listen instead of speak to those for whom they create policies. In the case of much social welfare policy, electoral politics is not proving an effective channel for the voices of those affected. We must create new ones if we honestly care about the democratic project.

On the issue of democracy and professionalism, I confess a deeply personal investment. Although my study did not begin as such, it soon became for me a way of searching for some model for being a professional and a committed democrat, which was for me part and parcel of feminism. I was uneasy about the grant of authority I would receive from professional credentials, and I wondered how on earth I could square that authority with a feminist's commitment to non-hierarchical relationships, to participatory democracy. When I discovered that indeed some women in the Progressive era created a professionalism much more inclusive and cooperative than the professionalism I associated with doctors and lawyers and moreover a professionalism that *owned* its political agenda at least in some circumstances, I breathed a sigh of relief, thinking that I surely had found the model I was looking for, the reassurance that I could occupy a professional position without reducing someone else to dependency. As my study continued, however, I had to admit that even the female professionalism of women in the dominion was fraught with the arrogance of power. And so I continue to wonder if it is possible to reconcile professionalism and feminism, to bend the privilege of professionalism toward the empowerment of all.

Notes

Introduction

1. Quoted in Susan Ware, *Beyond Suffrage: Women in the New Deal* (Cambridge, Mass.: Harvard Univ. Press, 1981), 42.

2. Quotation is from Mrs. Elizabeth Tilton's manuscript autobiography, cited in Clarke A. Chambers, *Seedtime of Reform: American Social Service and Social Action, 1918–1933* (1963; Westport, Conn.: Greenwood Press, 1980), 2.

3. J. Stanley Lemons, *The Woman Citizen: Social Feminism in the 1920s* (Chicago: Univ. of Illinois Press, 1973).

4. Ware, *Beyond Suffrage*; and Susan Ware, *Partner and I: Molly Dewson, Feminism, and New Deal Politics* (New Haven: Yale Univ. Press, 1987).

5. Nancy Cott pointed out women's continuing participation in "voluntarist politics" during the 1920s in *The Grounding of Modern Feminism* (New Haven: Yale Univ. Press, 1987), 85–114; Linda Gordon, in *Heroes of Their Own Lives: The Politics and History of Family Violence* (New York: Viking, 1988), 297, claimed that "the whole welfare state . . . derived to a significant degree from the feminist agenda of the late nineteenth and early twentieth centuries." See also Joan Williams, Jacqueline Dirks, and Regina Kunzel, "Women in the Progressive Era," *Conference Group on Women's History Newsletter* 19 (April/May 1988), 11–15; and Elisabeth Israels Perry, *Belle Moskowitz: Feminine Politics and the Exercise of Power in the Age of Alfred E. Smith* (New York: Oxford Univ. Press, 1987). The most recent dissenter from this view is Elizabeth Anne Payne, *Reform, Labor, and Feminism: Margaret Dreier Robins and the Women's Trade Union League* (Urbana: Univ. of Illinois Press, 1988).

6. Most famous recanters included Herbert Croly, Walter Lippmann, and Lincoln Steffens. See, for example, William E. Leuchtenburg, *The Perils of Prosperity, 1914–32* (Chicago: Univ. of Chicago, 1958), 125.

7. On the Women's Bureau, see Judith Sealander, *As Minority Becomes Majority: Federal Reaction to the Phenomenon of Women in the Work Force, 1920–1963* (Westport, Conn.: Greenwood Press, 1983). See also Eileen Boris, "Women's Networks and the Enactment of Legislation: Homework Laws in Depression America," paper

presented at the Eighth Berkshire Conference on the History of Women, New Brunswick, N.J., June 8, 1990; and work in progress by Sybil Lipschultz.

8. On discrimination and female strategies for coping, see Margaret W. Rossiter, *Women Scientists in America: Struggles and Strategies to 1940* (Baltimore: Johns Hopkins Univ. Press, 1982); Penina Migdal Glazer and Miriam Slater, *Unequal Colleagues: The Entrance of Women into the Professions, 1890–1940* (New Brunswick: Rutgers Univ. Press, 1987); Pnina G. Abir-Am and Dorinda Outram, eds., *Uneasy Careers and Intimate Lives Women in Science, 1789–1979* (New Brunswick: Rutgers Univ. Press, 1987); Elizabeth Fee, *Disease and Discovery: A History of the Johns Hopkins School of Hygiene and Public Health, 1916–1939* (Baltimore: Johns Hopkins Univ. Press, 1987), 173–76; Mary Roth Walsh, *"Doctors Wanted: No Women Need Apply": Sexual Barriers in the Medical Profession, 1835–1975* (New Haven: Yale Univ. Press, 1977); Gloria Moldow, *Women Doctors in Gilded-Age Washington: Race, Gender, and Professionalization* (Urbana: Univ. of Illinois Press, 1978).

9. On women in these traditionally female professions, see Barbara Melosh, *The Physician's Hand: Work, Culture, and Conflict in American Nursing* (Philadelphia: Temple Univ. Press, 1982); Nancy Tomes, "Little World of Our Own: The Pennsylvania Hospital Training School for Nurses, 1895–1907," *Journal of the History of Medicine and Allied Sciences* 33 (Oct. 1978), 507–30; Susan M. Reverby, *Ordered to Care: The Dilemma of American Nursing, 1850–1945* (New York: Cambridge Univ. Press, 1987); Darlene Clark Hine, *Black Women in Nursing: An Anthology of Historical Sources* (New York: Garland, 1984); Dee Garrison, *Apostles of Culture: The Public Librarian and American Society* (New York: Macmillan, 1979). See also Joan Jacobs Brumberg and Nancy Tomes, "Women in the Professions: A Research Agenda for American Historians," *Reviews in American History* (June 1982), 273–96; Barbara Kuhn Campbell, *The "Liberated" Woman of 1914: Prominent Women in the Progressive Era* (1976; Ann Arbor: UMI Research Press, 1979), chap. 3.

10. See especially Regina Morantz-Sanchez, *Sympathy and Science: Women Physicians in American Medicine* (New York: Oxford Univ. Press, 1985); Joyce Antler, *Lucy Sprague Mitchell: The Making of a Modern Woman* (New Haven: Yale Univ. Press, 1987), and Antler's *The Educated Woman and Professionalization: The Struggle for a New Feminine Identity, 1890–1920* (New York: Garland, 1987); Clarke A. Chambers, "Women in the Creation of the Profession of Social Work," *Social Service Review* 60 (March 1986), 1–33; Barbara Sicherman, *Alice Hamilton: A Life in Letters* (Cambridge, Mass.: Harvard Univ. Press, 1984); and Melosh, *The Physician's Hand*, chap. 4.

11. John H. Ehrenreich, *The Altruistic Imagination: A History of Social Work and Social Policy in the United States* (Ithaca: Cornell Univ. Press, 1985), 58–60; Judith A. Trolander, *Professionalism and Social Change: From the Settlement House Movement to Neighborhood Centers, 1886 to the Present* (New York: Columbia Univ. Press, 1987), 2.

12. Rosalind Rosenberg, *Beyond Separate Spheres: Intellectual Roots of Modern Feminism* (New Haven: Yale Univ. Press, 1982); Cott, *The Grounding of Modern Feminism*; William O'Neill, *Everyone Was Brave: A History of Feminism in America*

(New York: Quadrangle, 1969), esp. 250. See also Virginia G. Drachman, *Hospital With a Heart: Women Doctors and the Paradox of Separatism at the New England Hospital, 1862–1969* (Ithaca: Cornell Univ. Press, 1984); Judy Jolley Mohraz, "The Equity Club: Community Building Among Professional Women," *Journal of American Culture* 5 (Winter 1982), 34–39; Patricia M. Hummer, *The Decade of Elusive Promise: Professional Women in the United States, 1920–1930* (Ann Arbor: UMI Research Press, 1979), esp. 49, 113, 125.

13. Mary O. Furner, *Advocacy and Objectivity: A Crisis in the Professionalization of American Social Science, 1865–1905* (Lexington: Univ. of Kentucky Press, 1975). See also Dorothy Ross, "The Development of the Social Sciences," in *The Organization of Knowledge in Modern America, 1860–1920*, eds. Alexandra Oleson and John Voss (Baltimore: Johns Hopkins Univ. Press, 1979), 107–38.

14. Here I believe I am in the company of Regina Morantz-Sanchez, Joyce Antler, Judith Trolander, and most especially Elizabeth K. Hartley, whose dissertation argues that for some women—like Julia Lathrop—professionalization actually increased the commitment to social welfare reform. See Judith Trolander, *Professionalism and Social Change*, 44–45, and E. K. Hartley, "Social Work and Social Reform: Selected Women Social Workers and Child Welfare Reforms, 1877–1932," Ph.D. dissertation, Univ. of Pennsylvania, 1985, esp. 429, 432.

15. This new literature on the formation of welfare states and especially on gender includes Mimi Abramovitz, *Regulating the Lives of Women: Social Policy from Colonial Times to the Present* (Boston: South End Press, 1988); Barbara J. Nelson, "The Gender, Race, and Class Origins of Early Welfare Policy and the Welfare State: A Comparison of Workmen's Compensation and Mothers' Aid," in *Women, Change, and Politics*, eds. Louise Tilly and Patricia Gurin (New York: Russell Sage Foundation, 1990), 226–38; Linda Gordon, "What Does Welfare Regulate?," *Social Research* 55 (Winter 1988), 609–30, and Gordon's *Heroes of Their Own Lives*; Elizabeth Pleck, *Domestic Tyranny: The Making of American Social Policy Against Family Violence from Colonial Times to the Present* (New York: Oxford Univ. Press, 1987); Seth Koven and Sonya Michel, "Gender and the Origins of the Welfare State," *Radical History Review* 43 (Winter 1989), 112–19; Gwendolyn Mink, "Welfare Mother," *Women's Review of Books* 7 (Dec. 1989), 19–20; Gwendolyn Mink, "The Lady and the Tramp: Gender, Race and the Origins of the American Welfare System," *Women, the State, and Welfare*, ed. Linda Gordon (Madison: Univ. of Wisconsin Press, 1990); Dorothy O. Helly and Susan M. Reverby, eds., *Connected Domains: Beyond the Public/Private Dichotomy in Women's History* (Ithaca: Cornell Univ. Press, forthcoming 1991); Virginia Sapiro, "The Gender Bias of American Social Policy," *Political Science Quarterly* 101 (1986), 221–38.

16. Linda Gordon has shown, for instance, that between 1910 and 1930, as child welfare work was being professionalized, social workers shifted the focus of their protective work from the "drunken immigrant father" to the "incompetent, insensitive, and possibly untrained mother in need of professional guidance." Gordon, *Heroes of Their Own Lives*, 61.

17. Daniel P. Rodgers, "In Search of Progressivism," *Reviews in American History* 10 (Dec. 1982), 111–32.

Chapter 1. Hull House, 1890–1910

1. Addams to Alice Addams Haldeman, Feb. 19, 1889, Stephenson County Illinois Historical Society, frames 1017–19, reel 2, *Jane Addams Papers on Microfilm*, ed., Mary Lynn McCree Bryan (Ann Arbor: Univ. of Michigan, 1984). All citations from this microfilmed edition of the Jane Addams Papers will indicate the collection from which editors pulled the original document and will be abbreviated JAP.

2. On the cult of true womanhood, see Barbara Welter, "The Cult of True Womanhood, 1820–1860," *American Quarterly* 18 (Summer 1966), 151–74. On the centrality of self-sacrifice to this cult, see especially Kathryn Kish Sklar, *Catharine Beecher: A Study in American Domesticity* (New Haven: Yale Univ. Press, 1973).

3. Numerous studies have analyzed these voluntary associations. Sklar's biography of Beecher tells the story of how they moved women into elementary school teaching. On female missionaries, see Polly Welts Kaufman, *Women Teachers on the Frontier* (New Haven: Yale Univ. Press, 1984), and Jane Hunter, *The Gospel of Gentility: American Women Missionaries in Turn-of-the-Century China* (New Haven: Yale Univ. Press, 1984). On the temperance movement, see esp. Ruth Bordin, *Woman and Temperance: The Quest for Power and Liberty, 1873–1900* (Philadelphia: Temple Univ. Press, 1981), and Barbara Leslie Epstein, *The Politics of Domesticity: Women, Evangelism and Temperance in Nineteenth-Century America* (Middletown, Conn.: Wesleyan Univ. Press, 1981). On women in the antislavery societies, see Ellen Carol DuBois, *Feminism and Suffrage: The Emergence of an Independent Women's Movement in America, 1848–1869* (Ithaca: Cornell Univ. Press, 1978), and Gerda Lerner, *The Grimké Sisters from South Carolina: Rebels Against Slavery* (Boston: Houghton, Mifflin, 1967). For more general approaches, see Nancy F. Cott, *The Bonds of Womanhood: "Woman's Sphere" in New England, 1780–1835* (New Haven: Yale Univ. Press, 1977); Estelle B. Freedman, *Their Sisters' Keepers: Women's Prison Reform in America, 1830–1930* (Ann Arbor: Univ. of Michigan, 1981); Keith E. Melder, *Beginnings of Sisterhood: The American Woman's Rights Movement, 1800–1850* (New York: Schocken Press, 1977); Mary Ryan, "The Power of Women's Networks: A Case Study of Female Reform in Antebellum America," *Feminist Studies* 5 (Spring 1979), 66–85; Anne Firor Scott, *Making the Invisible Woman Visible* (Chicago: Univ. of Illinois Press, 1984), 259–94; Dorothy Sterling, ed. *We Are Your Sisters: Black Women in the Nineteenth Century* (New York: Norton, 1984), esp. 104–213; Lori D. Ginzberg, *Women and the Work of Benevolence: Morality, Politics, and Class in the Nineteenth-Century United States* (New Haven: Yale Univ. Press, 1990).

4. Lynn Gordon, "Women With Missions: Varieties of College Life in the Progressive Era," Ph.D. dissertation, Univ. of Chicago, 1980, pp. 5–7. See also Lynn Gordon's *Gender and Higher Education in the Progressive Era* (New Haven: Yale Univ.

Press, 1990); Barbara Miller Solomon, *In the Company of Educated Women: A History of Women and Higher Education in America* (New Haven: Yale Univ. Press, 1985).

5. Carroll Smith-Rosenberg, "The Female World of Love and Ritual: Relations Among Women in Nineteenth-Century America," *Signs* 1 (Autumn 1975), 1–29.

6. In addition to Gordon and Solomon, see Roberta Frankfort, *Collegiate Women: Domesticity and Career in Turn-of-the-Century America* (New York: New York Univ. Press, 1977); Patricia A. Palmieri, "Here Was Fellowship: A Social Portrait of Academic Women at Wellesley, 1895–1920," *History of Education Quarterly* 23 (Summer 1983), 195–214; Nancy Sahli, "Smashing: Women's Relationships Before the Fall," *Chrysalis* 8 (Summer 1979), 17–27; Helen Lefkowitz Horowitz, *Alma Mater: Design and Experience in Women's Colleges from Their Nineteenth-Century Beginnings to the 1930s* (1984; Boston: Beacon Press, 1986).

7. Frankfort, *Collegiate Women*, 85–98.

8. Allen F. Davis, *American Heroine: The Life and Legend of Jane Addams* (New York: Oxford Univ. Press, 1973), 3–10.

9. Jane Addams, "Bread Givers," speech delivered before the Junior Exhibition at Rockford Female Seminary, 1880, printed in Jane Addams, *A Centennial Reader* (New York: Macmillan, 1960), 103–4.

10. Addams to Starr, May 15, 1880, Ellen Gates Starr Papers, Smith College, frames 504–6, reel 1, JAP.

11. Addams to Starr, Sept. 3, 1881, Starr Papers, Smith College, frames 762–63, reel 1, JAP.

12. Starr to Addams, Aug. 11, 1878, Starr Papers, Smith College, frames 322–29, reel 1, JAP.

13. Starr to Addams, July 27, 1879, Jane Addams Papers, Swarthmore College Peace Collection, frames 374–85, reel 1, JAP.

14. Starr to Addams, Jan. 1, 1882, Jane Addams Papers, Swarthmore College Peace Collection, frames 857–66, reel 1, JAP.

15. Starr to Addams, Oct. 22, 1882, Jane Addams Papers, Swarthmore College Peace Collection, frames 1005–18, reel 1, JAP.

16. Addams to Starr, Jan. 7, 1883, Starr Papers, Smith College, frames 1037–40, reel 1, JAP.

17. Quotation is from Addams to Starr, Feb. 13, 1881, Starr Papers, Smith College, frames 584–88, reel 1, JAP.

18. Davis, *American Heroine*, 31–32, 41. Edward T. James et al., eds., *Notable American Women, 1607–1950*, 3 vols. (Cambridge, Mass.: Belknap Press, 1971), 3: 351–52.

19. Davis, *American Heroine*, 24–27.

20. Starr to Addams, July 3, 1883, Jane Addams Papers, Swarthmore College Peace Collection, frame 1112, reel 1, JAP.

21. Starr to Addams, Jan. 31, 1886, Jane Addams Papers, Swarthmore College Peace Collection, frames 192–200, reel 2; Addams to Starr, Sept. 3, 1881, Starr Papers, Smith College, frames 762–63, reel 1; JAP.

22. Addams to Starr, Aug. 12, 1883, Starr Papers, Smith College, frames 1140–41, reel 1, JAP.

23. Davis, *American Heroine*, 44.

24. Starr to Addams, March 17, 1888, Mrs. S. A. Haldeman MSS, Lilly Library, Indiana Univ., frames 877–85, reel 2, JAP.

25. Davis, *American Heroine*, 50. Allen F. Davis, *Spearheads for Reform: The Social Settlements and the Progressive Movement, 1890–1914* (New York: Oxford Univ. Press, 1967), 3–7.

26. Solomon, *In the Company of Educated Women*, 119. Davis, *Spearheads for Reform*, 10–11. John P. Rousmaniere, "Cultural Hybrid in the Slums: The College Woman and the Settlement House, 1889–1894," *American Quarterly* 22 (Spring 1970), 45–66.

27. See, in addition to the above, Carl N. Degler, *At Odds: Women and the Family in America from the Revolution to the Present* (New York: Oxford Univ. Press, 1980), 321.

28. Other authors have noted this same reversal in other contexts. See, for example, Penina Migdal Glazer and Miriam Slater in their discussion of Mount Holyoke College in the early twentieth century in *Unequal Colleagues: The Entrance of Women into the Professions, 1890–1940* (New Brunswick: Rutgers Univ. Press, 1987), 36.

29. Statistics compiled from information in Robert A. Woods and Albert J. Kennedy, eds., *Handbook of Settlements* (New York: Charities Publication Committee, 1911).

30. Quoted in Allen F. Davis and Mary Lynn McCree, eds., *Eighty Years at Hull-House* (Chicago: Quadrangle, 1969), 66.

31. "List of Hull-House Residents, 1889–1929," Hull-House Association Records, Univ. of Illinois–Chicago, frame 311, reel 50; *Hull-House Bulletin*, Dec. 1, 1896, Hull-House Association Records, frame 561, reel 53; *Hull-House Bulletin*, June 1897, Hull-House Association Records, frame 611, reel 53; JAP. Davis, *American Heroine*, 75. Newspaper Clipping, n.d., City Club of Chicago file, box 306, Series 1E, Anita McCormick Blaine Papers, State Historical Society of Wisconsin, Madison. Davis and McCree, *Eighty Years*, 118. Barbara Sicherman, *Alice Hamilton: A Life in Letters* (Cambridge, Mass.: Harvard Univ. Press, 1984), 123.

32. See Karen J. Blair, *Clubwoman as Feminist: True Womanhood Redefined, 1868–1914* (New York: Holmes and Meier, 1980).

33. Addams to Anna Haldeman Addams, May 9, 1889, Jane Addams Papers, Univ. of Illinois–Chicago, frames 1064–66, reel 2, JAP.

34. Addams to Anna Haldeman Addams, May 9, 1889, Jane Addams Papers, Univ. of Illinois–Chicago, frames 1064–66, reel 2, JAP.

35. "To Meet on Common Ground: A Project to Bring Rich and Poor Together," *Chicago Tribune*, March 8, 1889, p. 8. Addams to Mary Addams Linn, Feb. 12, 1889, Jane Addams Papers, Swarthmore College Peace Collection, frames 1008–16, reel 2, JAP.

36. Jane Addams, *Twenty Years at Hull-House* (1910; reprint, New York: New American Library, 1981), 94.

37. Addams, *Twenty Years*, 72.

38. Ibid., 98.

39. Ray Ginger, *Altgeld's America, 1890-1905* (New York: Funk and Wagnalls, 1958), 95.

40. Richard C. Wade and Harold M. Mayer, *Chicago: Growth of a Metropolis* (Chicago: Univ. of Chicago, 1969), 152.

41. Bessie Louise Pierce, *A History of Chicago*, 3 vols. (Chicago: Univ. of Chicago, 1957), 3: 235.

42. Ibid., 3: 237. See also Joanne J. Meyerowitz, *Women Adrift: Independent Wage Earners in Chicago, 1880-1930* (Chicago: Univ. of Chicago, 1988).

43. See, for example, Wade and Mayer, *Chicago*, 146, 252.

44. For the number of strikes, see U.S. Commissioner of Labor, *Twenty-first Annual Report* (Washington, D.C.: Government Printing Office, 1906), 15.

45. "To Meet on Common Ground." Davis, *American Heroine*, 59-60.

46. David Swing, "A New Social Movement," 1889, newspaper clipping, Jane Addams Papers, Univ. of Illinois–Chicago, frame 6, reel 10, Addendum, JAP.

47. Addams to George Haldeman, Nov. 24, 1889, Jane Addams Papers, Univ. of Illinois–Chicago, frames 1129-30, reel 2, JAP.

48. Mary A. Porter, "A Home on Halsted Street," *Advance*, July 11, 1889, Jane Addams Papers, Univ. of Illinois–Chicago, frame 6, reel 10, Addendum, JAP. Davis, *American Heroine*, 67-68.

49. Addams, *Twenty Years*, 56, 98, 101, 167-69, 206, 211-12.

50. Addams to Alice Addams Haldeman, March 6, 1890, Mrs. S. A. Haldeman MSS, Lilly Library, Indiana Univ., frames 1157-59, reel 2, JAP.

51. Minutes of Residents' Meeting, March 1, 1894, Hull-House Association Records, Univ. of Illinois–Chicago, frame 384, reel 50; *Hull-House Bulletin*, Dec. 1, 1896, Hull-House Association Records, frame 561, reel 53; *Hull-House Yearbook*, Jan. 1, 1916, Hull-House Association Records, frame 1114, reel 53; JAP. Addams, *Twenty Years*, 308.

52. Minutes of Residents' Meeting, March 1, 1894, Hull-House Association Records, Univ. of Illinois–Chicago, frame 384, reel 50; *Hull-House Bulletin*, Dec. 1, 1896, Hull-House Association Records, frame 561, reel 53; *Hull-House Bulletin*, April and May 1899, Hull-House Association Records, frame 700, reel 53; JAP.

53. Minutes of Residents' Meetings, 1893-94, Hull-House Association Records, Univ. of Illinois–Chicago, frames 301-86, reel 50, JAP. On the settlement spirit, see Addams to Mary Rozet Smith, Feb. 3, 1895, Jane Addams Papers, Swarthmore College Peace Collection, frames 1647-55, reel 2, JAP. On probation and its results, see Francis Hackett, "Hull-House–A Souvenir," *Survey* (June 1, 1925), 275-79, reprinted in Davis and McCree, *Eighty Years*, 72-74.

54. Minutes of Residents' Meetings, 1893-94, Hull-House Association Papers, Univ. of Illinois–Chicago, frames 301-86, reel 50, JAP.

55. Hackett, "Hull-House—A Souvenir," 74.

56. Alice Hamilton to Grace Abbott, May 20, 1935, folder 1, box 55, Grace and Edith Abbott Papers, Special Collections, Univ. of Chicago Library.

57. Davis, *American Heroine*, 76–78, 105. Edith Abbott, "Grace Abbott and Hull House, 1908–21," *Social Service Review* 24 (Sept. 1950), 380.

58. Jane Addams, *My Friend, Julia Lathrop* (New York: Macmillan, 1935), 60.

59. Milligan to Addams, Nov. 19, 1932, Esther Loeb Kohn Papers, Univ. of Illinois—Chicago, frames 447–52, reel 24, JAP.

60. See, for example, Dorothy Detzer to Addams, July 22, 1925, Women's International League for Peace and Freedom Papers, Swarthmore College, frames 745–46, reel 17; Rose Gyles to Addams, June 29, 1904, Rockford College Archives, frames 855–57, reel 4; Addams to Stanley Linn, Feb. 2, 1929, Jane Addams Papers, Univ. of Illinois—Chicago, frame 776, reel 20; Deknatels, Hooker, Yarroses, Benedict, Nancrede, Byrons, Donaldson, Cairos to Addams, Dec. 25, 1931, Jane Addams Papers, Swarthmore College Peace Collection, frame 236, reel 23; JAP.

61. Alice Hamilton to Margaret Hamilton, March 19, 1917, reprinted in Sicherman, *Alice Hamilton*, 197. On life in the settlement and relationships formed, see Edith Abbott, "Grace Abbott and Hull House, 1908–1921," *Social Service Review* 24 (Sept. 1950), 374–94; Addams, *Twenty Years*, 308–9; Kathryn Kish Sklar, "Hull House in the 1890s: A Community of Women Reformers," *Signs* 10 (Summer 1985), 658–77; Dorothea Moore, "A Day at Hull-House," reprinted in Davis and McCree, *Eighty Years*, 52–58.

62. Edith Abbott, "Grace Abbott and Hull House, 1908–1921," *Social Service Review* 24 (Sept. 1950), 377.

63. Starr to Addams, April 12, 1935, Jane Addams Papers, Swarthmore College Peace Collection, frames 1320–27, reel 26, JAP.

64. Louise de Koven Bowen, *Open Windows: Stories of People and Places* (Chicago: Ralph Fletcher Seymour, 1946), 227.

65. Smith to Addams, Sept. 3, 1933, Jane Addams Papers, Swarthmore College Peace Collection, frames 125–28, reel 25, JAP.

66. Janet Grieg Post to Smith, April 20, 1932, Jane Addams Papers, Swarthmore College Peace Collection, frames 1155–57, reel 23, JAP. See also Davis, *American Heroine*, 84–91.

67. Solomon, *In the Company of Educated Women*, 118.

68. Blanche Weisen Cook, "Female Support Networks and Political Activism: Lillian Wald, Crystal Eastman, and Emma Goldman," *Chrysalis* 3 (1977), 43–61.

69. "She Gave Up Her Home," *Chicago Journal*, May 17, 1890, newspaper clipping, Jane Addams Papers, Univ. of Illinois—Chicago, frame 6, reel 10, Addendum, JAP.

70. Addams to Blaine, Dec. 11, 1895, Jane Addams file, box 6, Blaine Papers.

71. Creche Account, 1891–92; Fellowships Account, 1894–95; Kindergarten Account, 1891–95; Relief Office Account, 1893–95; Labor Bureau Account,

1892–95; Classes Account, 1891–95; Hull-House General Journal, Hull-House Association Records, Special Collections, Univ. of Illinois–Chicago. Enclosure, Addams to Edward Barton, Nov. 6, 1896, Rockford College Archives, frame 1467, reel 49, JAP.

72. Before the late nineteenth century, a few women had earned a living as charity workers, but most were certainly volunteers. See Carroll Smith-Rosenberg, *Religion and the Rise of the American City* (Ithaca: Cornell Univ. Press, 1971), 6; Christine Stansell, *City of Women: Sex and Class in New York, 1789–1860* (1982; Urbana: Univ. of Illinois, 1987), 212–14. On the process of winning incorporation of services into existing institutions, see Judith A. Trolander, *Professionalism and Social Change: From the Settlement House Movement to Neighborhood Centers, 1866 to the Present* (New York: Columbia Univ. Press, 1987), 18; Jane Addams, *Democracy and Social Ethics* (1902; New York: Macmillan, 1916), 163–64.

73. Louise de Koven Bowen, *Growing Up With a City* (New York: Macmillan, 1926), 103–13. Bowen, *Open Windows*, 142–43. Davis, *American Heroine*, 150–51.

74. Bowen, *Growing Up*, 58–60.

75. Robert L. Duffus, *Lillian Wald: Neighbor and Crusader* (New York: Macmillan, 1938), 1–59.

76. On Wald's contribution to public health nursing, see Paul U. Kellogg, "Settler and Trailblazer," *Survey*, March 15, 1927, pp. 777–80. Other sources on Wald now include Doris Groshen Daniels, *Always a Sister: The Feminism of Lillian D. Wald* (New York: Feminist Press, 1989), and Clare Coss, ed., *Lillian D. Wald: Progressive Activist* (New York: Feminist Press, 1989).

77. Margaret Rossiter, *Women Scientists in America: Struggles and Strategies to 1940* (Baltimore: Johns Hopkins Univ. Press, 1982), 29–50.

78. Elizabeth K. Hartley, "Social Work and Social Reform: Selected Women Social Workers and Child Welfare Reforms, 1877–1932," Ph.D. dissertation, Univ. of Pennsylvania, 1985, p. 126. Joyce Antler, *Lucy Sprague Mitchell: The Making of a Modern Woman* (New Haven: Yale Univ. Press, 1987), 130, 219, 239, 243–44, 257, 301, 307.

79. See also Glazer and Slater, *Unequal Colleagues*, 101, 145.

80. On professionalization in the Progressive era, see, for example, Robert H. Wiebe, *The Search for Order, 1877–1920* (New York: Hill and Wang, 1967); Burton J. Bledstein, *The Culture of Professionalism: The Middle Class and the Development of Higher Education in America* (New York: Norton, 1976); Thomas L. Haskell, *The Emergence of Professional Social Science: The American Social Science Association and the Nineteenth-Century Crisis of Authority* (Urbana: Univ. of Illinois, 1977); Don S. Kirschner, *The Paradox of Professionalism: Reform and Public Service in Urban America, 1900–1940* (Westport, Conn.: Greenwood Press, 1986).

81. Joan Jacobs Brumberg and Nancy Tomes, "Women in the Professions: A Research Agenda for American Historians," *Reviews in American History* 10 (June 1982), 285. Sally Gregory Kohlstedt, "In From the Periphery: American Women in

Science, 1830–1880," *Signs* 4 (Autumn 1978), 81–96, and by the same author, "Maria Mitchell and the Advancement of Women in Science," in *Uneasy Careers and Intimate Lives: Women in Science, 1789–1979*, eds. Pnina G. Abir-Am and Dorinda Outram (New Brunswick: Rutgers Univ. Press, 1987), 129–46.

82. Regina M. Morantz-Sanchez, *Sympathy and Science: Women Physicians in American Medicine* (New York: Oxford Univ. Press, 1985), 60–61, 182–83, 283–89.

83. On male popularizers, see John A. Thompson, *Reformers and War: American Progressive Publicists and the First World War* (New York: Cambridge Univ. Press, 1987), 29; Elizabeth Fee, *Disease and Discovery: A History of the Johns Hopkins School of Hygiene and Public Health, 1916–1939* (Baltimore: Johns Hopkins Univ. Press, 1987), 126–32; Clarke A. Chambers, *Paul U. Kellogg and the Survey: Voices for Social Welfare and Social Justice* (Minneapolis: Univ. of Minnesota Press, 1971); Furner, *Advocacy and Objectivity*, esp. 317–18; Kirschner, *The Paradox of Professionalism*, esp. 63–74; Samuel P. Hays, *Conservation and the Gospel of Efficiency: The Progressive Conservation Movement, 1890–1920* (1959; New York: Atheneum, 1972), 29, 138–39.

84. Barbara Melosh, *The Physician's Hand: Work, Culture and Conflict in American Nursing* (Philadelphia: Temple Univ. Press, 1982), 24.

85. Davis, *Spearheads*, 95.

86. Addams to Blaine, Feb. 13, 1913, Jane Addams file, box 6, Blaine Papers. Davis, *Spearheads*, 95.

87. Gloria Moldow, *Women Doctors in Gilded-Age Washington: Race, Gender, and Professionalization* (Urbana: Univ. of Illinois, 1987), 130.

88. Ibid., 167.

89. Addams to Smith, Jan. 15, 1895, Jane Addams Papers, Swarthmore College Peace Collection, frames 1624–29, reel 2, JAP.

90. Addams to Smith, Feb. 3, 1895, Jane Addams Papers, Swarthmore College Peace Collection, frames 1647–55, reel 2, JAP.

91. Addams to Smith, Feb. 3, 1895, Jane Addams Papers, Swarthmore College Peace Collection, frames 1647–55, reel 2, JAP.

92. Addams to Smith, Jan. 15, 1895, Jane Addams Papers, Swarthmore College Peace Collection, frames 1628–29, reel 2, JAP.

93. Addams to Smith, [1895], Jane Addams Papers, Swarthmore College Peace Collection, frames 1617–18, reel 2, JAP.

94. Harriet A. Rice to Addams, Dec. 7, 1928, Jane Addams Papers, Supplement, Swarthmore College Peace Collection, frame 608, reel 20, JAP.

95. Harriet A. Rice to Smith, June 12, 1933, Jane Addams Papers, Supplement, Swarthmore College Peace Collection, frame 1286, reel 24, JAP.

96. Alice Hamilton to Agnes Hamilton, June 23, 1899, reprinted in Sicherman, *Alice Hamilton*, 132–34.

97. Sicherman, *Alice Hamilton*, 135–37.

98. Ibid., 156–58, 166, 182, 200, 237. See also James Weber Linn, *Jane Addams: A Biography* (New York: 1935), 144–46.

99. Addams, *Twenty Years*, 163.

100. Edward T. James et al., eds., *Notable American Women, 1607–1950*, 3 vols. (Cambridge, Mass.: Belknap Press, 1974), 2: 316–18.

101. Clarke A. Chambers, *Seedtime of Reform: American Social Service and Social Action, 1918–1933* (1963; Westpoint, Conn.: Greenwood Press, 1980), 4.

102. Quoted in ibid., 4.

103. Quoted in Hartley, "Social Work and Social Reform," 370.

104. Ibid., 281; Florence Kelley, *Notes of Sixty Years: The Autobiography of Florence Kelley*, ed. and intro., Kathryn Kish Sklar (Chicago, 1986), 25–30.

105. Hartley, "Social Work and Social Reform," 287; Sklar, Introduction to Kelley's *Autobiography*, 10.

106. Labor Bureau Account, 1892, Hull-House General Journal of Accounts, Hull-House Association Records.

107. Quoted in Hartley, "Social Work and Social Reform," 290.

108. Addams, *Twenty Years*, 150. James et al., *Notable American Women*, 2: 317.

109. Meredith Tax, *The Rising of the Women: Feminist Solidarity and Class Conflict, 1880–1917* (New York: Monthly Review Press, 1980), 21, 56, 87, 301. Adade M. Wheeler and Marlene S. Wortmann, *The Roads They Made: Women in Illinois History* (Chicago: Charles Kerr, 1977), 85.

110. Addams, *Twenty Years*, 150.

111. Ibid., 151. Guide to Anita McCormick Blaine Papers.

112. Quoted in Hartley, "Social Work and Social Reform," 293.

113. Addams, *Twenty Years*, 154. Florence Kelley, "I Go to Work," *Survey*, June 1, 1927, pp. 271–74.

114. My understanding of Progressivism is hardly original, and it is impossible fully to cite the works contributing to my understanding, but they include the following: Wiebe, *The Search for Order*; Samuel P. Hays, *The Response to Industrialism, 1885–1914* (Chicago: Univ. of Chicago Press, 1957); Daniel T. Rodgers, "In Search of Progressivism," *Reviews in American History* 10 (Dec. 1982), 111–32; Elizabeth A. Payne, *Reform, Labor, and Feminism: Margaret Dreier Robins and the Women's Trade Union League* (Urbana: Univ. of Illinois Press, 1988); Samuel Haber, *Efficiency and Uplift: Scientific Management in the Progressive Era, 1890–1920* (Chicago: Univ. of Chicago Press, 1964); Lawrence Goodwyn, *The Populist Moment: A Short History of the Agrarian Revolt in America* (New York: Oxford Univ. Press, 1978); Leon Fink, *Workingmen's Democracy: The Knights of Labor and American Politics* (Urbana: Univ. of Illinois Press, 1983); Stephen Skowronek, *Building a New American State: The Expansion of National Administrative Capacities, 1877–1920* (New York: Cambridge Univ. Press, 1982); Ruth Bordin, *Woman and Temperance: The Quest for Power and Liberty, 1873–1900* (Philadelphia: Temple Univ. Press, 1981).

115. Davis, *American Heroine*, 77; Sklar, "A Community of Reformers."

116. For the experience of early social scientists, see Furner, *Advocacy and Objectivity*; Haskell, *The Emergence of Professional Social Science*; James Leiby, *Carroll Wright and Labor Reform: The Origins of Labor Statistics* (Cambridge, Mass.: Harvard Univ. Press, 1960); Dorothy Ross, "The Development of the Social Sciences," in *The Organization of Knowledge in Modern America, 1860–1920*, eds. Alexandra Oleson and John Voss (Baltimore: Johns Hopkins Univ. Press, 1979), 107–38. On Kelley's approach, see Sklar, "A Community of Reformers." On the eventual generalization of this approach, see, for example, Elisabeth Israels Perry, *Belle Moskowitz: Feminine Politics and the Exercise of Power in the Age of Alfred E. Smith* (New York: Oxford Univ. Press, 1987), 45.

117. Davis, *American Heroine*, 99–101.

118. Ibid., 97, 101. For the change in personnel, see Davis, *Spearheads for Reform*, 38–39. For the change in personnel and the use of settlements by new departments of social science, see Madeline Wallin to Family, March 13, 1896, folder 1; Daily Themes, 1894, folder 12; Madeline Wallin to Mama, Jan. 15, 1893, folder 16; Madeline Wallin Papers, Special Collections, Univ. of Chicago Library.

119. Josephine Goldmark, *Impatient Crusader: Florence Kelley's Life Story* (Urbana: Univ. of Illinois Press, 1953), 47.

120. James et al., *Notable American Women*, 2: 370. Davis, *American Heroine*, 75–76. Addams, *My Friend*, 44–45. Linn, *Jane Addams*, 133.

121. Addams to Alice Addams Haldeman, Dec. 28, 1891, Mrs. S. A. Haldeman MSS, frames 1294–96, reel 2, JAP.

122. Addams, *My Friend*, 117–19. Linn, *Jane Addams*, 136.

123. Addams, *My Friend*, 84. Linn, *Jane Addams*, 135. James et al., *Notable American Women*, 2: 370.

124. Quoted in Addams, *My Friend*, 73. Edith Abbott, "Julia Lathrop," *Social Service Review* 6 (Sept. 1932), 336.

125. Edith Abbott, "Julia Lathrop," 336. Addams, *My Friend*, 109, 113, 163.

126. Davis, *American Heroine*, 92–93. Woods, *Handbook*, 1. Davis, *Spearheads for Reform*, 234.

127. Davis, *American Heroine*, 94–95, 185.

128. Goldmark, *Impatient Crusader*, 51–57. Florence Kelley, *On Industrial Legislation: Some Ethical Gains Through Legislation* (New York: Macmillan, 1905), vii.

129. Davis, *Spearheads for Reform*, 138–47. For the more complete history of the WTUL see Payne, *Reform, Labor, and Feminism*; and Nancy Schrom Dye, *As Equals and As Sisters: Feminism, the Labor Movement, and the Women's Trade Union League of New York* (Columbia: Univ. of Missouri Press, 1980).

130. Addams, *Twenty Years*, 202–4.

131. Rheta Childe Dorr, *What Eighty Million Women Want* (1919; New York: Kraus, 1971), 327.

Chapter 2. The Children's Bureau, 1903–1917

1. Florence Kelley, *On Industrial Legislation: Some Ethical Gains Through Legislation* (New York, 1905), 3.

2. Dorothy E. Bradbury, "The Children's Advocate: The Story of the Children's Bureau, 1900–1946," Ms. history, pp. 1–2, Special Collections, Univ. of Chicago Library. Edward Devine to Lillian Wald, Sept. 16, 1903, folder 1, box 38, Grace and Edith Abbott Papers, Special Collections, Univ. of Chicago Library.

3. The legend appears in a variety of forms in several sources. Robert L. Duffus, *Lillian Wald: Neighbor and Crusader* (New York, 1938), 93–95. Lillian Wald, "The Idea of the Children's Bureau," *Proceedings of the National Conference of Social Work* (Philadelphia, 1932), 33–35. "Notes and Comments," *Social Service Review* 25 (Sept. 1951), 384. Josephine Goldmark, *Impatient Crusader: Florence Kelley's Life Story* (Urbana, 1953), 99–107.

4. Duffus, *Lillian Wald*, 96. Letters and articles of endorsement abound in folder 1, box 38, Abbott Papers. Julia Lathrop, "Remarks at a Founders' Day Luncheon of the National Congress of Mothers" (Washington, D.C., Feb. 17, 1913), Julia Lathrop File, box 366, Anita McCormick Blaine Papers, Series 1E, State Historical Society of Wisconsin, Madison. Alice Elizabeth Padgett, "The History of the Establishment of the United States Children's Bureau," M.A. thesis, Univ. of Chicago School of Social Service Administration, 1936, pp. 8–11. Louis J. Covotsos, "Child Welfare and Social Progress: A History of the United States Children's Bureau, 1912–1935," Ph.D. dissertation, Univ. of Chicago, 1976, p. 23.

5. Walter I. Trattner, *Crusade for the Children: A History of the National Child Labor Committee and Child Labor Reform in America* (Chicago: Quadrangle, 1970), 55–58.

6. "National Child Labor Committee," *Charities* 13 (Oct. 8, 1904), 48.

7. Trattner, *Crusade for the Children*, 61–63, 257.

8. Ibid., 96.

9. Bradbury, "The Children's Advocate," 22–37.

10. *Proceedings of the Conference on the Care of Dependent Children*, Washington, D.C., Jan. 25–26, 1909 (Washington, D.C.: Government Printing Office, 1909), esp. 9–10, 17–18.

11. Jane Addams, *The Second Twenty Years at Hull-House* (New York: Macmillan, 1930), 18.

12. *Proceedings of the Conference on the Care of Dependent Children*, 202.

13. In addition to the conference proceedings, see Nancy P. Weiss, "Save the Children: A History of the Children's Bureau, 1903–1918," Ph.D. dissertation, Univ. of California at Los Angeles, 1974, pp. 59–69.

14. Quotation of James E. West, *Proceedings*, 174.

15. Ibid., 173–74. Weiss, "Save the Children," 59–69.

16. Quotation of Homer Folks, *Proceedings*, 173.

17. Mary O. Furner, *Advocacy and Objectivity: A Crisis in the Professionalization of American Social Science, 1865-1905* (Lexington, Ky.: 1975), 56, 59–77, 313–24.

18. Ibid., 317, 322, 324. Carroll Wright was one of the early social scientists who believed in the combination of advocacy and research, but even he seemed to believe at least in the 1880s that advocacy should not be the job of a government bureau. James Leiby, *Carroll Wright and Labor Reform: The Origins of Labor Statistics* (Cambridge, Mass.: 1960), 76–80, 89.

19. James T. Kloppenberg, *Uncertain Victory: Social Democracy and Progressivism in European and American Thought, 1870-1920* (New York: Oxford Univ. Press, 1986), esp. 3, 7, 299–385.

20. On the varieties of opinion on the proper role of the state within the middle way, see, in addition to Kloppenberg, Joan Hoff-Wilson, *Herbert Hoover: Forgotten Progressive* (Boston: Little, Brown, 1975), esp. 57–75; and Ellis W. Hawley, *The Great War and the Search for a Modern Order: A History of the American People and Their Institutions, 1917-1933* (New York: St. Martin's Press, 1979), esp. 104–23.

21. "Testimony before the Committee on Expenditures in the Interior Department of the House of Representatives," Jan. 27, 1909, folder 1, box 38, Abbott Papers. Bradbury, "The Children's Advocate," 23–31.

22. A. J. McKelway to Lillian Wald, Jan. 31, 1912; A. J. McKelway to Lillian Wald, no date; folder 2, box 38, Abbott Papers. Bradbury, "The Children's Advocate," 39, 52–54. Covotsos, "Child Welfare and Social Progress," 37–38. Weiss, "Save the Children," 104–5.

23. Addams, *Second Twenty Years*, 40.

24. Ibid., 39.

25. Eugene M. Tobin, *Organize or Perish: America's Independent Progressives, 1913-1933* (Westport, Conn.: Greenwood Press, 1986), 17.

26. David Burner, *The Politics of Provincialism: The Democratic Party in Transition, 1918-1932* (New York: Knopf, 1968), 29–30. David M. Kennedy, *Over Here: The First World War and American Society* (New York: Oxford Univ. Press, 1980), 95. Tobin, *Organize or Perish*, 34, 44–45.

27. Burner, *The Politics of Provincialism*, 30.

28. Children's Bureau, *First Annual Report* (Washington, D.C.: Government Printing Office, 1914), 2.

29. "Notes and Comments," *Social Service Review* 25 (Sept. 1951), 384. Trattner, *Crusade for the Children*, 119. Bradbury, "The Children's Advocate," 57. Covotsos, "Child Welfare and Social Progress," 40–41. Weiss, "Save the Children," 106.

30. Addams to Wald, April 12, 1912, folder 2, box 38, Abbott Papers.

31. Secretary of Labor Charles Nagel to Wald, April 17, 1912, folder 2, box 38, Abbott Papers. Bradbury, "The Children's Advocate," 57. Weiss, "Save the Children," 106.

32. Lathrop to John Glenn, April 24, 1912, folder 2, box 57, Abbott Papers.

33. Jane Addams, *My Friend, Julia Lathrop* (New York, 1935), 79–84, 163.

34. For sparkling and full of humor, see James Weber Linn, *Jane Addams: A Biography* (New York: D. Appleton-Century, 1935), 133–34; for brilliant, see Addams, *My Friend*, 119.

35. Addams, *My Friend*, 86.

36. Ibid., 88.

37. Lathrop to Grace Abbott, [1921], folder 7, box 57, Abbott Papers. Emphasis in the original.

38. Children's Bureau, *Third Annual Report* (Washington, D.C.: Government Printing Office, 1916), 6.

39. Ibid., 5–6.

40. Caroline Fleming to Henry P. Collin, Feb. 4, 1920, file 3-0-0, Central File 1914–20, Children's Bureau Records, (hereafter CBR), National Archives, Washington, D.C.

41. Cindy Sondik Aron, *Ladies and Gentlemen of the Civil Service: Middle-Class Workers in Victorian America* (New York: Oxford Univ. Press, 1987), 108. Margaret Rossiter, *Women Scientists in America: Struggles and Strategies to 1940* (Baltimore, 1982), 221.

42. Memo re Civil Service Examination, 1914, file 3-0, Central File 1914–20, CBR.

43. Children's Bureau, *First Annual Report*, 8.

44. Civil Service Commissioner to Secretary of Labor, July 31, 1914, file 3-0, Central File 1914–20, CBR.

45. See, for example, Helen Sumner to Assistant Secretary, May 13, 1918; Lathrop to Acting Secretary, Aug. 29, 1918; Acting Chief to Assistant Secretary, June 11, 1918; Acting Chief to Assistant Secretary, April 29, 1918; Acting Chief to Assistant Secretary, May 13, 1918; file 3-1-1-4-1, Central File 1914–20, CBR.

46. Lathrop to Acting Secretary, Sept. 4, 1918; Helen Sumner to Assistant Secretary, May 13, 1918; Lathrop to Acting Secretary, Aug. 29, 1918; Acting Chief to Assistant Secretary, June 11, 1918; Acting Chief to Assistant Secretary, April 29, 1918; Acting Chief to Assistant Secretary, May 13, 1918; file 3-1-1-4-1, Central File 1914–20, CBR.

47. Fanny Fiske to Lathrop, Oct. 19, 1913, folder 1, box 59, Abbott Papers.

48. "Children's Bureau Staff," March 1, 1919, file 3-0-0, Central File 1914–20, CBR.

49. See, for example, Jacqueline K. Parker, "Why Study the Early Children's Bureau?," Working Paper Number 14, Center for the Study of Women in Society, Eugene, Ore., 1983, pp. 11–12.

50. Lathrop to Secretary of Labor, July 31, 1914, file 3-0, Central File 1914–20, CBR. Children's Bureau, *Third Annual Report*, 6.

51. Katharine Lenroot, Transcript Interview, Social Security Project, Oral History Research Office, Columbia Univ., 1965, pp. 3–15.

52. Jacqueline K. Parker and Edward M. Carpenter, "Julia Lathrop and the Children's Bureau: The Emergence of an Institution," *Social Service Review* 55 (May 1981), 65–66. Grace Abbott to Momma, Nov. 2, 1912, folder 1, box 6, Addendum, Abbott Papers.

53. Parker, "Why Study the Early Children's Bureau?," 14.

54. Paul P. Van Riper, *History of the United States Civil Service* (Evanston, Ill.: Row, Peterson, 1958), 327.

55. For examples of the marginalization of men in other female-dominated institutions, see Penina Migdal Glazer and Miriam Slater, *Unequal Colleagues: The Entrance of Women into the Professions, 1890–1940* (New Brunswick, 1987), 36.

56. Children's Bureau, *First Annual Report*, 8.

57. Lathrop to Ann [Case], Feb. 19, 1920; Lathrop to Ann [Case], Aug. 14, 1921; folder 6, box 58, Abbott Papers. Lathrop to Grace Abbott, 1921; Lathrop to Kelley, Dec. 13, 1924; Lathrop to Grace Abbott, Nov. 25, 1921; folder 1, box 57, Abbott Papers. Edith Abbott, "Grace Abbott and Hull-House, 1908–1921," *Social Service Review* 24 (Dec. 1950), 516–17. Parker, "Why Study the Early Children's Bureau?," 18. *Official Congressional Directory* (Washington, D.C.: Government Printing Office, 1922), 289–90.

58. Katharine Lenroot to Lathrop, Jan. 1916; Lathrop to Emma O. Lundberg, Jan. 14, 1916; folder 3, box 59, Abbott Papers.

59. JCL to Belden, March 20, 1916, folder 3, box 59, Abbott Papers.

60. See, for example, A. C. P. to Lathrop, Oct. 19, 1916, folder 10, box 62, Abbott Papers. Mrs. E. to Lathrop, May 1915; Lathrop to E., May 6, 1915; Mrs. Max West to E., May 11, 1915; Mrs. Max West to Lathrop, May 21, 1915; folder 3, box 59, Abbott Papers. See also Mrs. G. S. to Lathrop, March 30, 1916; Lathrop to S., April 4, 1916; folder 3, box 59, Abbott Papers. Many other examples may be found in folder 4, box 59, Abbott Papers, and in files 4-0-1, 9-4-4-1, 1-4-2-4, and 1-4-2-5; Central File 1914–20, CBR. See also Molly Ladd-Taylor, ed., *Raising a Baby the Government Way: Mothers' Letters to the Children's Bureau, 1915–1932* (New Brunswick: Rutgers Univ. Press, 1986).

61. Mrs. G. S. to Lathrop, March 30, 1916, folder 3, box 59, Abbott Papers.

62. Weiss, "Save the Children," 194–96. See also notes 57–60.

63. I am certainly not the first to notice the similarities between Hull House and the Children's Bureau. See especially Weiss, "Save the Children," 53, who calls the Bureau a "national settlement house." See also Morantz-Sanchez, *Sympathy and Science*, 299.

64. In agreement with this view of the Children's Bureau is Weiss, "Save the Children," 290.

65. Emma O. Lundberg to Lathrop, Jan. 17, 1916, folder 3, box 59, Abbott Papers. See also Lundberg to Lathrop, May 17, 1917; Lundberg to Lathrop, July 8, 1916; Lundberg to Lathrop, July 11, 1916; folder 3, box 59, Abbott Papers. For biographical information, see Lathrop to Secretary of Labor, July 31, 1914, file 3-0,

Central File 1914–20, CBR; Emma O. Lundberg and Mary E. Milburn, *Child Dependency in the District of Columbia* (Washington, D.C.: Government Printing Office, 1924); Lela B. Costin, *Two Sisters for Social Justice: A Biography of Grace and Edith Abbott* (Urbana: Univ. of Illinois Press, 1983), 128.

66. Parker, "Why Study the Early Children's Bureau?," 18–19.

67. Lathrop to Staff, May 26, 1918, file 3-6-0-1, Central File 1914–20, CBR.

68. Parker and Carpenter, "Julia Lathrop and the Children's Bureau," 61–62.

69. Lathrop to Wald, Oct. 26, 1912, folder 1, box 59, Abbott Papers.

70. Weiss, "Save the Children," 198.

71. *Prenatal Care*, first ed. (Washington, D.C.: Government Printing Office, Aug. 1913); second ed. (October 1913); fourth ed. (May 1915). Lathrop to Walter Evans, Oct. 24, 1914, file 4-0-1, Central File 1914–20, CBR. Lewis Meriam to Lathrop, Oct. 6, 1913, folder 1, box 59, Abbott Papers. Lathrop to Graham Taylor, April 14, 1914, folder 2, box 59, Abbott Papers.

72. Fanny Fiske to Lathrop, Oct. 19, 1913, folder 1, box 59, Abbott Papers.

73. Ladd-Taylor, *Raising a Baby*, 2.

74. Children's Bureau, *Tenth Annual Report* (Washington, D.C.: Government Printing Office, 1922), 28.

75. Sheila M. Rothman, *Woman's Proper Place: A History of Changing Ideals and Practices, 1870 to the Present* (New York: Basic Books, 1978), 98–111.

76. Quoted in Elizabeth Kennedy Hartley, "Social Work and Social Reform: Selected Women Social Workers and Child Welfare Reforms, 1877–1932," Ph.D. dissertation, Univ. of Pennsylvania, 1985, p. 217.

77. Don S. Kirschner, *The Paradox of Professionalism: Reform and Public Service in Urban America, 1900–1940* (Westport, Conn., 1986), 65–67. Harold D. Lasswell, *Propaganda Technique in World War I* (1927; Cambridge, Mass.: MIT Press, 1971). Elisabeth Israels Perry, *Belle Moskowitz: Feminine Politics and the Exercise of Power in the Age of Alfred E. Smith* (New York, 1987), 140–41.

78. Quoted in Hartley, "Social Work and Social Reform," 261.

79. Edith B. Lowry to Grace Meigs, Jan. 10, 1918, file 4-12-4, Central File 1914–20, CBR. Renee B. Stern to Lathrop, June 23, 1916; Alice Grant to Lathrop, Oct. 27, 1920; L. Myra Harbeson to Children's Bureau, Nov. 24, 1920; file 8-2-2-0-1, Central File 1914–20, CBR. W. L. Porter to Harriet Anderson, Dec. 11, 1919, file 8-2-2-0, Central File 1914–20, CBR.

80. R. R. Wright to Lathrop, April 5, 1917; Bernard Bell to Lathrop, Jan. 16, 1917; file 8-2-2-0-1, Central File 1914–20, CBR.

81. Hight C. Moore to Harriet Anderson, Jan. 8, 1920, file 8-2-2-0-1, Central File 1914–20, CBR.

82. Wilma K. McFarland to Harriet Anderson, Dec. 17, 1919, file 8-2-2-0, Central File 1914–20, CBR.

83. Ladd-Taylor, *Raising a Baby*, 2 and the letters published in her book. In addition, see Lathrop to Mrs. G. A., July 31, 1917; Lathrop to Mrs. F. D., April

24, 1917; Lathrop to N. B., June 13, 1917; M. A. M. to Lathrop, Feb. 17, 1916; folder 4, box 59, Abbott Papers.

84. Marguerite G. Rosenthal, "The Children's Bureau and the Juvenile Court: Delinquency Policy, 1912–1940," *Social Service Review* (June 1986), 305.

85. Quotation from Lathrop's 1912 speech before the National Conference of Charities and Corrections, quoted in Hartley, "Social Work and Social Reform," 175.

86. Memo to File, Jan. 1918, file 8-4-1-1, Central File 1914–20, CBR.

87. See speeches of Lathrop to women's organizations in folder 9, box 60, Abbott Papers, and Julia Lathrop File, box 366, Blaine Papers. Parker and Carpenter, "Julia Lathrop and the Children's Bureau," 62, 68–69. Gertrude B. Knipp to Lathrop, Sept. 3, 1918, file 4-0-1, Central File 1914–20, CBR.

88. Mary Webb to Lathrop, Nov. 23, 1916, file 8-4-1-1-6; Alice T. Kurtz to Grace Meigs, March 30, 1917, file 4-12-4; Central File 1914–20, CBR.

89. Alice T. Kurtz to Grace Meigs, March 30, 1917, file 4-12-4, Central File 1914–20, CBR.

90. Parker and Carpenter, "Julia Lathrop and the Children's Bureau," 67–68.

91. *Birth Registration: An Aid in Protecting the Lives and Rights of Children* (Washington, D.C.: Government Printing Office, 1913).

92. Kelley to Lathrop, Aug. 17, 1913, file 4-0-1, Central File 1914–20, CBR.

93. Children's Bureau, *First Annual Report*, 10. Etta R. Goodwin to Lathrop, Sept. 19, 1916; Mrs. Frances Waite Leiter to Children's Bureau, Sept. 20, 1916; file 4-12-4, Central File 1914–20, CBR.

94. Laura C. Whitten to Mrs. Max West, Jan. 29, 1918; Lathrop to Whitten, Feb. 2, 1918; file 4-0-1, Central File 1914–20, CBR.

95. Alice Day Marston to Lathrop, Nov. 27, 1914; file 4-0-1, Central File 1914–20, CBR.

96. Lathrop to Marston, Jan. 12, 1915; file 4-0-1, Central File 1914–20, CBR.

97. Senator L. M. Enger to Lathrop, March 8, 1915, file 4-0-1, Central File 1914–20, CBR.

98. Marston to Lathrop, Sept. 27, 1915, file 4-0-1, Central File 1914–20, CBR.

99. Etta R. Goodwin to Mrs. Maud Hemingway, Aug. 5, 1915, file 4-0-1, Central File 1914–20, CBR.

100. Lathrop to Walter Evans, Oct. 24, 1914, file 4-0-1, Central File 1914–20, CBR.

101. Lathrop to Mrs. Herbert T. Johnson, Oct. 31, 1914, file 4-0-1, Central File 1914–20, CBR.

102. Etta R. Goodwin to Maud Hemingway, Aug. 5, 1915, file 4-0-1, Central File 1914–20, CBR.

103. Etta R. Goodwin to Lathrop, Sept. 19, 1916, file 4-12-4, Central File 1914–20, CBR.

104. Lathrop to Thomas C. Quinn, Feb. 11, 1915; Acting Chief to P. W. Beasley, Nov. 3, 1915; Lathrop to Director of the Census, March 7, 1916; Lathrop to Mrs. C. W. Bland, Feb. 29, 1916; Mrs. J. K. Codding to Lathrop, Sept. 11, 1916; file 4-0-1, Central File 1914–20, CBR.

105. Cressy L. Wilbur to Lathrop, Nov. 15, 1915, file 4-0-1, Central File 1914–20, CBR.

106. Lathrop to Gates F. Young, Aug. 26, 1916, file 4-0-1, Central File 1914–20, CBR.

107. Children's Bureau, *First Annual Report*, 12; *Second Annual Report* (Washington, D.C.: Government Printing Office, 1915), 13–14.

108. For example, J. N. Hurty to Lathrop, Oct. 31, 1916; Ellsworth Farris to Mary Titzel, Jan. 10, 1919; Edward F. Glaser to Anna Rude, June 5, 1919; Lathrop to L. W. Hutchcroft, Dec. 12, 1914; file 4-0-1, Central File 1914–20, CBR.

109. For example, see Mrs. Harry E. Canty to Lathrop, Aug. 2, 1919; and other personal requests in file 4-0-1, Central File 1914–20, CBR.

110. Etta R. Goodwin to File, Jan. 23, 1917; Lathrop to W. W. Harris, April 7, 1919; file 4-0-1, Central File 1914–20, CBR. Children's Bureau, *Tenth Annual Report*, 30.

111. Laura C. Whitten to Mrs. Max West, Jan. 29, 1918, file 4-0-1, Central File 1914–20, CBR. Elizabeth Hawley Everett to Lathrop, Aug. 5, 1914, folder 3, box 59, Abbott Papers.

112. H. Hayward to Lathrop, April 20, 1915, file 7424.1; "Tentative Plans," Feb. 12, 1916, file 7424.2; Central File 1914–20, CBR.

113. "Tentative Outline of Investigation of Mental Defectives in Delaware," Oct. 29, 1915, file 7424.2, Central File 1914–20, CBR.

114. Lundberg to Mrs. Frank M. Jones, Aug. 19, 1915; Memo re Persons Interested in Problem; file 7424.6, Central File 1914–20, CBR.

115. Lathrop to Mrs. Selden Deemer, Dec. 14, 1916; Lundberg to Governor Charles Miller, Dec. 2, 1916; Lundberg to Mrs. Selden Deemer, Dec. 6, 1916; Lundberg to Mrs. Selden Deemer, Dec. 14, 1916; Lundberg to Mrs. F. M. Jones, March 16, 1917; file 7424.6, Central File 1914–20, CBR.

116. Daniel T. Rodgers, "In Search of Progressivism," *Reviews in American History* 10 (Dec. 1982), 121.

117. Robert D. Cuff, *The War Industries Board: Business-Government Relations During World War I* (Baltimore: Johns Hopkins Univ. Press, 1973), 158.

118. For other examples and discussions of the intimate relationships between government agencies and private groups, see, in addition to Cuff, Samuel P. Hays, *Conservation and the Gospel of Efficiency: The Progressive Conservation Movement, 1890-1920* (1959; New York, 1972), esp. 29–35, 134–35; Robert H. Wiebe, *Businessmen and Reform: A Study of the Progressive Movement* (Cambridge, Mass.: Harvard Univ. Press, 1962), esp. 5, 44–66, 216; Tobin, *Organize or Perish*, 43–44, 53–60.

119. Children's Bureau, *Second Annual Report*, 5. Wald and Kelley to Owen Lovejoy, April 3, 1914, folder 2, box 38, Abbott Papers.

120. Wald and Kelley to Lovejoy, April 3, 1914, folder 2, box 38, Abbott Papers. Lovejoy to Lathrop, April 9, 1914, file 2-1-2-3, Central File 1914–20, CBR.

121. Wald to Lathrop, April 3, 1914, folder 2, box 59, Abbott Papers.

122. Henry Moskowitz to Lathrop, April 17, 1914, file 2-1-2-3, Central File 1914–20, CBR.

123. Wald to Addams, April 13, 1914, folder 2, box 38, Abbott Papers.

124. All articles are in folder 3, box 38, Abbott Papers.

125. Lathrop to Wald, April 15, 1914, folder 2, box 59, Abbott Papers. Walter Sumner to Lathrop, May 8, 1914; Charles Welsh to Lathrop, May 8, 1914; Edwin Solenberger to Lathrop, April 30, 1914; Louise de Koven Bowen to Lathrop, April 16, 1914; Ira C. Copley to Emily W. Dean, April 9, 1914; Edward Devine to Lathrop, April 17, 1914; Ben Lindsay to Lathrop, April 22, 1914; John Glenn to Lathrop, April 25, 1914; James Wolfe to Lathrop, April 24, 1914; Mrs. John Blodgett to Lathrop, April 21, 1914; John O'Connor to Lathrop, April 20, 1914; W. P. Smith to Lathrop, April 17, 1914; Paul Furman to Lathrop, April 13, 1914; file 2-1-2-3, Central File 1914–20, CBR.

126. Lathrop to Wald, April 15, 1914, folder 2, box 59, Abbott Papers. Weiss, "Save the Children," 183. Bradbury, "Children's Advocate," 82.

127. Lathrop to Wald and Kelley, Dec. 16, 1916; Lathrop to Mrs. Joseph T. Bowen, Dec. 16, 1916; Lovejoy to Lathrop, Dec. 14, 1916; Lovejoy to Lathrop, Dec. 18, 1916; folder 3, box 59, Abbott Papers.

128. Elizabeth Hawley Everett to Lathrop, July 7, 1916, folder 3, box 59, Abbott Papers.

129. Gertrude S. Martin to Lathrop, Sept. 16, 1916; Kristine Mann to Lathrop, Dec. 20, 1919; Helen Louise Johnson to Mrs. Max West, June 29, 1917; file 4-12-4, Central File 1914–20, CBR. Gertrude B. Knipp to Lathrop, Sept. 3, 1918, file 4-0-1; Kristine Mann to Caroline Fleming, Dec. 29, 1919, file 8-2-2-0-1; Central File 1914–20, CBR.

130. Addams, *My Friend*, 172.

Chapter 3. The School of Social Service Administration, 1903–1930

1. Louise de Koven Bowen, *Growing Up With a City* (New York, 1926), 102.

2. Walter I. Trattner, *From Poor Law to Welfare State*, 2nd ed., (New York: Free Press, 1979), 80–87.

3. Ibid., 87–88.

4. Especially good on this split is John H. Ehrenreich, *The Altruistic Imagination: A History of Social Work and Social Policy in the United States* (Ithaca, 1985).

5. *Charities* 13 (Oct. 8, 1904), 48–49; *Charities* 13 (March 11, 1905), 564; *Charities* 21 (Oct. 10, 1908), 84; Irene Farnham Conrad, "Education for Social Work," in *Social Work Year Book*, ed., Fred S. Hall (New York, 1930), 150; James Leiby, *A History of Social Welfare and Social Work in the United States* (New York: Columbia Univ. Press, 1978), 187–89. Trattner, *From Poor Law*, 196–97.

6. *City Welfare Aids and Opportunities*, Bulletin of the Chicago School of Civics and Philanthropy, Oct. 1911, p. 2, box 2, Chicago School of Civics and Philanthropy section, Graham Taylor Papers, Special Collections, Newberry Library, Chicago.

7. Quotations from "Institute of Social Science and Arts Training for Philanthropic and Social Work," 1904, folder 1, Chicago School of Civics and Philanthropy Records, Special Collections, Univ. of Chicago Library (hereafter, CSCPR). General history in Edith Abbott to Julius Rosenwald, June 5, 1924, bound volume, box 19, Grace and Edith Abbott Papers, Special Collections, University of Chicago Library. Louise Wade, *Graham Taylor: Pioneer for Social Justice, 1851-1938* (Chicago: Univ. of Chicago Press, 1964), 166–69.

8. *City Welfare Aids and Opportunities*, 2.

9. *Charities* 21 (Oct. 10, 1908), 81–83. Conrad, "Education for Social Work," 150.

10. Leiby, *A History of Social Welfare*, 187. Wade, *Graham Taylor*, 168–71.

11. Edward T. James et al., eds., *Notable American Women, 1607-1958*, 3 vols. (Cambridge, Mass.: Belknap Press, 1971), 1: 233–36. Ellen Fitzpatrick, *Endless Crusade: Women Social Scientists and Progressive Reform* (New York: Oxford Univ. Press, 1990), 3–5.

12. Breckinridge quoted in James C. Klotter, *The Breckinridges of Kentucky, 1760-1981* (Lexington: Univ. of Kentucky Press, 1986), 197. Charles Merriam called her "sweetness and light" in "A Member of the University Community," *Social Service Review* 12 (Dec. 1948), 424.

13. Quoted in Klotter, *The Breckinridges*, 196.

14. Quoted in ibid., 197. For other biographical details, see also James et al., *Notable American Women*, 1: 233–36.

15. Quotation in Edith Abbott, "Are Women Business Failures?," *Harper's Weekly* 49 (April 8, 1905), 496. Biographical information is in Barbara Sicherman et al., eds., *Notable American Women: The Modern Period* (Cambridge, Mass.: Belknap Press, 1980), 1–3; Lela B. Costin, *Two Sisters for Social Justice: A Biography of Grace and Edith Abbott* (Urbana, 1983), 3–40.

16. On difficulties after college for the generation in general, see Roberta Frankfurt, *Collegiate Women: Domesticity and Career in Turn-of-the-Century America* (New York, 1977), 85–98; and Joyce Antler, "After College, What? New Graduates and the Family Claim," *American Quarterly* 32 (Fall 1980), 409–34.

17. James et al., *Notable American Women*, 233–35.

18. Ibid., 1: 233–35. Edith Abbott, "Sophonisba Preston Breckinridge Over the Years," *Social Service Review* 22 (Dec. 1948), 417–23, esp. 418. On discrimina-

tion among faculty in higher education, see Margaret W. Rossiter, *Women Scientists in America: Struggles and Strategies to 1940* (Baltimore, 1982), esp. 110.

19. On the breaks between generations of educated women, see Joyce Antler, "Review," *Signs* 12 (Winter 1987), 386–90, esp. 387. For biographical information, see Costin, *Two Sisters*, 26–38, and J. Laurence Laughlin to Abbott, June 13, 1905; Laughlin to Abbott, Jan. 9, 1906; Carroll Wright to Breckinridge, June 17, 1905; folder 8, box 1; Laughlin to Abbott, April 7, 1906, folder 9, box 1; Abbott Papers.

20. Rossiter, *Women Scientists*, 110. Penina Migdal Glazer and Miriam Slater, *Unequal Colleagues: The Entrance of Women into the Professions, 1890–1940* (New Brunswick, 1987), 26.

21. James et al., *Notable American Women*, 1: 233–35.

22. Abbott, "Sophonisba," 417–23, esp. 419–20. Steven J. Diner, *A City and Its Universities: Public Policy in Chicago, 1892–1919* (Chapel Hill: Univ. of North Carolina Press, 1980), 131.

23. Mary O. Furner, *Advocacy and Objectivity: A Crisis in the Professionalization of American Social Science, 1865–1905* (Lexington, Ky., 1975), 56, 77. Fitzpatrick, *Endless Crusade*, 47–49, 66–69.

24. Furner, *Advocacy and Objectivity*, 56, 59–77, 313–24.

25. Nancy Cott has provided a brilliant analysis of this tension among feminists in the 1910s and 1920s in her *Grounding of Modern Feminism* (New Haven, 1987). For the same tension in an earlier generation, see Regina Morantz-Sanchez, *Sympathy and Science: Women Physicians in American Medicine* (New York, 1985), esp. 185–202.

26. Sicherman et al., *Notable American Women*, 1–2; Costin, *Two Sisters*, 31–35; Fitzpatrick, *Endless Crusade*, 87–91.

27. Abbott to O. A. Abbott, June 6, 1907, folder 1, box 2, Addendum, Abbott Papers.

28. Breckinridge to Abbott, Oct. 23, 1907, folder 10, box 1, Abbott Papers. Sicherman et al., *Notable American Women*, 1.

29. Abbott, "Julia Lathrop and the Public Social Services," *Social Service Review* 6 (June 1932), 301–6, esp. 305. Science enjoyed such prestige in the Progressive era that, despite Abbott's qualification of her own understanding of social research as scientific, she and her colleagues continued to use the term to refer to their research. It was always a problematic word, denoting various—and inconsistent—characteristics and understandings. But its primary purpose was to cloak their work in the authority that only a claim to scientific method could provide in the Progressive era.

30. None of this is in the least to cast aspersions on the sincerity of Breckinridge, Abbott, or other women like them. Once professional opportunity had encouraged them to reconsider their own convictions—political, professional, personal—these women genuinely, fervently committed themselves to various progressive causes. This line of argument simply attempts to find priorities among the range of motives that congealed to produce political activists in the Progressive era, to

acknowledge the multi-dimensionality of these women, and to begin to uncover an explanation for the persistence of reform commitments among middle-class women.

Neither is this to accuse the older generation of misusing its power to coerce younger women into commitments not of their own choosing. Addams, Kelley, and Lathrop certainly did not think of their job offers as ways to lure unsuspecting women into reform. They matter-of-factly recruited talent to bolster their causes as any effective reformers must. Given the restricted range of professional options for women in the early twentieth century and the larger structure of professional job markets, this recruitment nevertheless granted significant power to the first generation of reformers.

31. Graham Taylor, "President's Statement," May 8, 1918, folder 1917–18, box 2, Chicago School of Civics and Philanthropy section, Taylor Papers. Roy Lubove, *The Professional Altruist: The Emergence of Social Work as a Career* (Cambridge, Mass.: Harvard Univ. Press, 1965), 157–59. Trattner, *From Poor Law*, 193. On bureaucratization as a central value of early-twentieth-century reformers, see Robert H. Wiebe, *The Search for Order, 1877–1920* (New York, 1967), 133–63.

32. Stenographic Report, Meeting of Trustees of Chicago School of Civics and Philanthropy, Feb. 13, 1920, folder 1920–22, box 2, Chicago School of Civics and Philanthropy section, Taylor Papers.

33. Graham Taylor, *Religion in Social Action* (New York: Dodd, Mead, 1913), vii.

34. See James T. Kloppenberg, *Uncertain Victory: Social Democracy and Progressivism in European and American Thought, 1870–1920* (New York, 1986), 28–46, 91–99, 373–94.

35. Taylor, *Religion*, 165. One is reminded here of Maria C. Lugones and Elizabeth V. Spelman, "Have We Got a Theory for You! Feminist Theory, Cultural Imperialism and the Demand for 'The Women's Voice,'" *Women's Studies International Forum* 6, no. 6 (1983), 573–81. See also Jane Addams, *Democracy and Social Ethics* (1902; New York, 1916), esp. 272; *Twenty Years at Hull House* (1910; New York, 1981), esp. 98, 253–54.

36. Taylor, *Religion*, 159.

37. Spring Quarter Courses, n.d., folder 1903–08, box 2, Chicago School of Civics and Philanthropy section, Taylor Papers.

38. Taylor, *Religion*, 4.

39. Taylor's position mirrored that of many other male participants in the founding of social work, and most men in the profession were in the higher-paid, executive positions. See for example Breckinridge, Draft of Public Announcement, [Aug. 1920], folder 10, box 20, Abbott Papers. See also Conrad, "Education for Social Work," 151; James H. Tufts, *Education and Training for Social Work* (New York: Holt, 1923), 220–21. Interestingly, at the New York School of Social Work, men also taught the casework courses while female instructors taught social research. Clarke A. Chambers, "Women in the Creation of the Profession of Social Work," *Social Service Review* (March 1986), 1–33, esp. 7–8.

40. Quotation in Abbott to Mr. Laing, May 22, 1924; bound volume, box 19, Abbott Papers. On expectations of their students, *Chicago School of Civics and Philanthropy Bulletin*, July 1909; 1910; 1913–14; 1914–15; no folder; *The Department of Social Investigation*, Special Bulletin of the Chicago School, Jan. 1912, folder 12; CSCPR.

41. Abbott, "Are Women Business Failures?"

42. Sophonisba P. Breckinridge, *Family Welfare Work in a Metropolitan Community: Selected Case Records* (Chicago: Univ. of Chicago Press, 1924), 31.

43. Edith Abbott to Editor, *Chicago Daily Tribune*, April 26, 1937, folder 1, box 4, Abbott Papers.

44. Abbott to Julia Lathrop, Aug. 7, 1920, folder 11, box 3, Abbott Papers.

45. Breckinridge to Mrs. A. D. Kohn, Aug. 15, 1920, folder 3, box 4, Abbott Papers.

46. Stenographic Report, Meeting of the Trustees of Chicago School of Civics and Philanthropy, Feb. 13, 1920, folder 1920–22, box 2, Chicago School of Civics and Philanthropy section, Taylor Papers.

47. Abbott, *Woman in Industry: A Study of American Economic History* (New York: Appleton, 1910); *The Real Jail Problem* (Chicago: Juvenile Protective Association, 1915). Abbott and Breckinridge, *The Delinquent Child and the Home* (New York: Charities Publication Committee, 1912); *Truancy and Non-Attendance in the Chicago Schools: A Study of the Social Aspects of the Compulsory Education and Child Labor Legislation in Illinois* (Chicago: Univ. of Chicago, 1917).

48. *Chicago School of Civics and Philanthropy Bulletin*, July 1909; 1910; 1911; no folder, CSCPR. *The Department of Social Investigation*, Special Bulletin of the Chicago School, Jan. 1912; folder 12, CSCPR.

49. Edith Abbott to Lathrop, Sept. 7, 1920, folder 11, box 3, Abbott Papers.

50. Taylor's quotation is from Taylor to Victor Lawson, Aug. 10, 1920, folder 1920, box 2, Outgoing Correspondence section, Taylor Papers. See also Taylor to John Glenn, July 27, 1920, folder 1920, box 2, Outgoing Correspondence section, Taylor Papers. Paul Harder Werner, "The Emergence of a Profession: Social Work Education in Chicago, 1903–1920," Oct. 1976, p. 14, CSCPR. Wade, *Graham Taylor*, 179.

51. Memo Re History of the Graduate School of Social Service Administration, bound volume, box 19; Memo Concerning the Future of the Chicago School, 1919–20, folder 10, box 20; Abbott Papers.

52. Memo Re History of the Graduate School of Social Service Administration, bound volume, box 19; Memo Concerning the Future of the Chicago School, 1919–20, folder 10, box 20; Abbott Papers.

53. Taylor to Ken, July 29, 1920, folder 1920, box 2, Outgoing Correspondence section, Taylor Papers. Breckinridge to Julia Lathrop, July 15, 1920, folder 10, box 20, Abbott Papers. Minutes of Meeting of the Board, July 9, 1920, folder 1920–22, box 2, Chicago School of Civics and Philanthropy section, Taylor Papers.

Breckinridge to President Judson, Aug. 6, 1920; Breckinridge to Morton D. Hull, Aug. 12, 1920; folder 10, box 20, Abbott Papers.

54. Wade, *Graham Taylor*, 178. James et al., *Notable American Women*, 1: 235. Annual Report to the President of the University, 1923–24, bound volume, box 19, Abbott Papers.

55. *Chicago School of Civics and Philanthropy Bulletin*, 1915–16, folder 16; *Chicago School of Civics and Philanthropy Bulletin*, July 1909; 1910; 1911; no folder, CSCPR. *Alumni Register*, 1903–13, folder 13, CSCPR. Compare Wade, *Graham Taylor*, 172, with Registrar's Report Re Number of Students Earning Certificates, [1920], folder 1920–22, box 2, Chicago School of Civics and Philanthropy section, Taylor Papers.

56. Breckinridge to President Judson Re Cost, July 5, 1920; Memo Concerning the Future of the Chicago School, 1919–20; folder 10, box 20, Abbott Papers.

57. Morantz-Sanchez, *Sympathy and Science*, 254–62.

58. Breckinridge, Suggested Form of Public Announcement of Merger, Aug. 1920, folder 10, box 20, Abbott Papers.

59. Abbott to Julia Lathrop, Aug. 7, 1920, folder 11, box 3, Abbott Papers. On the early marriage and later divorce between sociology and social work, see Trattner, *From Poor Law*, 194–95. On the increasing distance between the two in the 1920s, see Rosalind Rosenberg, *Beyond Separate Spheres: Intellectual Roots of Modern Feminism* (New Haven, 1982), 241. See also Furner, *Advocacy and Objectivity*, 313.

60. Costin, *Two Sisters*, 193. The *Social Service Review* was, of course, not the only journal of social work. Paul Kellogg had long edited the *Survey*, and other groups published *Social Casework* beginning in 1920 and *Child Welfare* in 1922. Trattner, *From Poor Law*, 202. On the ritualized formation of new professions, see Furner, *Advocacy and Objectivity*, 312.

61. See, for instance, Abbott, *Social Welfare and Professional Education* (Chicago: Univ. of Chicago, 1931), 52.

62. "American Association of Schools of Social Work," 1925–26, bound volume, box 18, Abbott Papers.

63. Abbott, Speech Manuscript [1924–25?], folder 12, box 1, Abbott Papers.

64. Charles Merriam, "A Member of the University Community," esp. 425. Katharine Lenroot, "Friend of Children and the Children's Bureau," *Social Service Review* 22 (Dec. 1948), 427–30, esp. 429. See also Fitzpatrick, *Endless Crusade*, 195–200.

65. Trattner, *From Poor Law*, 213–15, 218–19. On the founding of psychiatric social work, see for instance, Glazer and Slater, *Unequal Colleagues*, chap. 5.

66. Breckinridge, *Public Welfare Administration in the United States Select Documents* (Chicago: Univ. of Chicago Press, 1927), 3, 708–9.

67. Abbott, *Welfare and Professional Education*, 52.

68. Graduate School of Social Service Administration, 1924–26, pp. 15, 25, bound volume, box 19, Abbott Papers. Abbott, *Welfare and Professional Education*, 78–79.

69. Abbott, *Welfare and Professional Education*, 88.

70. Abbott to President Hutchins, Nov. 1929, bound volume, box 19, Abbott Papers. Abbott, Report on Local Community Research, Autumn 1925, Appendix 1, folder 12, box 1, Abbott Papers. Graduate School of Social Service Administration, 1923–24, bound volume, box 19, Abbott Papers.

71. Edith Abbott to President Hutchins, Nov. 1929, bound volume, box 19, Abbott Papers.

72. Abbott to Leonard White, Dec. 19, 1929, folder 12, box 1, Abbott Papers.

73. Edith Abbott to Grace Abbott, Nov. 10, 1930, folder 2, box 3, Abbott Papers.

74. Edith Abbott to Grace Abbott, April 1, 1926, folder 2, box 3, Abbott Papers.

75. Edith Abbott to Grace Abbott, Nov. 10, 1930, folder 2, box 3, Abbott Papers.

76. Rockefeller Report, 1926–31, bound volume, box 19; Graduate School of Social Service Administration, 1923–24, bound volume, box 19; Abbott Papers.

77. See, for example, Barbara Melosh, *The Physician's Hand: Work, Culture, and Conflict in American Nursing* (Philadelphia, 1982), esp. 113–55; and Susan M. Reverby, *Ordered to Care: The Dilemma of American Nursing, 1850–1945* (New York, 1987), esp. 109–10.

78. Breckinridge to Taylor, n.d., folder 3, box 4; Breckinridge to Taylor, Oct. 13, 1920, folder 13, box 20; Contract between Children's Bureau and Chicago School, June 30, 1919, folder 11, box 3; Abbott Papers. Memo Concerning the Future of the Chicago School of Civics, 1919–20, folder 10, box 4, Addendum, Abbott Papers.

79. Abbott to Julia Lathrop, Aug. 7, 1920, folder 11, box 3, Abbott Papers.

80. Abbott to Julia Lathrop, Aug. 7, 1920, folder 11, box 3; Graduate School of Social Service Administration, 1923–24, bound volume, box 19; Abbott Papers. Jacqueline K. Parker, "Why Study the Early Children's Bureau?," Working Paper Number Fourteen, Center for the Study of Women in Society, Eugene, Ore., 1983, pp. 14–16.

81. Stenographic Report, Feb. 13, 1920, folder 1920–22, box 2, Chicago School of Civics and Philanthropy section, Taylor Papers.

82. Charles Nagel to Lillian Wald, Sept. 12, 1912; Lathrop to Wald, Jan. 15, 1913; folder 1, box 59, Abbott Papers. Lathrop to Grace Abbott, Oct. 24, April 1, Feb. 9, April 6, 8, 15, May 3, 1921; folder 5, box 57, Abbott Papers.

83. Costin, *Two Sisters*, 120, 122–24.

84. Ibid.

85. Ibid., 121.

86. Ibid., 120, 122–24.

87. James et al., *Notable American Women*, 1: 2–3.

88. Edith Abbott to Lathrop, June 7, 1922, folder 5, box 57, Abbott Papers. Regarding her sick headaches, see Edith Abbott to Brother, Sept. 12, 1910, folder 2, box 2, Addendum, Abbott Papers.

89. See Edith Abbott's book of quotations, folder 4, box 2, Abbott Papers.

90. Lathrop to Edith Abbott, Oct. 13, 1921, folder 11, box 3, Abbott Papers.

91. Molly Dewson to Grace Abbott, Dec. 2, 1935, folder 8, box 68, Abbott Papers. See also Alice Hamilton to Grace Abbott, May 20, 1935, folder 1, box 55, Abbott Papers.

92. Grace Abbott to Edith Abbott, Nov. 20, 1932, folder 2, box 3, Abbott Papers.

93. James et al., *Notable American Women*, 1: 2–3.

94. See Costin, *Two Sisters*, 103.

95. Ibid., 102–4. A. J. McKelway to Owen R. Lovejoy, Nov. 8, 1917; Wald to Lovejoy, Nov. 30, 1917; Lovejoy to Members of the Executive Committee, Nov. 27, 1917; Children 1917 File, box 40, Lillian Wald Papers, Special Collections, Butler Library, Columbia Univ., New York. Lathrop to Grace Abbott, April 21, 1917, folder 7, box 57, Abbott Papers.

96. James et al., *Notable American Women*, 1: 3.

97. Quoted in Costin, *Two Sisters*, 121–22.

98. Helen Wright, "Three Against Time: Edith and Grace Abbott and Sophonisba P. Breckinridge," *Social Service Review* 28 (March 1954), 45.

99. Graduate School of Social Service Administration, 1923–24; Edith Abbott to Tufts, Jan. 5, 1925; bound volume, box 19, Abbott Papers.

100. Edith Abbott to Grace Abbott, April 4, 1929, folder 2, box 3, Abbott Papers.

101. Children's Bureau, *Third Annual Report* (Washington, D.C., 1916), 6–7. Grace Abbott to Edith Abbott, Feb. 2, 1926, folder 12, box 1, Abbott Papers.

102. Edith Abbott to Grace Abbott, Feb. 11, 1924; Edith Abbott to Grace Abbott, Oct. 28, 1930; folder 2, box 3, Abbott Papers. Doctoral Dissertation and Masters Theses Under Way, Graduate School of Social Service Administration, 1923–24, bound volume, box 19, Abbott Papers.

Chapter 4. The Sheppard-Towner Maternity and Infancy Act, 1918–1924

1. "War Will Kill Our Men; Don't Let Sun Kill Our Babies!," *Gazette* (Niagara Falls, N.Y.), Aug. 2, 1917, bound volume, box 43, Grace and Edith Abbott Papers, Special Collections, Univ. of Chicago Library.

2. See David M. Kennedy, *Over Here: The First World War and American Society* (New York, 1980), 3–44. On Addams in particular, see Allen F. Davis, *American Heroine: The Life and Legend of Jane Addams* (New York, 1973), 212–50, and Jane

Addams, *Peace and Bread in Time of War* (New York: Macmillan, 1922), 111. See also Barbara Steinson, *American Women's Activism in World War I* (New York: Garland, 1982).

3. See especially Robert D. Cuff, *The War Industries Board: Business-Government Relations During World War I* (Baltimore, 1973), and Kennedy, *Over Here*, 93–143.

4. Neva R. Deardorff, "The Demise of a Highly Respected Doctrine," *The Survey* 39 (Jan. 12, 1918), 416.

5. Gertrude Seymour, "The Health of Soldier and Civilian: Some Aspects of the American Health Movement in War-Time," *The Survey* 39 (April 27, 1918), 89.

6. Kennedy, *Over Here*, 279–87. Allen F. Davis, "Welfare, Reform and World War I," *American Quarterly* 19 (Fall 1967), 516–23. Nancy F. Cott, *The Grounding of Modern Feminism* (New Haven, 1987), 62–63.

7. Lathrop to Florence King, July 15, 1918, folder 6, box 59, Abbott Papers.

8. Kennedy, *Over Here*, 26–27, 66–75.

9. Cott, *Grounding of Modern Feminism*, 63–64. William E. Leuchtenburg, *The Perils of Prosperity, 1914–32* (Chicago, 1958), 66–83, 204–24. Robert H. Wiebe, *The Search for Order, 1877–1920* (New York, 1967), 286–93.

10. Evidence for Lathrop's opposition to the war is found in Alice Hamilton, *Exploring the Dangerous Trades: The Autobiography of Alice Hamilton* (Boston: Little, Brown, 1943), 192.

11. Lathrop was quoted in "War Will Kill Our Men; Don't Let Sun Kill Our Babies!," *Gazette* (Niagara Falls, N.Y.), Aug. 2, 1917, bound volume, box 43, Abbott Papers. Lathrop herself quoted Wilson in her Memo on a Statement Before Conference on Children's Year, May 16, 1918, folder 9, box 60, Abbott Papers.

12. Helen Sumner to Professor Walter Willcox, Jan. 17, 1918, folder 5, box 59, Abbott Papers.

13. Lathrop, Speech Before Alabama Educational Union, March 28, 1918, folder 9, box 60, Abbott Papers.

14. William J. Breen, *Uncle Sam at Home: Civilian Mobilization, Wartime Federalism, and the Council of National Defense, 1917–1919* (Westport, Conn.: Greenwood Press, 1984), 4–5, 9, 94, 115–17.

15. Mrs. J. F. Hooper to Lathrop, Aug. 30, 1918, file 12-8-0, Central File 1914–20, Children's Bureau Records, National Archives, Washington, D.C. (hereafter CBR).

16. Lathrop, Speech Before Alabama Educational Union, March 28, 1918, folder 9, box 60, Abbott Papers.

17. Lathrop, Memo on Statement Before Conference on Children's Year, May 16, 1918, folder 9, box 60, Abbott Papers.

18. Lathrop quoted in "To Abolish Poverty Task for Women," *Philadelphia Record*, May 4, 1918, bound volume, box 43, Abbott Papers.

19. L. Clarke and Anna Rochester, Advance Publicity on Children's Year, Jan. 23, 1918, bound volume, box 43; Lathrop, Speech Before Alabama Educational Union, March 28, 1918, folder 9, box 60; Abbott Papers.

20. Children's Bureau, *Third Annual Report* (Washington, D.C., 1915), 9–10.

21. A. C. Phelps to Lathrop, Oct. 19, 1916, folder 10, box 62, Abbott Papers.

22. *Third Annual Report*, 12–13. Children's Bureau, *Eleventh Annual Report* (Washington, D.C.: Government Printing Office, 1923), 3. Louis J. Covotsos, "Child Welfare and Social Progress: A History of the United States Children's Bureau, 1912–1935," Ph.D. dissertation, Univ. of Chicago, 1976, p. 115.

23. Lathrop to Anna Rochester, Aug. 26, 1918, file 12-8-0, Central File 1914–20, CBR.

24. Children's Bureau, *Third Annual Report*, 8–13. Covotsos, "Child Welfare and Social Progress," 116.

25. Breen, *Uncle Sam at Home*, 128; Molly Ladd-Taylor, ed., *Raising a Baby the Government Way: Mothers' Letters to the Children's Bureau, 1915–1932* (New Brunswick, N.J., 1986), 20–21.

26. Breen, *Uncle Sam at Home*, 127.

27. Children's Bureau, *Fifth Annual Report* (Washington, D.C.: Government Printing Office, 1918), 466–71. Caroline Fleming to Mary Woods, May 16, 1919, folder 5, box 62, Abbott Papers.

28. Anna Rude to Dr. Martha Tracy, Nov. 10, 1920, file 4-15-2-0, Central File 1914–20, CBR.

29. Anna Rude to Martha Tracy, Nov. 10, 1920, file 4-15-2-0, Central File 1914–20; Secretary to Ellen C. Babbitt, Nov. 24, 1924, file 4-11-1-3, Central File 1921–24; CBR. Lathrop to Mary Reed, Sept. 14, 1916; Mrs. Max West to Gertrude Knipp, Jan. 13, 1919; file 4-15-2-0, Central File 1914–20, CBR. See for example, A. R. Lewis to Anna Rude, July 11, 1921, file 10-6-3-2, Central File 1921–24, CBR. Acting Chief to Jeannette F. Throckmorton, July 6, 1920, file 4-15-2-1-0, Central File 1914–20, CBR. On Lathrop's lobbying, see for instance, Lathrop to W. H. Kellogg, April 20, 1918, file 4-15-2-1-6; Lathrop to Guilford Sumner, Nov. 27, 1918, file 4-15-2-1-17; Central File 1914–20, CBR.

30. Newsletter for Directors of State Child Hygiene Division, April 1920, file 4-15-2-1-0, Central File 1914–20, CBR. Regina Markell Morantz-Sanchez, *Sympathy and Science: Women Physicians in American Medicine* (New York, 1985), 314; Children's Bureau, *The Promotion of the Welfare and Hygiene of Maternity and Infancy*, Pamphlet Number 146 (Washington, D.C., 1925), 19; Children's Bureau, *The Promotion of the Welfare and Hygiene of Maternity and Infancy*, Pamphlet Number 178 (Washington, D.C., 1927), 7.

31. See, for example, Mrs. W. S. Jennings to Grace Abbott, Sept. 2, 1922, file 4-11-1-3, Central File 1921–24; Helen Guthrie Miller to Anna Rude, Oct. 21, 1920, file 4-15-2-1-0; Nannie J. Lackland to Anna Rude, Sept. 8, 1920, file 9-1-2-3, Central File 1914–20; CBR.

32. Dr. Frances M. Hollingshead to Dr. Grace Meigs, Nov. 24, 1915; Dr. Grace Meigs to Dr. Frances Hollingshead, Dec. 1, 1915; Frances Hollingshead to Grace Meigs, Dec. 6, 1915; Hollingshead to Meigs, March 2, 1916; file 4-12-4, Central File 1914–20, CBR.

33. Dr. Dorothy Child to Lathrop, June 25, 1919, file 4-0-1, Central File 1914–20, CBR.

34. Dr. Lydia Allen DeVibliss to Lathrop, July 16, 1918, file 4-0-1, Central File 1914–20, CBR.

35. Mary M. West to Caroline Fleming, June 7, 1920, file 9-1-2-3, Central File 1914–20, CBR.

36. See also, Nannie J. Lackland to Anna Rude, Sept. 8, 1920; Report from Zoe LaForge to Anna Rude, Nov. 21, 1919; file 9-1-2-3; Dr. J. N. Hurty to Caroline Fleming, June 27, 1919; file 4-15-2-1-16; Lathrop to Dr. W. H. Cox, Nov. 27, 1918; file 4-15-2-1-11; Central File 1914–20, CBR.

37. Dorothy Child to Anna Rude, Nov. 7, 1920, file 4-15-2-1-0; Newsletter for Directors of State Child Hygiene Divisions, April 1920, file 4-15-2-1-0; Central File 1914–20, CBR. Anna Rude to Florence Brown Sherbon, Feb. 1, 1921; Estelle Mathews to Grace Abbott, Sept. 16, 1921; Florence McKay to Linnie Beauchamp, April 5, 1921; Maude Howe to Anna Rude, Feb. 2, 1921; Jessie Marriner to Anna Rude, Jan. 14, 1921; file 4-11-1-3, Central File 1921–24, CBR.

38. Breen, *Uncle Sam at Home*, 195–97.

39. Ibid., 195.

40. "Standardize Care of Babies" *Union* (Walla Walla, Wash.), June 5, 1918, bound volume, box 43, Abbott Papers.

41. Josephine Baker to Mrs. Whitman Cross, June 10, 1919, file 9-1-2-0-1, Central File 1914–20, CBR.

42. Sophonisba P. Breckinridge, *Women in the Twentieth Century: A Study of Their Political, Social and Economic Activities* (1933; New York: McGraw Hill, 1972), 264–68.

43. Breckinridge, *Women in the Twentieth Century*, 262–65. Lela B. Costin, *Two Sisters for Social Justice: A Biography of Grace and Edith Abbott* (Chicago, 1983), 101–18, 150–58.

44. Ellis W. Hawley, *The Great War and the Search for a Modern Order: A History of the American People and Their Institutions, 1917–1933* (New York, 1979), 60.

45. Cf. Joan Hoff Wilson, *Herbert Hoover, Forgotten Progressive* (Boston, 1975), 270.

46. Hawley's analysis of the position of the NCLC and the Federation of Settlements lacks gender as a category, which might change his conclusions on 121–22.

47. Mrs. Albion Fellows Bacon to Lathrop, May 26, 1919, folder 6, box 62, Abbott Papers.

48. David Burner, *The Politics of Provincialism: The Democratic Party in Transition, 1918-1932* (New York, 1968), 161–66.

49. Eugene M. Tobin, *Organize or Perish: America's Independent Progressives, 1913-1933* (Westport, Conn.: 1986), 107–24, 132.

50. See, for instance, J. Stanley Lemons, *The Woman Citizen: Social Feminism in the 1920s* (Chicago, 1973), 155–57; Joseph B. Chepaitis, "The First Federal Social Welfare Measure: The Sheppard-Towner Maternity and Infancy Act, 1918–1932," Ph.D. dissertation, Georgetown Univ., 1968, pp. 40–50. Cott, *Grounding of Modern Feminism*, 97–98.

51. Breckinridge, *Women in the Twentieth Century*, 259–61. Chepaitis, "The First Federal Social Welfare Measure," 89–92.

52. Lathrop to Mrs. Ella L. Blair, April 28, 1919; Mary Wood to Lathrop, June 9, 1919; Lathrop to Mrs. Josiah Cowles, May 24, 1919; News Release, Aug. 1921; folder 5, box 62, Abbott Papers.

53. Lathrop to Mrs. Charles H. Brooks, May 26, 1919; Helen T. Woolley to Carrie Chapman Catt, May 10, 1919; folder 5, box 62, Abbott Papers. Mrs. Ira Couch Wood to Lathrop, Feb. 18, 1920, folder 6, box 62, Abbott Papers.

54. Lathrop to Margaret Dreier Robins, July 21, 1919; Robins to Lathrop, June 23, 1919; folder 5, box 62, Abbott Papers.

55. Lathrop to Mrs. Elmer L. Blair, April 28, 1919, folder 5, box 62, Abbott Papers.

56. Lathrop to Mrs. Elmer Blair, Aug. 2, 1919, folder 5, box 62, Abbott Papers.

57. Chepaitis, "The First Federal Social Welfare Measure," 92.

58. Edith Abbott, "Grace Abbott," MS biography, folder 2, box 10, Addendum, Abbott Papers. Chepaitis, "The First Federal Social Welfare Measure," 93.

59. Quoted in Lemons, *The Woman Citizen*, 155.

60. Ibid., 167.

61. Lathrop to File, Oct. 14, 1919, folder 5, box 62, Abbott Papers.

62. Lathrop to Ella Phillips Crandall, March 26, 1919; Crandall to Lathrop, March 28, 1919; folder 5, box 62, Abbott Papers.

63. Chepaitis, "The First Federal Social Welfare Measure," 85–89.

64. Quoted in ibid., 84. Similar quotations in Lemons, *The Woman Citizen*, 166–67; Breckinridge, *Women in the Twentieth Century*, 260.

65. Florence Kelley to Lathrop, Oct. 11, 1920, folder 6, box 62, Abbott Papers.

66. See, for example, Edith Brown Kirkwood to Eleanor Marsh, June 5, 1924, file 11-0, Central File 1921–24, CBR.

67. League of Women Voters, "Reasons Why the Administration of the Sheppard-Towner Maternity and Infancy Bill Should Be Vested in the Children's Bureau," file 11-0-11, Central File 1921–24, CBR.

68. Mary M. Roberts to Grace Abbott, March 25, 1924; Maria W. Bates to Grace Abbott, March 10, 1924; Grace Anderson to Grace Abbott, April 14, 1924; file 11 0, Central File 1921–24, CBR. Anna Rude to Martha Tracy, Nov. 10, 1920, file 4-15-2-0, Central File 1914–20, CBR. Mary Morgan to Anna Rude, Feb. 8, 1922, file 11-53-1, Central File 1921–24, CBR.

69. For Rankin's proposal, see Covotsos, "Child Welfare and Social Progress," 124.

70. Chepaitis, "The First Federal Social Welfare Measure," 66–69.

71. Lathrop to File, Oct. 14, 1919, folder 5, box 62, Abbott Papers. "An Act for the Promotion of the Welfare and Hygiene of Maternity and Infancy," 43 Stat. 135 (Nov. 23, 1921).

72. "An Act for the Promotion of the Welfare and Hygiene of Maternity and Infancy."

73. Chepaitis, "The First Federal Social Welfare Measure," 58, 70–76. Lemons, *The Woman Citizen*, 156–57.

74. Quoted in Lemons, *The Woman Citizen*, 167–68.

75. "An Act for the Promotion of the Welfare and Hygiene of Maternity and Infancy."

76. Lathrop to Grace Abbott, Jan. 15, [1922]; Lathrop to Grace Abbott, Jan. 22, [1922]; folder 7, box 57, Abbott Papers. Lathrop to Grace Abbott, June 24, 1923, folder 9, box 57, Abbott Papers.

77. Costin, *Two Sisters*, 135.

78. Mrs. Willis G. Mitchell to Katharine Lenroot, March 28, 1923, file 11-34-2; Mary Morgan to Anna Rude, Feb. 4, 1921, file 10-6-3-0; Central File 1921–24, CBR. Kelley to Lathrop, June 1924, folder 1, box 57, Abbott Papers.

79. Children's Bureau, *The Promotion of the Welfare and Hygiene of Maternity and Infancy*, Pamphlet Number 137 (Washington, D.C.: Government Printing Office, 1924), 4–5.

80. Ibid., 5–6.

81. Children's Bureau, *The Promotion of the Welfare and Hygiene of Maternity and Infancy*, Pamphlet Number 178 (Washington, D.C.: Government Printing Office, 1927), 1.

82. Anna Rude to File, July 21, 1922, file 11-7, Central File 1921–24, CBR. Children's Bureau, Pamphlet Number 137, 1924, pp. 5, 6–8. John J. Tigert to Anna Rude, April 3, 1922, file 11-1-5, Central File 1921–24, CBR.

83. Anna Rude to Estella Ford Warner, Dec. 15, 1922, file 11-39-1, Central File 1921–24, CBR. Children's Bureau, Pamphlet Number 137, 1924, p. 23.

84. Estelle Mathews to Ethel Watters, March 6, 1923, file 11-7; Anna Rude to Estella Ford Warner, Dec. 15, 1922, file 11-39-1; Ethel M. Watters to Estelle Mathews, Oct. 13, 1922, file 11-7; Central File 1921–24, CBR.

85. Children's Bureau, Pamphlet Number 137, 1924, p. 27. Children's Bureau, *The Promotion of the Welfare and Hygiene of Maternity and Infancy*, Pamphlet Number 146 (Washington, D.C., 1925), 12, 44.

86. Statistics compiled from letters, Anna Rude to Directors of Divisions of Child Hygiene, Jan. and Feb. 1921, file 10-6-3-0, Central File 1921–24, CBR.

87. Children's Bureau, Pamphlet Number 178, 1927, p. 7.

88. Sheila M. Rothman, *Woman's Proper Place: A History of Changing Ideals and Practices, 1870 to the Present* (New York, 1978), 140, 303. Mary Roth Walsh *"Doctors Wanted: No Women Need Apply": Sexual Barriers in the Medical Profession, 1835–1975* (New Haven, 1977), 185.

89. Report of the Division of Maternity, Infancy and Child Hygiene of the New York State Department of Health, 1923, file 11-34-8, Correspondence and Reports File 1917–1954, CBR.

90. Children's Bureau, Pamphlet Number 137, 1924, pp. 8–9.

91. Rosalind Rosenberg, *Beyond Separate Spheres: Intellectual Roots of Modern Feminism* (New Haven, 1982), 244–46. Virginia Drachman, "Female Solidarity and Professional Success: The Dilemma of Women Doctors in Late Nineteenth-Century America," *Journal of Social History* 15 (Summer 1982), 607–20. Judy Jolley Mohraz, "The Equity Club: Community Building Among Professional Women," *Journal of American Culture 5* (Winter 1982), 34–39.

92. Children's Bureau, Pamphlet Number 137, 1924, pp. 9–12, 16–18.

93. I have been helped enormously and obviously by Linda Gordon's *Heroes of Their Own Lives: The Politics and History of Family Violence* (New York, 1988), esp. 6, 12, 29–30, 293–99; and by Judith A. Trolander, *Professionalism and Social Change: From the Settlement House Movement to Neighborhood Centers, 1866 to the Present* (New York, 1987), 11.

94. Thanks to Lucie White and Molly Ladd-Taylor, who convinced me that a client's freedom to say no really counted for something in these cases.

95. Children's Bureau, Pamphlet Number 146, 1925, pp. 5, 9, 13–14.

96. Children's Bureau, Pamphlet Number 137, 1924, pp. 16–17. For similar information, see Arkansas Bureau of Child Hygiene, Semi-Annual Report of Maternity and Infancy Work, Jan. 1, 1924–July 1, 1924, file 11-5-8, Correspondence and Reports File 1917–54, CBR. This procedure varied among states depending largely on the amount of money available for the work. Where funds were scarce, a state might employ only one or two nurses. These nurses often went directly to county officials and lobbied for the employment of a county nurse, whom the state nurse could then train to conduct conferences. Other state's staffs depended on women's groups to organize the conferences so that a nurse could simply travel to each town only for the days of the conferences. See, for example, Elena Crough to Florence E. Kraker, Sept. 25, 1924; Ethel M. Watters to File, Oct. 5, 1922; file 11-31-1, Central File 1921–24, CBR. For a huge operation that allowed a terrific degree of specialization, on the other hand, see New York State Department of Health, Report on the Division of Maternity, Infancy and Child Hygiene, 1923, file 11-34-8, Correspondence and Reports File 1917–54, CBR.

97. Children's Bureau, Pamphlet Number 146, 1925, p. 6.

98. Children's Bureau, Pamphlet Number 178, 1927, p. 12.

99. Ibid.

100. Nancy Weiss, "Save the Children: A History of the United States Children's Bureau, 1912–1918," Ph.D. dissertation, Univ. of California–Los Angeles, 1974, pp. 199–200. On diet, see, for example, Children's Bureau, Pamphlet Number 178, 1927, p. 78; and Children's Bureau, Pamphlet Number 137, 1924, pp. 19–20. On breastfeeding, see, for example, Children's Bureau, *Tenth Annual Report* (Washington, D.C.: Government Printing Office, 1922), 10. On immunization, see Children's Bureau, Pamphlet 178, 1927, p. 12. On play, *Tenth Annual Report*, 18.

101. Quotation from "The Minor Third," Press Release through the Committee on Public Information, July 1, 1918, bound volume, box 43, Abbott Papers. The references to regularity are everywhere, but see for instance Children's Bureau, Pamphlet Number 178, 1927, p. 80.

102. Children's Bureau, Pamphlet Number 178, 1927, p. 80. Children's Bureau, *Eleventh Annual Report* (Washington, D.C., 1923), 8.

103. See, for example, Lathrop's introduction to Sophonisba P. Breckinridge and Edith Abbott, *The Delinquent Child and the Home* (New York, 1912); Addams, *Twenty Years*, 210.

104. Quotation is from "Standardize Care for Babies," *Union* (Walla Walla, Wash.), June 5, 1918, bound volume, box 43, Abbott Papers.

105. Quoted in Weiss, "Save the Children," 204.

106. Ibid., 198–204. Children's Bureau, Pamphlet Number 137, 1924, p. 19. Children's Bureau, Pamphlet Number 178, 1927, pp. 8, 20, 28, 80. Children's Bureau, Pamphlet Number 146, 1925, p. 46. Arkansas Bureau of Child Hygiene, Semi-Annual Report, Jan. 1, 1924–July 1, 1924, file 11-5-8; Kentucky Bureau of Maternal and Child Health, Semi-Annual Report, July 1, 1923–Jan. 1, 1924, file 11-19-8; Minnesota Bureau of Child Hygiene, Semi-Annual Report, July 1, 1924–Dec. 31, 1924, file 11-25-8; Correspondence and Reports File 1917–54, CBR.

107. Children's Bureau, Pamphlet Number 146, 1925, pp. 6–7. Children's Bureau, Pamphlet Number 178, 1927, pp. 12, 78. Children's Bureau, Pamphlet Number 137, 1924, p. 19.

108. See, for example, Arkansas Bureau of Child Hygiene, Semi-Annual Report of Maternity and Infancy Work, Jan. 1–July 1, 1924, file 11-5-8, Correspondence and Reports File 1917–54, CBR; and Molly Ladd-Taylor, "Federal Help for Mothers: The Rise and Fall of the Sheppard-Towner Act in the 1920s," expanded version of a paper presented at the Seventh Berkshire Conference on the History of Women, Wellesley, Mass., June 19, 1987, p. 25. See a different version in Dorothy Helly and Susan Reverby, eds., *Connected Domains: Beyond the Public/Private Dichotomy in Women's History* (Ithaca: Cornell Univ. Press, forthcoming 1991).

109. Ladd-Taylor, "Federal Help for Mothers," 25.

110. The second quotation is from Tennessee's annual report as cited in Children's Bureau, Pamphlet Number 178, 1927, p. 67. The first, quoting Alabama's annual report, is cited in Children's Bureau, Pamphlet Number 146, 1925, p. 21.

111. See, for example, Semi-Annual Report, Arkansas Bureau of Child Hygiene, Jan. 1–July 1, 1924, file 11-5-8, Correspondence and Reports File, CBR.

112. See Ladd-Taylor, "Federal Help for Mothers," 24–25.

113. Semi-Annual Report, Kentucky Bureau of Maternal and Child Health, July 1, 1923–Jan. 1, 1924, file 11-19-8, Correspondence and Reports, CBR.

114. Children's Bureau, Pamphlet Number 146, 1925, p. 6.

115. Ibid.

116. Ladd-Taylor, "Federal Help for Mothers," 28.

117. Minnesota Bureau of Child Hygiene, Semi-Annual Report, July 1–Dec. 31, 1924, file 11-25-8, Correspondence and Reports File 1917–54, CBR. For an analysis of the race and gender components of epistemologies based on personal experience and those based on statistics, see Patricia Hill Collins, "The Social Construction of Black Feminist Thought," *Signs* 14 (Summer 1989), esp. 759–62.

118. Kentucky Bureau of Maternal and Child Health, Semi-Annual Report, July 1, 1923–Jan. 1, 1924, file 11-19-8; Minnesota Bureau of Maternal and Child Health, Semi-Annual Report, July–Dec. 1924, file 11-25-8; Correspondence and Reports File 1917–54, CBR. Children's Bureau, Pamphlet Number 146, 1925, p. 14. Children's Bureau, Pamphlet Number 178, 1927, pp. 19–20.

119. "Play and Americanization," Press Release, Aug. 19, 1918, bound volume, box 43, Abbott Papers.

120. Grace Abbott, "The Midwife in Chicago," *American Journal of Sociology* 20 (March 1915), 684–99. See also Morantz-Sanchez, *Sympathy and Science*, 297–98.

121. Children's Bureau, Pamphlet Number 137, 1924, pp. 14–15; Children's Bureau, Pamphlet Number 146, 1925, pp. 5, 9, 11–13. For the name of Dr. Ionia Whipper, I thank Susan Smith of the Department of History at the Univ. of Wisconsin – Madison, whose exciting work on the black women's health movement cannot appear soon enough.

122. Children's Bureau, Pamphlet Number 137, 1924, pp. 14–15.

123. Kentucky Bureau of Maternal and Child Health, Semi-Annual Report, July 1, 1923–Jan. 1, 1924, file 11-19-8, Correspondence and Reports File 1917–54, CBR.

124. Children's Bureau, Pamphlet Number 178, 1927, p. 44.

125. See, for example, Mississippi's report as quoted in Children's Bureau, Pamphlet Number 178, 1927, p. 47.

126. Quoted in Children's Bureau, Pamphlet Number 137, 1924, p. 16.

127. Children's Bureau, Pamphlet Number 178, 1927, p. 58.

128. Ibid., 18.

129. Molly Ladd-Taylor, "'Grannies' and 'Spinsters': Midwife Education Under the Sheppard-Towner Act," *Journal of Social History* 22 (Winter 1988), 270.

130. Semi-Annual Report, California Bureau of Child Hygiene, Jan. 1–June 30, 1924, file 11-6-8, Correspondence and Reports 1917–54, CBR.

131. Children's Bureau, Pamphlet Number 178, 1927, p. 15.

132. Children's Bureau, Pamphlet Number 137, 1924, p. 14.

133. Abbott, "The Midwife in Chicago," 684–99.

134. For evidence of the degree to which black women believed that race determined whether an occupation was classified as a profession or not, see Elsa Barkley Brown, "Womanist Consciousness: Maggie Lena Walker and the Independent Order of Saint Luke," *Signs* 14 (Spring 1989), esp. footnote 31.

135. Quoted in Ladd-Taylor, "Grannies and Spinsters," 260.

136. Quotation is from Children's Bureau, Pamphlet Number 178, 1927, p. 67.

137. Children's Bureau, Pamphlet Number 146, 1925, p. 17. Elena M. Crough to Ethel Watters, Jan. 22, 1924, file 11-31-1, Central File 1921–24; Colorado Bureau of Child Welfare, Semi-Annual Report, 11-7-1, Correspondence and Reports File 1917–54; CBR.

138. Children's Bureau, Pamphlet Number 146, 1925, pp. 10, 12, 16. Minnesota Bureau of Maternal and Child Health, Semi-Annual Report, July–Dec. 1924, file 11-25-8, Correspondence and Reports File 1917–54; Ethel M. Watters to File, Oct. 5, 1922, file 11-31-1, Central File 1921–24; CBR. Children's Bureau, Pamphlet Number 137, 1924, p. 15.

139. Children's Bureau, Pamphlet Number 178, 1927, pp. 75, 77. Alabama's Semi-Annual Report on Maternity and Infancy Work, file 11-2-1, Correspondence and Reports File 1917–54, CBR. Children's Bureau, Pamphlet Number 146, 1925, p. 12. For the name of Vinita Lewis, I again thank Susan Smith of the Department of History at the University of Wisconsin–Madison.

140. Ladd-Taylor, "Grannies and Spinsters," 255–75.

141. Kentucky Bureau of Maternal and Child Hygiene, Semi-Annual Report, July 1, 1923–Jan. 1, 1924, file 11-19-8, Correspondence and Reports File 1917–54, CBR.

142. Kentucky Bureau of Maternal and Child Hygiene, Semi-Annual Report, July 1, 1923–Jan. 1, 1924, file 11-19-8; Division of Maternity, Infancy and Child Hygiene, New York State Department of Health, Annual Report, 1923, file 11-34-8; Correspondence and Reports File 1917–54, CBR. Children's Bureau, Pamphlet Number 137, 1924, pp. 24–25. Jessie L. Marriner to Anna Rude, Dec. 28, 1921, file 11-2-1; Florence McKay to Florence Kraker, Aug. 22, 1924, file 11-34-1; Plan of Bureau of Public Health Nursing and Child Hygiene of Oregon State Board of Health, 1921, file 11-39-1; Ethel Watters to Grace Abbott, Aug. 22, 1922, file 11-53-1; Central File 1921–24, CBR.

143. Children's Bureau, Pamphlet Number 146, 1925, pp. 18, 19–20, 29. Children's Bureau, Pamphlet Number 178, 1927, p. 23.

144. Estella Ford Warner to Anna Rude, Nov. 29, 1922; Plan of Bureau of Public Health Nursing and Child Hygiene of Oregon State Board of Health, 1921; file 11-39-1, Central File 1921–24, CBR.

Chapter 5. *Federal Child Welfare Policy, 1924–1935*

1. Rodney Dutcher, "Delegates Angered at Treatment They Received at Child Health Conference," *Washington Star*, Nov. 23, 1930, quoted in Lela B. Costin, "Women and Physicians: The 1930 White House Conference on Children," *Social Work* 28 (March/April 1983), 111.

2. Grace Abbott to Mary Murphy, Nov. 16, 1925, folder 7, box 62, Grace and Edith Abbott Papers, Special Collections, Univ. of Chicago Library. Joseph Benedict Chepaitis, "The First Federal Social Welfare Measure: Sheppard-Towner Maternity and Infancy Act, 1918–1932," Ph.D. dissertation, Georgetown Univ., 1968, pp. 214–15. J. Stanley Lemons, *The Woman Citizen: Social Feminism in the 1920s* (Chicago, 1973), 172.

3. Chepaitis, "The First Federal Social Welfare Measure," 218–24.

4. Ibid., 227–40.

5. Quotation is from Grace Abbott to Florence McKay, Jan. 18, 1927, folder 7, box 62, Abbott Papers. For further evidence of confidence in ultimate renewal of the law, see Kelley to Lathrop, March 22, 1927, folder 1, box 57, Abbott Papers; Lela B. Costin, *Two Sisters for Social Justice: A Biography of Grace and Edith Abbott* (Urbana, 1983), 148; Lemons, *The Woman Citizen*, 173.

6. Chepaitis, "The First Federal Social Welfare Measure," 278.

7. Ibid., 333–37.

8. Sophonisba Preston Breckinridge, *Women in the Twentieth Century: A Study of Their Political, Social, and Economic Activities* (1933; reprint, New York, 1972), 245–56. William H. Chafe, *The American Woman: Her Changing Social, Economic and Political Roles, 1920–1970* (New York: Oxford Univ. Press, 1972), 30. See also Paul Kleppner, "Were Women to Blame? Female Suffrage and Voter Turnout," *Journal of Interdisciplinary History* 12 (Spring 1982), 621–43; Sara Alpern and Dale Baum, "Female Ballots: The Impact of the Nineteenth Amendment," *Journal of Interdisciplinary History* 16 (Summer 1985), 43–67.

9. Nancy F. Cott, *The Grounding of Modern Feminism* (New Haven, 1987), esp. 117–42. Alice Kessler-Harris, *Out to Work: A History of Wage-Earning Women in the United States* (New York: Oxford Univ. Press, 1982), esp. 180–214. Chafe, *The American Woman*, 112–32. See also Susan D. Becker, *The Origins of the Equal Rights Amendment: American Feminism Between the Wars* (Westport, Conn.: Greenwood Press, 1981).

10. See Cott, *Grounding of Modern Feminism*, 85–114.

11. The phrase is in Robert Wiebe to Robyn Muncy, July 21, 1989, in author's possession.

12. Lathrop to Grace Abbott, June 2, 1923, folder 9, box 57, Abbott Papers. For her continued ambition for a seat in Congress, see Lathrop to Grace Abbott, Jan. 4, 1924, folder 9, box 57, Abbott Papers.

13. Eugene M. Tobin, *Organize or Perish: America's Independent Progressives, 1913-1933* (Westport, Conn.: 1986), 70–88. William E. Leuchtenberg, *Perils of Prosperity, 1914-1932* (Chicago, 1958), 101–2. For an analysis of the relationship between the granting of women's suffrage and the shift to interest group politics, see Paula Baker, "The Domestication of Politics: Women and American Political Society, 1780–1920," *American Historical Review* 89 (June 1984), 620–47. On the shift to interest group politics see especially Richard L. McCormick, "The Party Period and Public Policy: An Exploratory Hypothesis," *Journal of American History* 66 (Sept. 1979), 279–98; and the essays in his *The Party Period and Public Policy: American Politics from the Age of Jackson to the Progressive Era* (New York: Oxford Univ. Press, 1986).

14. Cott, *Grounding of Modern Feminism*, 99. See also Baker, "The Domestication of Politics."

15. Cott, *Grounding of Modern Feminism*, 110–11. For other discussions of these issues surrounding women's participation in politics in the 1920s, see Elisabeth I. Perry, *Belle Moskowitz: Feminine Politics and the Exercise of Power in the Age of Alfred E. Smith* (New York, 1987), esp. xi–xii; Felice D. Gordon, *After Winning: The Legacy of the New Jersey Suffragists* (New Brunswick, Rutgers Univ. Press, 1986), esp. 122–23.

16. Sophonisba Breckinridge noted the irony of this transformation: "[T]hese daughters of rebels have allied themselves with the militaristic theory of national defense, and with what was there recognized as the Tory, rather than the revolutionary, attitude toward political theories." Breckinridge, *Women in the Twentieth Century*, 46.

17. Quoted in Chepaitis, "The First Federal Social Welfare Measure," 253. For general information on female opponents, see ibid., 250–56; Costin, *Two Sisters*, 143–44; Cott, *Grounding of Modern Feminism*, 243–65; William L. O'Neill, *Everyone Was Brave: A History of Feminism in America* (New York, 1969), 228–31; Grace Abbott to John F. Hall, Aug. 28, 1924, folder 3, box 36, Abbott Papers.

18. See, for example, Leuchtenburg, *Perils of Prosperity*, 66–83; John A. Thompson, *Reformers and War: American Progressive Publicists and the First World War* (New York, 1987), 258–86.

19. See, for example, Cott, *Grounding of Modern Feminism*, 248–51; Allen Davis, *American Heroine: The Life and Legend of Jane Addams* (New York, 1973), 263–65.

20. Grace Abbott to Mother, March 1, 1924, folder 2, box 6, Addendum, Abbott Papers.

21. Cott, *Grounding of Modern Feminism*, 250.

22. Arthur S. Link, "What Happened to the Progressive Movement in the 1920s?," *American Historical Review* 64 (1959), 833–51, reprinted in *Progressivism: The Critical Issues*, ed. David M. Kennedy (Boston: Little, Brown, 1971), 147–64, esp. 158.

23. David Burner, *The Politics of Provincialism: The Democratic Party in Transition, 1918-1932* (New York, 1968), 169–71. See also Tobin, *Organize or Perish*, 161; Chepaitis, "The First Federal Social Welfare Measure," esp. 275.

24. Burner, *Politics of Provincialism*, 161–66.

25. Ibid. See also Leuchtenburg, *Perils of Prosperity*, 204–40. For a recent consideration of the urban-rural split in politics during the 1920s, see Charles Eagles, "Urban-Rural Conflict in the 1920s: A Historiographical Assessment," *Historian* 49 (Nov. 1986), 26–48; and his "Congressional Voting in the 1920s: A Test of Urban-Rural Conflict," *Journal of American History* 76 (Sept. 1989), 528–34.

26. Ellis W. Hawley, *The Great War and the Search for a Modern Order: A History of the American People and Their Institutions, 1917-1933* (New York, 1979), 100–107, 120–23; Joan Hoff Wilson, *Herbert Hoover: Forgotten Progressive* (Boston, 1975), 82–102.

27. Sophonisba P. Breckinridge, ed., *Public Welfare Administration in the United States: Select Documents* (Chicago: Univ. of Chicago Press, 1927), 366–67. For a discussion of the role of gender in determining positions along the spectrum from classical liberalism to socialism, see chap. 2.

28. Lathrop to Grace Abbott, June 24, 1923, folder 9, box 57, Abbott Papers.

29. For evidence of the relative inexpense of the maternal and infant health programs, cf. Hoff Wilson, *Herbert Hoover*, 86, and Children's Bureau, *The Promotion of the Welfare and Hygiene of Maternity and Infancy*, Pamphlet Number 178 (Washington, D.C., 1927), 1–2.

30. Quoted in Costin, *Two Sisters*, 142.

31. For infant mortality rates, see Children's Bureau, Pamphlet Number 178, 1927, p. 83; Molly Ladd-Taylor, ed., *Raising a Baby the Government Way: Mothers' Letters to the Children's Bureau, 1915-1932* (New Brunswick, N.J., 1986), 29. For maternal mortality rates, see 28–29.

32. For babies as "wonderful little mechanisms," see Chap. 4, p. 113, and for the other quotations, see Chap. 4, p. 91.

33. Lemons, *The Woman Citizen*, 174.

34. Calvin Coolidge, Presidential Message Transmitting the Budget, Dec. 7, 1927, pp. 164–65, folder 7, box 62, Abbott Papers.

35. Quoted in Chepaitis, "The First Federal Social Welfare Measure," 127.

36. Quoted in ibid.

37. Costin, *Two Sisters*, 139–40. Chepaitis, "The First Federal Social Welfare Measure," 177–204.

38. Sheila M. Rothman, *Woman's Proper Place: A History of Changing Ideals and Practices, 1870 to the Present* (New York, 1978), 145, 149. Lemons, *The Woman Citizen*, 163.

39. Lemons, *The Woman Citizen*, 166.

40. Ibid., 164. Breckinridge, *Women in the Twentieth Century*, 260. Patricia M. Hummer, *The Decade of Elusive Promise: Professional Women in the United States, 1920–1930* (Ann Arbor: UMI Research Press, 1979), 119. Regina M. Morantz-Sanchez, *Sympathy and Science: Women Physicians in American Medicine* (New York, 1985), 302.

41. Chepaitis, "The First Federal Social Welfare Measure," 61, 262. Lemons, *The Woman Citizen*, 164–65.

42. On the Pediatrics Sections' endorsement, see Rothman, *Woman's Proper Place*, 148–49; Chepaitis, "The First Federal Social Welfare Measure," 104. For the Children's Bureau's report on support from volunteer doctors, see Children's Bureau, *The Promotion of the Welfare and Hygiene of Maternity and Infancy*, Pamphlet Number 178, 1927, p. 7. For evidence that many of these doctors were male, see Mary Morgan to Grace Abbott, June 2, 1924; Mary Morgan to Grace Abbott, June 5, 1924; file 11-53-1, Central File 1921–24, Children's Bureau Records, National Archives, Washington, D.C. (hereafter CBR). On the state boards of health and hiring of male doctors, see Chepaitis, "The First Federal Social Welfare Measure," 262; Breckinridge, *Women in the Twentieth Century*, 321; Division of Maternity, Infancy, and Child Hygiene of the New York State Department of Health, Annual Report, 1923, file 11-34-8, Correspondence and Reports File 1917–54, CBR.

43. *Journal of the American Medical Association* 79 (Oct. 7, 1922), 1261.

44. Ibid.

45. Information compiled from the inside covers of the *Journal of the American Medical Association*, vols. 80–86 (1923–28); *Directory of the American Medical Association* (Chicago, 1927).

46. Books cited in Mary Roth Walsh, *"Doctors Wanted: No Women Need Apply": Sexual Barriers in the Medical Profession, 1835–1975* (New Haven, 1977), 139. Penina Glazer and Miriam Slater have also noticed the importance of fee-paying clients to male doctors and their relative unimportance to so many female doctors. See their *Unequal Colleagues: The Entrance of Women into the Professions, 1890–1940* (New Brunswick, N.J., 1987), 101. They have also seen the more frequent reliance of female doctors on the "ideology of service" (esp. p. 117).

47. *Journal of the American Medical Association* 79 (Sept. 16, 1922), 962–63. The quotation on prussianization of the medical profession may be found, for example, in Stenographic Report of Meetings of the Public Health Committee of the Chicago Woman's City Club, April 5 and 12, 1921, p. 45, Woman's City Club file, box 764, Anita McCormick Blaine Papers, State Historical Society of Wisconsin, Madison.

48. *Journal of the American Medical Association* 79 (Sept. 16, 1922), 963.

49. Stenographic Report of Meetings of the Public Health Committee of the Chicago Woman's City Club, April 5 and 12, 1921, pp. 45–48, Woman's City Club file, box 764, Blaine Papers.

50. Children's Bureau, *The Promotion of the Welfare and Hygiene of Maternity and Infancy*, Pamphlet Number 178, 1927, pp. 11, 13–14. Elena Crough to Florence Kraker, Sept. 25, 1924, file 11-31-1; Oregon State Board of Health, Plan of Action, 1921, file 11-39-1; Florence McKay to Florence Kraker, Aug. 22, 1924, file 11-34-1; Central File 1921–24, CBR. Chepaitis, "The First Federal Social Welfare Measure," 350.

51. See, for example, Stenographic Report, 43. Chepaitis, "The First Federal Social Welfare Measure," 102.

52. See, for instance, the story of Harriet Rice in chap. 1. See also Rothman, *Woman's Proper Place*, 140; Morantz-Sanchez, *Sympathy and Science*, 145–46, 153–56.

53. Morantz-Sanchez, *Sympathy and Science*, 151, 282, 285.

54. Ibid., 282–85.

55. See chap. 1.

56. Breckinridge, *Public Welfare Administration*, 7. Breckinridge, ed., *Medical Social Case Records* (Chicago: Univ. of Chicago Press, 1928), vii.

57. Lathrop to Abbott, June 27, 1926, folder 11, box 57, Abbott Papers.

58. Elizabeth Fee, *Disease and Discovery: A History of the Johns Hopkins School of Hygiene and Public Health, 1916–1939* (Baltimore, 1987), 22. For other information on the development of the public health profession, see esp. 2–7, 22–24, 37, 86. On male/female differences in the public health profession, see also Barbara Sicherman, "Gender, Professionalism and Reform in the Career of Alice Hamilton," in *Women in the Progressive Era*, eds. Noralee Frankel and Nancy Schrom Dye (Lexington: Univ. of Kentucky Press, 1990). See also Morantz-Sanchez, *Sympathy and Science*, 281–85.

59. Fee, *Disease and Discovery*, 86.

60. "After Miss Lathrop's Scalp," *Washington Herald*, May 30, 1914, newspaper clipping, folder 3, box 38, Abbott Papers.

61. Lathrop to Ann Case, 1920, folder 6, box 58; Lathrop to Secretary of Labor, July 19, 1921, folder 6, box 62; Abbott Papers. League of Women Voters, "Reasons Why the Administration of the Sheppard-Towner Bill Should Be Vested in the Children's Bureau," file 11-0-11, Central File 1921–24, CBR.

62. Lathrop, Testimony before House Committee on Interstate and Foreign Commerce, Dec. 1920, 19, clipping, folder 2, box 10, Addendum, Abbott Papers.

63. Lathrop, Notes on Interview with Surgeon General Rupert Blue, May 24, 1919, folder 5, box 62, Abbott Papers.

64. Lathrop, Notes on Interview with Surgeon General, 1919, folder 5, box 62, Abbott Papers.

65. Lathrop to Florence Kelley, 1914, folder 2, box 59, Abbott Papers.

66. Lathrop, Notes on Interview with Surgeon General, 1919, folder 5, box 62, Abbott Papers.

67. Memo to File, Oct. 14, 1919, folder 5, box 62, Abbott Papers.

68. Hearings of House Committee on Interstate and Foreign Commerce, Dec. 1920, clippings, folder 2, box 10, Addendum, Abbott Papers.
69. See, for instance, League of Women Voters, "Reasons Why the Administration of the Sheppard-Towner Bill Should Be Vested in the Children's Bureau."
70. Ibid.
71. Children's Bureau, *Fifth Annual Report* (Washington, D.C.: Government Printing Office, 1918), 49. Lathrop, Notes for Speech on Maternity and Infancy Act, 1921, folder 8, box 62, Abbott Papers.
72. Quoted in Edith Abbott, "Grace Abbott," MS biography, folder 2, box 10, Addendum, Abbott Papers.
73. League of Women Voters, "Reasons Why the Administration of the Sheppard-Towner Bill Should Be Vested in the Children's Bureau."
74. Helen T. Woolley to Carrie Chapman Catt, May 10, 1919, folder 5, box 62, Abbott Papers.
75. Chepaitis, "The First Federal Social Welfare Measure," 290–93.
76. On Hoover and the completely undemocratic purposes of conferences, see Hoff Wilson, *Herbert Hoover: Forgotten Progressive*, 82, 90–91.
77. Lela B. Costin, "Women and Physicians," esp. 110. Chepaitis, "The First Federal Social Welfare Measure," 295–302. Information on Ray Lyman Wilbur in *Journal of the American Medical Association* 79 (Oct. 7, 1922), inside cover.
78. Costin, "Women and Physicians," 111.
79. Quoted in ibid.
80. Rodney Dutcher, "Delegates Angered at Treatment They Received at Child Health Conference," *Washington Star*, Nov. 23, 1930, quoted in Costin, "Women and Physicians," 111.
81. Martha May Eliot, Oral History Transcript, Schlesinger-Rockefeller Oral History Project, 1974, p. 64, transcript in Special Collections, Butler Library, Columbia Univ.
82. Costin, "Women and Physicians," 112. Martha May Eliot, Oral History, 64–68.
83. Lathrop to Grace Abbott, Nov. 3, 1929, folder 3, box 58, Abbott Papers.
84. Kathryn Kish Sklar, "How Can We Explain the Decline in Power of American Women's Political Culture in the 1920's?," presented at the American History Seminar, Syracuse Univ., Feb. 16, 1989, esp. 11–22; Peggy Pascoe, *Relations of Rescue: The Search for Female Moral Authority in the American West, 1874–1939* (New York: Oxford Univ. Press, 1990), 177–207.
85. Costin, *Two Sisters*, 205–12. Lathrop to Grace Abbott, Nov. 3, 1929; Lathrop to Grace Abbott, Nov. 5, 1929; folder 3, box 58, Abbott Papers.
86. Grace Abbott quoted by Edith Abbott in "Grace Abbott," MS biography, 5–9, folder 9, box 11, Addendum, Abbott Papers.
87. Katharine Lenroot, "Presidential Address," *Conference Bulletin of the National Conference of Social Work*, 37, no. 4 (July 1934), 3, folder 3, box 61, Abbott Papers.

88. Susan Ware, *Beyond Suffrage: Women in the New Deal* (Cambridge, Mass., 1982), 1, 151. Winifred D. Wandersee, "Frances Perkins and the Twentieth-Century Reform Tradition: A Biographical View," unpublished paper presented at the American Historical Association Convention, Cincinnati, Ohio, Dec. 29, 1988, pp. 3–7.

89. Costin, *Two Sisters*, 176–77, 216. Lathrop to Grace Abbott, March 29, 1929, folder 3, box 58, Abbott Papers.

90. Ware, *Beyond Suffrage*, 146. See also Susan Ware, *Partner and I: Molly Dewson, Feminism, and New Deal Politics* (New Haven, 1987).

91. Ware, *Beyond Suffrage*, 145.

92. Ibid., 151–52. *United States Government Manual* (Washington, D.C.: Government Printing Office, Fall 1940), 310–11.

93. Edwin E. Witte, *The Development of the Social Security Act* (Madison: Univ. of Wisconsin Press, 1962), 42–45, 48–63.

94. Martha May Eliot, Oral History, 46.

95. Ware, *Beyond Suffrage*, 100. Costin, *Two Sisters*, 221–23. Katharine Lenroot to Grace Abbott, Aug. 17, 1934; Edwin Witte to Grace Abbott, Aug. 22, 1934; Witte to Grace Abbott, Sept. 11, 1934; folder 1, box 54, Abbott Papers. Edwin E. Witte to Edith Abbott, Oct. 18, 1939, folder 11, box 11, Addendum, Abbott Papers. Katharine Lenroot to Witte, Sept. 13, 1934, folder 3, box 61, Abbott Papers.

96. Grace Abbott to Mrs. A. M. Tunstall, Feb. 14, 1935; Witte to Grace Abbott, Feb. 21, 1935; folder 2, box 54, Abbott Papers. See also Witte, *The Development of the Social Security Act*, 85.

97. Witte's plea for advice is in Witte to Grace Abbott, Feb. 21, 1935, folder 2, box 54, Abbott Papers. Further movement on the organizing of such help is in Katharine Lenroot to Grace Abbott, March 3, 1935; Grace Abbott to Katharine Lenroot, March 6, 1935; folder 2, box 54, Abbott Papers. Quotation is in Witte to Edith Abbott, Oct. 18, 1939, folder 11, box 11, Addendum, Abbott Papers. See also Witte, *The Development of the Social Security Act*, 97.

98. See, for example, all the lobbying correspondence in folders 4 and 5, box 54, Abbott Papers. For report on the amount of mail to congressmen, see Katharine Lenroot to Grace Abbott, Feb. 26, 1935, folder 2, box 54, Abbott Papers.

99. Witte, *The Development of the Social Security Act*, 97. Witte to Edith Abbott, Oct. 18, 1939, folder 11, box 11, Addendum, Abbott Papers.

100. For the broader agenda of the child welfare establishment, see, for example, Katharine Lenroot's quotation of a 1919 report from Breckinridge to the Children's Bureau in Katharine Lenroot, "Friend of Children and of the Children's Bureau," *Social Service Review* 22 (Dec. 1948), 429. See also Charles Merriam, "A Member of the University Community," *Social Service Review* 22 (Dec. 1948), 425. Chepaitis, "The First Federal Social Welfare Measure," 144–46. See also Marguerite Rosenthal, "The Children's Bureau and the Juvenile Court: Delinquency Policy, 1912–1940," *Social Service Review* (June 1986), 312–13.

210 *Notes*

101. Ware, *Beyond Suffrage*, 103. Grace Abbott to Edward Costigan, March 7, 1938; Grace Abbott to Theodore Keeps, March 7, 1938; Grace Abbott to Samuel Levin, March 7, 1938; Grace Abbott to Charlotte Carr, March 7, 1938; Grace Abbott to Henry Harriman, March 7, 1938; Grace Abbott to Edwin Witte, March 10, 1938; Beatrice McConnell to Grace Abbott, March 16, 1938; folder 11, box 54, Abbott Papers.

102. Their mentor, Florence Kelley, had been convinced of the necessity of minimum wages and legislation to prevent child labor for decades, of course. See, for example, Elizabeth K. Hartley, "Social Work and Social Reform: Selected Women Social Workers and Child Welfare Reforms, 1877–1932," Ph.D. dissertation, Univ. of Pennsylvania, 1985, pp. 309, 342.

103. See, for example, Edith Abbott, *The Tenements of Chicago, 1908–1935* (Chicago: Univ. of Chicago Press, 1936), xii. Costin, *Two Sisters*, 227–30.

104. Edith Abbott, "Child Welfare in Review," May 9, 1950, folder 9, box 3, Addendum, Abbott Papers. On Grace Abbott's views, see especially Grace Abbott to Robert Keenan, Feb. 20, 1935; Frank Graham to Grace Abbott, Oct. 22, 1936; folder 2, box 54, Abbott Papers.

105. Edith Abbott, "Child Welfare in Review," May 9, 1950, folder 9, box 3, Addendum, Abbott Papers.

106. Costin, *Two Sisters*, 224. Witte, *The Development of the Social Security Act*, 162–63. Katharine Lenroot to Grace Abbott, Jan. 10, 1935; Grace Abbott to Katharine Lenroot, Feb. 21, 1935; Katharine Lenroot to Grace Abbott, April 25, 1935; Grace Abbott to Katharine Lenroot, April 26, 1935; folder 4, box 61, Abbott Papers. Katharine Lenroot to Secretary Perkins, Sept. 21, 1936, folder 6, box 61, Abbott Papers.

107. Ware, *Beyond Suffrage*, 10–11.

108. Ibid., 147.

109. *Official Register of the United States* (Washington, D.C.: Government Printing Office, 1940), 175.

110. *Official Congressional Directory* (Washington, D.C.: Government Printing Office, 1940), 362. Walsh, *Doctors Wanted*, 264.

111. Katharine Lenroot to Frederich W. Brown [1936], folder 5, box 61, Abbott Papers.

112. Cott, *Grounding of Modern Feminism*, 218.

113. Morantz-Sanchez, *Sympathy and Science*, 336.

114. Cott, *Grounding of Modern Feminism*, 224–25.

115. The story of these appointments is told in detail in Ware, *Beyond Suffrage*, esp. 45–86.

116. Barbara Sicherman et al., eds., *Notable American Women: The Modern Period* (Cambridge, Mass., 1980), 341–43. Ware, *Beyond Suffrage*, 193.

117. *United States Government Manual* (Washington, D.C.: Government Printing Office, 1948), 394.

Conclusion

1. *Congressional Record*, 69th Congress, 1st Session (1926), 12946-47. Quoted in Allen F. Davis, *American Heroine: The Life and Legend of Jane Addams* (New York, 1973), 266.

2. Mimi Abramovitz, *Regulating the Lives of Women: Social Welfare Policy from Colonial Times to the Present* (Boston: South End Press, 1988). See also Linda Gordon, *Heroes of Their Own Lives: The Politics and History of Family Violence* (New York, 1988), for example, 5, 166–67; Elizabeth Pleck, *Domestic Tyranny: The Making of American Social Policy Against Family Violence from Colonial Times to the Present* (New York, 1987), for example, 11–13; and Seth Koven and Sonya Michel, "Gender and the Origins of the Welfare State," *Radical History Review* 43 (Winter 1989), 112–19; Virginia Sapiro, "The Gender Bias of American Social Policy," *Political Science Quarterly* 101 (1986), 221–38.

3. Barbara Nelson in her essay, "The Gender, Race, and Class Origins of Early Welfare Policy and the Welfare State: A Comparison of Workmen's Compensation and Mothers' Aid," in *Women, Change, and Politics*, eds. Louise Tilly and Patricia Gurin (New York: Russell Sage Foundation, 1990), 226–38, does both. See also Koven and Michel.

4. Quoted in Elizabeth Kennedy Hartley, "Social Work and Social Reform: Selected Women Social Workers and Child Welfare Reforms, 1877–1932," Ph.D. dissertation, Univ. of Pennsylvania, 1985, p. 180.

5. On attempts of married women to pursue careers in the 1920s, see, for example, Virginia Collier, *Marriage and Careers* (New York: Channel Bookshop, 1926); Chase Woodhouse, ed., *After College—What?* (Greensboro, N.C.: Institute of Women's Professional Relations, 1932); Frank Stricker, "Cookbooks and Law Books: The Hidden History of Career Women in Twentieth Century America," *Journal of Social History* 10 (Fall 1976) 1–19; Joyce Antler, "Feminism as Life Process: The Life and Career of Lucy Sprague Mitchell," *Feminist Studies* 7 (Spring 1981), 135, 155; Barbara Solomon, *In the Company of Educated Women: A History of Women and Higher Education in America* (New Haven, 1985), 172–82.

Index

Abbott, Edith: employment, 68–70, 72; and reform, 68, 71–74, 83–86, 147; and social work, 68, 74–83, 103, 141; character, 69, 89; education, 69–70; research projects, 78, 84; victory over Taylor, 79; and the Children's Bureau, 86–88, 91–92, 147; and Grace Abbott, 89, 91; attitude towards New Deal, 153

Abbott, Grace: character, 89; early career, 89; and Immigrants' Protective League, 89; research projects, 89–90; as head of Child Labor Division, 90, 102; recruited to head the Children's Bureau, 90–91, 162; relationship with School of Social Service Administration, 91–92; as Chief of the Children's Bureau, 91–93, 151; implementing Sheppard-Towner Act, 107, 112, 116–18, 125–27, 141; approach to midwifery, 116–18; accused of communism, 129; participation in White House Conference (1930), 147–48; considered for Secretary of Labor, 150; and New Deal, 151–53

Addams, Jane: motive for founding Hull House, 3, 7–9, 11–12, 36; at Rockford Female Seminary, 6, 32; character, 6–7, 25, 49; relationship with Ellen Starr, 7–8, 16; trips to Europe, 8; founding Hull House, 10–14; as dominant figure at Hull House, 14–15, 23–24, 26; relationship with Mary Rozet Smith, 16–17; and social research, 31; and publicity, 33, 63; as a leader in the settlement movement, 33–34; as a leader in reform, 34–36, 40, 43, 46–48, 63, 88, 92, 103; and social work, 66, 73, 75; view of education, 75; opposes World War I, 95; accused of communism, 129; death, 153

Addams, John Huy, 6

Aid to Dependent Children, 152–54, 156–57

American Association for the Study and Prevention of Infant Mortality, 64

American Association of University Women, 104, 120

American Child Hygiene Association, 105–6, 144

American Federation of Labor, 35, 63, 105

American Medical Association, 109, 135–42, 145, 147

American Public Health Association, 105–6, 144

Anderson, Sara, 8

Armour, Joseph, 12

Armour, Philip, 12

Association of Collegiate Alumnae, 5, 59–60, 64

Association Opposed to Woman Suffrage, 128

Baltimore, Md., 8

Barnard College, 4

Barnett, Samuel, 9

Belden, Evelina, 51–52

213

220 *Index*

Social Security Board, 151, 153–54, 156–
57
social work: general, xvi, 34, 150, 155; pro-
fessionalization of, 66–68, 74, 76–79, 81–
83, 86, 108–9, 121, 139–42; and reform,
68, 74, 77, 82–86, 150; and Sheppard-
Towner, 108–9, 115, 118, 124, 128, 139,
143, 147; and midwifery, 115; and the
New Deal, 147, 150, 154
social workers, as policymakers, 76–77, 82,
85
Socialist party, 95
Spider Web Chart, 129
St. Louis School for Social Work, 68
Starr, Eliza Allen, 7
Starr, Ellen Gates, 6–13, 16, 18, 33, 36
Starr, Rhoda Morgan, 85
State Charities Aid Association [New York],
44
Stevens, Alzina, 27
suffrage, *see* women's suffrage
Swope, Gerard, 10

Taft, William Howard, 46–47, 87
Talbot, Marion, 70
Taylor, Graham, 68, 74–79
Texas Federation of Women's Clubs, 60
Thrower, Pauline, 85
Towner, Horace, 103
Toynbee Hall, 9, 13
Trolander, Judith, 110

United States Congress, xii, 39–43, 46–47,
50, 63–64, 88, 90, 93, 97, 102–3, 105–
8, 125–27, 129–32, 134–36, 142, 144–
46, 148, 152–53, 162
University of California at Los Angeles,
10
University of Chicago, xii, xvi, 65, 70, 79–
81, 89, 159
University of Illinois, 79
University of Michigan, 23
University of Nebraska, 69
University of Pennsylvania, 25
University of Wisconsin, 51, 159
University of Zurich, 25

Vassar College, 4, 9, 32
Vermont Federation of Women's Clubs, 60
voluntary organizations, *see* female voluntary
organizations

Wald, Lillian: general, 19–20, 35, 140, 147;
campaign for Children's Bureau, 38–48;
vision of an active state, 43–45, 55, 60,
84, 104; in the dominion, 63–64, 73, 76,
84, 88, 103, 147
Walling, William English, 35
Ware, Susan, xi
Webb, Beatrice, 10, 72
welfare state, xiv, 83, 98, 108, 125, 160–61
Wellesley College, 4, 9, 69–70, 72
Wendell Phillips Settlement, 22, 71
West, Mary Mills, 55
Whipper, Ionia, 116
White House Conference on Child Health
and Protection (1930), 124, 146–47
White House Conference on the Care of
Dependent Children (1909), 42–44, 46
Wilbur, Ray Lyman, 147–48
Wilmarth, Mary, 17
Wilson, Woodrow, 46–47, 87, 94, 97, 99,
128
Wischnewetzky, Lazare, 25
Withington, Anne, 17
Witte, Edwin, 152
Woman Patriot Publishing Company, 128
Woman's Committee of the Council of Na-
tional Defense, 97, 99, 101, 103
Woman's Foundation for Health, 64, 105
Woman's Journal, 33
Woman's Medical School [Northwestern
University], 23
women's bloc, 103, 126, 128
Women's Bureau, xii, 150
Women's Christian Temperance Union
(WCTU), 28, 59, 104, 120
Women's Joint Congressional Committee
(WJCC), xii, 103–6, 121–22, 126, 159–
60
Women's Medical College [New York City],
19
Women's Press Club, 105